ADVANCES IN
HUMAN ECOLOGY

Volume 4 • 1995

EDITORIAL ADVISORS

ADVANCES IN
HUMAN ECOLOGY

Editor: LEE FREESE
Department of Sociology
Washington State University

Published in association with the
Society for Human Ecology

VOLUME 4 • 1995

 **JAI PRESS INC.**

Greenwich, Connecticut   *London, England*

CONTENTS

LIST OF CONTRIBUTORS

William R. Catton, Jr.

Department of Sociology
Washington State University

Lee Freese

Department of Sociology
Washington State University

Kenneth A. Gould

Department of Sociology
St. Lawrence University

Richard Machalek

Department of Sociology
University of Wyoming

Bonnie J. McCay

Department of Human Ecology
Rutgers University

Richard B. Norgaard

Energy and Resources
    Program
University of California,
    Berkeley

Allan Schnaiberg

Department of Sociology
Northwestern University

Jane Sell

Department of Sociology
Texas A&M University

Yeongi Son

Kangwon Development
    Research Institute
Seoul, Korea

Adam S. Weinberg

Department of Sociology
Northwestern University

PREFACE

EDITORIAL POLICY

This series publishes original theoretical, empirical, and review papers on scientific human ecology. Human ecology is interpreted to include structural and functional patterns and changes in human social organization and sociocultural behavior as these may be affected by, interdependent with, or identical to changes in ecosystemic, evolutionary, or ethological processes, factors, or mechanisms. Three degrees of scope are included in this interpretation: (1) the adaptation of sociocultural forces to bioecological forces; (2) the interactions between sociocultural and bioecological forces; (3) and the integration of sociocultural with bioecological forces.

The goal of the series is to promote the growth of human ecology as a transdisciplinary problem solving paradigm. Contributions are solicited without regard for particular theoretical, methodological, or disciplinary orthodoxies, and may range across ecological anthropology, socioecology, evolutionary ecology, environmental sociology, ecological economics, ecological demography, ecological geography, and other relevant fields of specialization. The editor will be especially receptive to contributions that promote the growth of general scientific theory in human ecology. No single volume will represent the full range the series is intended to cover.

CONTENTS OF VOLUME 4

Volume 4 begins with two theoretical papers from opposite ends of the spectrum of human ecological analysis. William R. Catton, Jr., using an ecosystemic-ecological point of view, analyzes the significance of symbiosis for human ecology. Catton describes how symbiosis, which extends from microbes to the biosphere, provides a model for the relationship of human societies to ecosystems. Richard Machalek, using an evolutionary-ecological point of view, develops a comparative sociology of exploitative behavior. In seeking to identify the conditions for resource expropriation, Machalek argues that the fundamental dimensions and forms of exploitation are cross-specific.

There follow five papers that address multifarious aspects of the human exploitation of resources. Several follow Garrett Hardin's model of a dilemma and tragedy of the commons, which they criticize and develop. Some wrestle extensively with the relationship between local and global economic-ecological processes.

Yeongi Son and Jane Sell seek to find a theoretical basis by which to distinguish resource dilemmas from dilemmas of public goods. Son and Sell examine economists' expected utility theory and prospect theory, as well as some pertinent evidence, to evaluate the distinctive properties of the different dilemmas and the conditions for solving them. Bonnie J. McCay argues that the metaphor of a tragedy of the commons is indiscriminate and misleading. McCay addresses the different kinds of "tragedies" (environmental and sociocultural) that can occur and the different kinds of responses to them that human cultures can adopt, and she argues that the tragedy interpretation alone does not permit the fine discriminations necessary to develop effective theories that link property rights to natural resource systems and their management. Like McCay, I argue that the tragedy of the commons is too simple a model for human ecological analysis, so I convert the problem of ecological commons into a problem of serial ecological traps. Then I argue that a concept of human-nature balance, which undergirds commons analyses, has little use for the understanding of macroscopic human ecological series that lead to trap conditions.

Richard B. Norgaard argues that some flawed assumptions of neoclassical economic theory have contributed to the growth of a global economy that has brought in its wake a degeneration of historically functional, community based commons institutions. Norgaard tries to show how economic logic in theory demands what many neoclassical interpretations seem to deny, namely, the existence of global intergenerational commons institutions. Adam S. Weinberg, Allan Schnaiberg, and Kenneth A. Gould also address failures of the institutional practice of necolcassical economics, but with application to a different problem. Weinberg, Schnaiberg, and Gould extensively document, with regard to recycling programs, the irony by which the structure of sociopolitical and economic interests can lead environmental conservation movements to promote policies that actually undermine their own objectives.

Lee Freese
Editor

FROM EUKARYOTIC CELLS TO GAIA:

THE RANGE OF SYMBIOSIS AND ITS RELEVANCE FOR HUMAN ECOLOGY

William R. Catton, Jr.

ABSTRACT

Mutual dependence of populations of differentiated organisms (symbiosis) permeates our world. This has great significance for human ecology. Division of labor in human society, a special case, has illuminating parallels in intracellular division of functions. Evidence assembled by Margulis strongly supports the theory of speciation by symbiogenesis which says microbes that were once independent came together as symbionts, as guest and host cells, and the guest cells eventually became organelles performing specialized functions within a new kind of cell. For Durkheim, occupational specialization was the human equivalent of speciation, making humans interdependent, giving their society "organic solidarity." A continuum of symbiosis extends from microbes to the entire biosphere. Profoundly multilateral, symbiosis can lead to effective homeostasis (both at the micro and macro levels). As Hawley recognized, humans can have other (differently specialized) humans as symbionts; it is important to extend this insight by seeing that the symbionts of humans may also include machines (Butler), all the biotic and abiotic components of ecosystems (Tansley),

Advances in Human Ecology, Volume 4, pages 1-34.
ISBN: 1-55938-874-9

and even the whole planet (Lovelock). If regarding society as an organism was heuristically useful in the past, but later taboo, now human society is best seen as an important subsystem (in symbiosis with other parts) of an ecosystem. Ecosystemic homeostasis can fail. Symbiosis can break down. Discovery that eukaryotic cells originated in microendosymbiosis sheds new light on the resemblance of human population growth to cancer, and calls for study of whatever pressures tend to convert mutualism to predation, as reflected in deceptive communication practices so endemic in modern society. If terminal derangement of Gaia is to be averted, clarification of such issues by human ecologists is essential.

We can never be certain beforehand which new observations, which yet-to-be-discovered fact will be most useful.
                                                    Prescott and Flexer (1982, p. 28)

It is not clear to me where ecology ends and the study of the ethics of nature begins, nor is it clear to me where biological ecology ends and human ecology begins.
                                                    Golley (1993, p. 205)

INTRODUCTION

Symbiosis is a concept that has been in the vocabulary of human ecology right from the start. Bioecology literature, beginning more than a century ago, defined symbiosis quite simply as the intimate living together of dissimilar organisms (Margulis 1991, p. 1). Organisms living in a symbiotic relationship are called symbionts (or symbiotes). Sometimes the adjective "dissimilar" is replaced by the phrase "of different species" (Margulis 1987, p. 103). But dissimilarity can occur within a species. As used in human ecology, symbiosis would not always have the symbionts be of different species.[1] Humans may be symbionts of each other. It is important for human ecologists to recognize, however, that not all symbionts of humans are human. One of the earliest textbooks to mention human ecology titled its third chapter "Symbiosis and Society" (Park and Burgess [1921] 1924). Materials reprinted therein from Alfred Espinas (1878), Eugenius Warming (1909), and William M. Wheeler (1910) afforded readers preparing to become sociologists some clear indications of the nature of assorted symbiotic relations. Even though, in most current biological literature, symbiosis is commonly taken to mean "mutualistic biotrophic associations" (Margulis 1991, p. 1), parasitism, predation, and commensalism, as well as mutualism, are all recognized as forms of symbiosis. Chapter 3 of Park and Burgess distinguished these types of interaction from each other but included them all. The collection of ecological writings those

Chicago sociologists assembled made it clear that symbiosis was an important concept for human ecology; symbiotic relations were by no means confined to a narrow portion of the organic world.

Now, however, it is turning out that mutualistic symbiosis is an even more extensive type of phenomenon than had been generally recognized. The aim of this paper is to highlight some converging developments in bioscience literature that make this evident, and then show how taking the pervasiveness of symbiosis more fully into account can open new avenues of inquiry for human ecologists. We shall see that there are both microsymbiosis and macrosymbiosis. Symbiosis can be not just bilateral but multilateral. It can be so multilateral, in fact, that Darwin's concept of "the web of life" takes on enhanced meaning.

SYMBIOGENESIS, DIVISION OF LABOR, AND MAN-MACHINE SYMBIOSIS

The idea that symbiosis was actually involved in the origin of new forms and new physiological processes was already present in the writings of Russian "symbiologists" early in the twentieth century (Golley 1993, pp. 169-174). These writings only belatedly reached Western scientists who write in English, but the Russians' view of mechanisms by which "geologically sudden" evolutionary change was generated is now recognized in the West (Margulis 1991, p. 1).

Transformation of the biosphere from one with no more than one part per million atmospheric oxygen to a biosphere bathed in a 21 percent oxygen atmosphere was a change that necessitated monumental adaptation. What has been aptly called "the oxygen holocaust" (Margulis and Sagan 1986, p. 99) extinguished much of the bacterial life of the planet, to which it was enormously more catastrophic than industrial pollution is to us today. To anaerobic life forms, oxygen was a serious pollutant; without a major evolutionary breakthrough it had to be lethal. Waves of bacterial speciation were set off (Margulis and Sagan 1986, p. 112):

> The energy dynamo created by cyanobacterial pollution was a prerequisite for a new unit of life—the nucleated cell which is the fundamental component of plant, animal, protist, and fungal life. In eukaryotes, genes are packaged in a nucleus and there is an elaborate orchestration of internal cell processes, including the presence in the area surrounding the nucleus (the cytoplasm) of mitochondria—special structures that metabolize oxygen for the rest of the cell.

In sum, the world made a huge transition, from being populated solely by prokaryotes to being home to many varieties of eukaryotes, many of which could use oxygen, the former pollutant.

Hutchinson (1970, p. 11) credits Margulis with having "assembled most convincingly the scattered but extensive evidence that this response was of a very special kind, involving a multiple symbiosis" with various prokaryotic cells combining to achieve "an evolutionary advance quite unlike any other known to have occurred." Margulis (1991, p. 7) credits Wallin (1927, pp. 8, 58) with developing the principle of "prototaxis," by which was meant an organism's (or cell's) innate tendency to react to another in a definite manner, positive or negative. The end result of positive prototaxis is "the establishment of intimate microsymbiotic complexes." Mainstream biologists of the time scoffed at Wallin's idea that microsymbiosis was the fundamental factor in the origin of species, but the theory has now become a preferred explanation for the origins of organelles within cells (Taylor 1987).

To anyone entering human ecology from one of the established social science disciplines, the question of how mitochondria and plastids came to be components of eukaryotic cells may seem at least peripheral (if not altogether irrelevant). I hope to show otherwise. The present paper is a result of an exciting adventure in reading. Just how the reading of a particular book or article (such as the writings of Margulis and others) will influence one's ideas, and what subsequent work it may stimulate, always depends on what other books and articles one has previously read, and what one's prior experiences have been (Golley 1993, pp. xi-xiv). This is as true of work in human ecology as in any field. What follows is therefore, in part, an account of a somewhat fortuitous literary odyssey. The sequence of encounters with works of various writers is important for understanding the combination of ideas aroused and nurtured thereby.

My attempts to become acquainted with recent biological literature on evolutionary theory stemmed from a particular interest that would probably not have been expected to lead to the unusually thought-provoking book, *Microcosmos*, by Lynn Margulis and Dorion Sagan (1986). Other scholars, pursuing other interests, would doubtless have read the same book very differently. It was while working on ideas pertaining to a classic sociological topic, the division of labor in human society, that I happened to come across a description by Margulis and Sagan of intracellular division of functions. This is a phenomenon few if any sociologists had previously had much occasion to think about. The description opened an entirely unforeseen line of thinking, and led to broadened and deepened consideration of symbiosis. This led to additional (variously related) works by the same authors—including Margulis (1974b, 1987, 1992), Margulis and Schwartz (1988), and Sagan (1990), which, in turn, required looking up some things cited in their bibliographies. The rapidly burgeoning list of previously unsought publications provided a wealth of important information about recent developments in biology, although much of it, I suspect, would have seemed to most human ecologists to be of as little import for human ecology as sociologists would have assumed.

Here, then from Margulis (1987, p. 103), is a succinct statement of the idea whose startlingly seminal quality was evident from the way Margulis and Sagan (1986) seemed to be generalizing from it:

> According to the symbiotic theory of the origin of eukaryotes, once-independent microbes came together, first casually as separate guest and host cells, then by necessity. Eventually, the guest cells became organelles of a new kind of cell.

Many outsiders to microbiology have, of course, previously learned about the lichen example of a symbiotic combination of species—an autotrophic algal species and a heterotrophic fungus living collaboratively. This fact had been established by the opening of the twentieth century (Margulis 1991, pp. 3-4). But it would hardly have occurred to most of us, before encountering this new body of biological literature, that the merging of symbionts into a new species could be so universal. According to Margulis and Sagan, and as succinctly restated by Margulis (1987, p. 103):

> Such a sequence of events can be found in the symbiotic relationships between many modern life forms. Many organisms live inside, on top of, or attached to other organisms. Hereditary symbioses—those in which the partners remain together throughout their life cycle—are surprisingly common.

This certainly was surprising to one who had entered human ecology by way of sociology. Oddly, though, a sociological background, it could be argued, ought to have made the idea unsurprising. To understand this, let us return to the topic of the division of labor. A hundred years ago, when Emile Durkheim ([1893] 1984) published his groundbreaking sociological treatise on the division of labor in human society, he differed from his contemporaries in one respect that was extremely important. He understood the then-seminal work by Charles Darwin very differently from the way it was being construed by many nineteenth-century social commentators. Many nineteenth-century writers had got hung up in reading about "survival of the fittest" by their automatically moralistic or chauvinistic misinterpretations of "fittest." Perhaps it was unfortunate that Darwin had chosen to embrace this phrase from Herbert Spencer as a shorthand expression for the natural selection process. Anyway, Durkheim avoided the common hang-up. He had instead drawn from Darwin the idea of speciation as niche-diversification.

What Durkheim saw as most significant in Darwin's study of the origin of species was the importance of what modern evolutionary ecologists would call "resource partitioning." (In the nineteenth century the phrasing was different.) The point was this: Organisms that differ from each other in the resources they require and the demands their lives make on their surroundings are in a less competitive relation to each other than are organisms that make identical demands. An environment can support a larger total biomass if that biomass consists of many diverse species than if it consists of just a few similar ones. In this respect, Durkheim saw occupational differentiation among humans as the intraspecific counterpart to speciation among nonhumans.

Thus, by his atypically perceptive reading of Darwin, Durkheim was able to see that resource partitioning by niche diversification had the effect of limiting the range of competition between coexisting organisms. Organisms in the same niche compete; organisms in different niches compete less or not at all. Durkheim's book, presenting a detailed analysis of the human parallel to *that* idea, remained uncontaminated by the more common but misguided perspective that came to be misleadingly known as Social Darwinism.

Occupational specialization was, for Durkheim, the human version of speciation. It achieved niche-diversification within a human society, so it was a means of resource partitioning among a human population. A person competes mainly with one's fellow practitioners of the same occupation, not with those in other (especially in more remote) occupations, using other materials, dealing with other markets. What Adam Smith ([1776] 1901, pp. 43-67) had depicted as division of labor's main function, increased productivity, Durkheim viewed as more peripheral.

But one has to depend on others in other specialties for products and services not produced by one's own specialized efforts, the more so the greater the division of labor. If there is specialization, exchange relations become necessary. Division of labor not only limited the range of competition, Durkheim contended, it made people interdependent. It thus achieved a new form of social cohesion. He called it "organic solidarity" to distinguish it from "mechanical solidarity" based on likeness and common identity. Another name for interdependence-based organic solidarity would be mutualism (or symbiosis). Although unknown to Durkheim, the endomicrosymbiosis that accounts, according to Margulis, for organelles within eukaryotic cells would be a prototypical case of "organic solidarity" (with "organic" taken quite literally). A previously "facultative" association of unlike microorganisms developed into such strong interdependence that it became "obligate" symbiosis—and the partners became one organism. The idea that symbionts could become one organism might nudge sociologists to rethink their earlier skepticism about "organismic" ideas in nineteenth-century sociology literature.

What was it precisely that brought about this encounter (a century after Durkheim) between a sociologist-turned-human-ecologist and the writings of Margulis and others about "symbiogenesis"? It came about because, knowing there had been much added by other researchers and theorists since Durkheim's time to Darwin's explanation for the origin of species, it seemed important to pursue the possibility that this more advanced knowledge of speciation processes might revise our understanding of the causes and effects of division of labor in human society. It turns out, for example, that modern speciation theory focuses much more on allopatric speciation, whereby a subpopulation of a species becomes geographically isolated, adapts by natural selection to its distinctive environment, and becomes sufficiently unlike the ancestral population so as to be reproductively isolated—a new species—even if, eventually, the geographic isolation ends. Durkheim's interpretation of Darwin seemed to regard speciation as sympatric—as if, without migration or dispersal, pressure for resource partitioning due to intense competition arising from overpopulation produced speciation which in turn limited competition, apart from any intervening period of geographic separation.

Be that as it may, there was another factor favoring receptivity to the idea of symbionts becoming one organism, namely the evolutionary views of Samuel Butler (see Jones 1911).[2] Butler's original enthusiasm for Darwin's theory (Jones 1919, pp. 42-47) degenerated later into antagonism toward Darwin. He became a severe critic of Darwin, and purported to have come up with an alternative theory of evolution. But Butler had been onto something important in his delightful essay for a New Zealand newspaper ("Darwin Among the Machines") and in his imaginative novel, *Erewhon*. He viewed machines (and tools) in a way that made them subject to evolution. It was as if, in more modern terms, he saw machines and their users as symbionts.

This idea was potentially valuable as an extension of Darwin's theory, not a repudiation of it. The artificial kidney machine is a device for performing external hemodialysis on patients suffering from failure of their natural kidneys. Various other, more familiar, objects function as detachable organs enabling humans to do things they could not do with their natural organic components. The wings of aircraft enable humans to fly, without being limited by exclusive adaptation of their forelimbs as feathered flight organs. The wings of birds (and of bats and butterflies) are useful for flight but not for much else. However, those of us humans who occasionally take to the air still retain the hands we inherited from simian ancestors and continue to find them useful as devices for manipulating other kinds of detachable organs, including screwdrivers, scalpels, the keyboards of typewriters (and pianos), needles and scissors, weapons, steering wheels, and cricket bats. Clearly, the flexibility gained by our reliance on detachable organs contributes immensely to our intraspecific occupational differentiation—to what has been called "quasi-speciation" (Hutchinson 1965; Catton 1980, 1987).

Computers and libraries, as detachable extensions (or symbionts) of human brains, make it unnecessary for us to have heads too large for passage through the birth canal, while enabling us to exceed the achievements of other large-brained animals. Thus our cultural-technological progress has accompanied rather than precluded the vast increase of our numbers and the perilous enlargement of our ecosystem impact.

Examples such as these seemed indicative of technology's essential place among the variables studied by human ecology (cf. Duncan 1959, 1961).

Butler's ideas about "Darwin Among the Machines" thus seemed to have effectively linked notions of cultural evolution with notions of biological evolution. His images were unusual but potentially incisive. They were better, it might be said, than attitudes expressed in social science literature seeking to embargo any consideration of connections between the two levels of evolution (e.g., see, Moore [1965] and Nisbet [1965], responding to Stebbins [1965]). Had Butler pursued his insight more wisely and without becoming antagonistic he might have made a real contribution to scientific knowledge. Instead, he fancied himself a clever David striking down Goliath (Darwin), so in scientific circles he is remembered (if at all) as a somewhat bizarre novelist and essayist. It was left to others to develop the insight he conceived and aborted (e.g., see, Leach 1968, pp. 16-30; Odum 1971; Lenski and Lenski 1982, pp. 46-47, 82-89). Knowing about Butler's foray into evolutionary thought made it a pleasure to read the opinion of Margulis and Sagan (1986, pp. 256-262) that even if "Butler was kidding" about the evolution of machines he may nevertheless have been "a visionary who saw an important aspect of the coming supercosm." Supercosm? The ultimate symbiosis of humans and technology?

To fathom what Margulis and Sagan meant by strange terms like that, a grasp of the unusual main theme of their book is required. They were writing about a revolution in the life sciences that elevated symbiosis from a minor curiosity to a central and pervasive aspect of nature. This scientific revolution was significantly altering previously accepted ideas about life's origin, about the appropriate classification of its types, and about the dynamics of evolution (Margulis 1987;Margulis and Schwartz 1988). It demanded a vocabulary enlargement.

Some of the words of Margulis and Sagan (1986) seem implicitly supportive of human ecology's inclusion within general ecology. New discoveries and new thinking, they wrote, "have shown the folly of considering people as special, apart and supreme" (p. 14). That statement implies the unwisdom of attempts to develop human ecology separately as a soft social science, set apart from biological science (cf. Hawley 1944; Catton 1992; Beus 1993). But it was merely preliminary to their succinct articulation of their book's central idea (p. 14):

> From the paramecium to the human race, all life forms are meticulously organized, sophisticated aggregates of evolving microbial life. Far from leaving microorganisms behind on an evolutionary 'ladder,' we are both surrounded by them and composed of them.

Hence the title of their book: *Microcosmos*. Each of us is not just an individual; as a eukaryotic organism, each of us is a population of (differentiated and interdependent) microbes. We have all known, of course, that our bodies consist of millions and millions of cells, but thinking of them as "microbes" in a symbiotic relation with each other, as Margulis and Sagan urged we do, puts us and symbiosis in a new light.

It was startling to be told by Margulis and Sagan (1986, p. 120) that all organisms consisting of eukaryotic cells

> are probably composites, mergers of once differentiated creatures. The human brain cells that conceived these creatures are themselves chimeras—no less fantastic mergers of several formerly independent kinds of prokaryotes that together coevolved.

The mention of coevolution, of course, stirs up various lines of ecological thought. But the idea that coevolving-but-separate cells eventually combined to form new kinds of integrated cells, which in turn combined into increasingly complex multicellular organisms, even those with brains capable of developing ecological insights, is an idea too pregnant to ignore. It extends Darwin no less truly than would a careful pursuit of Butler's insight about evolution of man-machine symbioses. As Margulis and Sagan (1986, p. 124) put it:

> If symbiosis is as prevalent and important in the history of life as it seems to be, we must rethink biology from the beginning. Life on earth is not really a game in which some organisms beat others and win. It is what in the mathematical field of game theory is known as a nonzero-sum game.

All large organisms, they argue, "came from smaller prokaryotes that together won a victory for cooperation, for the art of mutual living" (p. 125).

ENDOMICROSYMBIOSIS

To recognize the importance of this new view of symbiosis (and of evolution by symbiogenesis), one must appreciate the distinction between two basic cell types—prokaryotes and eukaryotes. The two terms were foreign to the lexicon of sociology so they had been quite absent from my working vocabulary before I read Margulis and Sagan. It turns out that they are worthy of becoming well-known among human ecologists. What makes this so evident is the image their book offers of symbiosis being not only ubiquitous but also leading to effective homeostasis, to self-regulation.

For sociologists of my generation, symbiosis first entered our vocabulary in graduate school, before most of us were prepared to appreciate its full significance. We read, just after its publication, Hawley's *Human Ecology: A Theory of Community Structure* (1950). Lacking at that time any significant acquaintance with the literature of the biological sciences (beyond faint memories some may have had of a high school biology textbook studied a decade earlier), we were in no position to evaluate Hawley's usage of terms from bioecology. (For most social scientists this limitation probably persists throughout their careers; who has time for potentially profitable but seemingly inessential reading outside one's own discipline?)

Hawley (1950, pp. 36-41) defined symbiosis as "a mutual dependence between unlike organisms" and went on to give examples of the kinds of cooperative interactions between species that are regarded by biologists as mutualism. Then he pointed out that there are also "many less sanguinary expressions of symbiosis" and mentioned more one-sidedly exploitative relations such as parasitism. What was most likely to be retained from a first reading of Hawley was mainly a distinction he emphasized (whether we understood the distinction or not) between two words: "symbiosis" and "commensalism." In a later rereading, when ecological thoughtways had become more central to my own work, I focused on his statement that "symbiosis may occur *within* a species" (Hawley 1950, p. 41, emphasis added). The importance of this for my later view of sociocultural differentiation—as a counterpart among humans of speciation among other organisms—had been blunted previously by Hawley's additional (and initially confusing to me) statement that "commensalism often reaches across two or more species." When eventually the early confusion was overcome, I focused much later on the final point in the same paragraph: "the speciation of importance in ecological study is occupational rather than morphological." Clarity and cogency became manifest by having read in the meantime the book *Animal Ecology* by Charles Elton (1927) that had served Hawley as the basis for making these points.

Later still, in my own writing, I had come to define symbiosis as "mutual dependence of populations of differentiated organisms" (Catton 1980, p. 281), which is Hawley's definition except for substitution of "differentiated" in place of "unlike" so as to convey a sense that the unlikeness is due to evolutionary (or sociocultural) selection pressures. Although I never felt a need to embrace Hawley's emphasis on a symbiosis-versus-commensalism contrast, until recently I had continued to perceive symbiosis as essentially a bilateral relationship, characteristic only between some types of organisms and some particular other types. I had not seen it as a pervasive condition of life. I suspect most human ecologists (whatever social science discipline they may have come from) have also been accustomed to this narrower view of it. Despite a readiness to insist on the importance of symbiosis within one species (*Homo sapiens*), an idea drawn from Hawley that has profound significance for human ecology, I was altogether astonished to encounter in the Margulis and Sagan book the idea of *symbiosis within one microorganism*—and hence within all organisms consisting of eukaryotic cells.

From the central idea that "plastids and mitochondria represent bacteria that got trapped inside other bacteria" and by about 1.4 billion years ago had begun spreading around the world as "intertwined communities of cells-within-cells" (Margulis and Sagan 1986, p. 117), an amazing array of further insights and hypotheses arises. First, this symbiotic view liberates the mind from its common prejudice against bacteria as nothing but pathogens, to be destroyed whenever, wherever, and however possible. Second, it enables the mind to see previously unseen similarities, as when Margulis and Sagan (1986, p. 156) define sex in a biological sense as

> ... simply the union of genetic material from more than one source to produce a new individual. ... According to this strict definition, the passing of nucleic acid into a cell from a virus, bacterium, or any other source is sex. The transfer of genetic particles such as viruses among different bacteria is sex. The fusion of two human germ cell nuclei is sex. Even the infection of humans by an influenza virus is a sexual act in that genetic material inserts itself in our cells. Symbiosis is like sex in that the genetic materials of different individuals eventually join in the formation of a new individual.

The "new individual" formed by symbiosis may thus range from one eukaryotic cell to a very large biotic community. And the point of all this is not what "is" sex, or merely the relabeling of these various DNA-transfer phenomena with one three-letter word; the point is to note what a variety of ways there are in which information (genetic, at least—but also symbolic?) may be brought together from two or more sources to produce an effect unlike that wrought by information from a single source (cf. Barnett 1953, pp. 181-224; Hart 1959, pp. 200-216; Allen 1971, pp. 258-269).

It becomes apparent, too, that symbiosis and coevolution are two facets of the same intellectual jewel. Margulis and Sagan (1986, p. 244) put it this way:

> In coevolution over thousands of years partners change genetically. Inherited partnerships evolve together as new proteins and developmental patterns emerge. Ultimately the partners become totally dependent on each other, and it is no longer valid to consider them individuals.

FROM MICROSYMBIOSIS TO MACROSYMBIOSIS

In order fully to comprehend both the legitimacy and the abundant implications of this new idea of symbiogenesis, one needs to explore some literature not otherwise likely to have seemed relevant to human ecology or pertinent to a sociological interest in division of labor (e.g., Benton 1991; deWaal and Harcourt 1992; Fenchel and Finlay 1994; Grene 1987; Harcourt and deWaal 1992; Stenseth and Maynard Smith 1984). One may find it enlightening also to look up material on prokaryotes and eukaryotes as such (e.g., see Sagan 1967; Margulis 1974a; Asimov 1989, pp. 184-195; Taylor 1974; Vidal 1984; and Koshland 1993). But does the symbiogenesis theory of eukaryote origins really prove symbiosis is so omnipresent?

It seemed dramatically so to me, largely due to an insight that remained tantalizingly inchoate and accounts for the odd title of the present paper.[3] James Lovelock's (1979) *Gaia: A New Look at Life on Earth* came to mind as an apparent representation of the opposite end of a continuum of symbiosis. Before elaborating on this conception of a continuum and to forestall misunderstanding, Michael Allaby's *A Guide to Gaia: A Survey of the New Science of Our Living Earth* has an excellent chapter titled "The Earth is not a God." Allaby wonders "why people bother to seek the supernatural when the natural world ... [has] marvels enough to satisfy the most voracious spirit" (p. 114). Some people in our time tend to construe as a personification Lovelock's application of the Greek proper name "Gaia" to his view of Earth as a global homeostatic system. They take this supposed personification as an excuse for imagining (as Lovelock does not) that Earth is something one can pray to or hope to influence by ritual and persuasion. Allaby deplores this tendency.[4]

Margulis (1988, p. 50) has also explicitly disavowed "the formulation that says Gaia is an organism," and has concurred instead with the idea that "Gaia is an extremely complex system with identifiable regulatory properties which are very specific to the lower atmosphere."

I had first thought Lovelock's idea of the whole biosphere being like one big organism, capable of homeostatically maintaining conditions on this planet conducive to ongoing life an intriguing notion, but one that was not to be taken altogether seriously. As a sociologist I had been expected to absorb in graduate school the prescribed aversion to "the organic analogy" used by Herbert Spencer (and others in the nineteenth century) to describe human society (see Spencer [1873] 1961, pp. 301-302; for criticisms, see Brodbeck 1959, p. 380; House 1936, pp. 120-131; Timasheff 1967, p. 39). So how could regarding the biosphere as a super-organism be scientifically admissible?

The legitimacy and relevance of the Gaia hypothesis becomes clear from reading not only the assortment of writings by Margulis previously mentioned, but also an assortment of other writings by Lovelock (1972, 1987, 1988, 1989; Hitchcock and Lovelock 1967). The influence of these works is enhanced by another line of study which can largely offset that once-standard sociological aversion to views tainted by "organicism." Bioecology literature of recent times makes clear the idea that (from an ecological perspective) it is ecosystems that are nature's units. If one is persuaded that human ecology is best not separated from general ecology, one then tends to accept the idea that the ecosystem concept, as understood among biologists (not as it is often misunderstood by sociologists), would be as basic to human ecology as to the rest of the field of ecology.

The word "ecosystem" first appeared in 1935, coined by Arthur Tansley, and has since become modern ecology's most fundamental concept, as reflected in the findings of a survey of the British Ecological Society's members (Cherrett 1989).[5] Tansley, who had been the first BES president some two decades before putting forth this new term, meant it to denote a more comprehensive and integrative concept than the older notion of a biotic community (Tansley 1935). Further, he meant it to avoid difficulties he saw arising from the tendency to treat biotic communities as "super-organisms" (Tansley 1939). These having been Tansley's intentions, one need feel no trepidation about using the ecosystem concept in moving to a really succinct definition of ecology: Ecology should be regarded as *the study of ecosystems.*

That is to say, ecologists study *systems* of interactions among differentiated organisms as well as interactions between them and the nonliving components of their environment. Tansley's point was that these systems are truly integral. As systems, they comprise both living and nonliving components. Ecological studies necessarily consider energy flows and materials cycling through ecosystems.

In view of all this, *human* ecology could now be defined simply as *the study of ecosystems that involve humans.*[6] Even though ecosystems in which humans are involved may be extremely diverse, Tansley's insistence on conceiving them as integral systems of interaction among living and nonliving components should be kept in mind. First, there are, of course, ecosystems of which humans are a very dependent part. Second, there are also ecosystems dominated in varying degrees by humans. Third, among these there are ecosystems (or fragments of ecosystems, such as cities) so extensively human dominated that they tend to be misperceived as cases of complete human autonomy and self-sufficiency.[7]

Equipped with knowledge of the ecosystem concept as Tansley meant it, one is prepared to benefit from studying the works of Margulis and of Lovelock. Thus equipped, sociologists who work as human ecologists can put aside their trained aversion to "organicism." It really should not have been surprising to find Margulis and Lovelock citing each other in their respective writings. In both *Microcosmos* and *Gaia* there are explicit citations of work by the other book's author. Further, Lovelock and Margulis have even coauthored some papers (Margulis and Lovelock 1974, 1989; Lovelock and Margulis 1974). The clear implication of this intertwining of their publications and citations is that they fully intended the notion of a continuum of symbiotic interdependence extending all the way from microbes to the whole biosphere (and beyond?). Careful comparison of the respective discussions by Margulis and by Lovelock of the symbioses observable at both the extreme micro and extreme macro ends of a continuum reveals the relationship of their ideas to some of the more familiar advances in ecological thought—for example, Tansley's concept, and uses thereof, such as Bennett's (1976), which indicate its importance. Lovelock's idea of Gaia is basically Tansley's idea of ecosystem projected onto a larger screen. The Gaia theory puts abiotic and biotic components into the system together, mutually affecting each other, just as does the ecosystem concept. The Gaia theory more explicitly attributes homeostatic properties to the system; they remain somewhat more implicit in Tansley's concept, though in a condition of ecological climax the homeostasis was fully recognized.

My generation of sociologists was probably right, at first, to acquire an aversion to "the organic analogy" as a description of human society. But we now have the ecosystem concept and can begin to see how a human society functions as a subsystem of an ecosystem. The vocabulary was not yet available for Spencer to see it that way. For him the organic analogy probably did enable him to advance a considerable distance along the path toward comprehension of what Tansley's term later brought into sharp focus. Indeed, Spencer appears to have influenced ecologists as they developed the ecosystem concept (Golley 1993, pp. 25, 33, 36, 211). But the "society is an organism" analogy is not helpful now. Also not helpful now is the tendency to persist in separating human society from its context. Human society does need to be seen as an important subsystem (in symbiosis with the other parts) of an ecosystem.

Whether approached from the vantage point of biological science or from the vantage point of social science, that is the way to understand what human societies are and what they do. That way of viewing them could become both plausible and advantageous, however, only insofar as we have indeed advanced in five important ways:

1. beyond thinking of a society as an abstraction only, with individual persons considered more real;
2. beyond thinking of humans as exempted by culture from ecological principles that apply to other species;
3. beyond thinking of human communities as single-species entities rather than as multi-species biotic communities in which humans are involved and sometimes dominant;
4. beyond thinking of biotic communities as being in, but distinct from, their abiotic environments; and
5. beyond thinking the Earth just happens to be fortuitously a suitable habitat for life.

MULTILATERAL SYMBIOSIS, ABIOTIC SYMBIONTS

There is another important aspect of the kind of symbiosis Lovelock seems to have envisioned. It is multilateral. Traditionally, symbiosis has been discussed almost as if it were always merely bilateral, a relation between just two organisms or two species. Occasionally one may encounter instances of trilateral symbiosis, or instances where predator A preys alternatively on species B or C, so that there is (indirectly) a relationship between B and C. Lovelock, however, describes a biosphere in which the web of interactions works to maintain the conditions of the planet that will be suitable for life. But this goes even farther than just recognizing that symbiosis applies to the whole web, that it is profoundly multilateral. As Lovelock sees it, the concept of symbiosis applies both within the web of life and between it and the abiotic world. If the abiotic world not only shapes life but is shaped by it, he sees that as a symbiotic relation. Perhaps it stretches (or dodges) the literal meaning of the middle part of the word sym-bio-sis, but recognition of intimate, mutual, reciprocal influence (symbiosis) between the biota and the abiotic planet is another consistent step along the path Tansley sought to chart. As Allaby (1989, p. 96) sums it up, "Gaia is the name that has been given to the Earth seen as a system, to contrast it with the more usual sense of Earth seen as a planet."

Butler extended the status of symbiont to machines. Tansley gave the status of symbiont to all the abiotic components of an ecosystem. Lovelock, following in their footsteps, regarded the whole planet as a symbiont of the whole biota. Fundamentally, that is what the concept of biosphere has come to mean, whether or not one calls it Gaia (cf. Gates 1962; Vernadsky [1926] 1986). Enlarging the perspective, *The Symbiotic Universe* (Greenstein 1988) considers the way laws of physics are such as to have made life possible; had they been different in any of a number of imaginable ways, life would have been impossible on this planet or anywhere else.

Harvard's L.J. Henderson recognized, as a biological chemist, that the "fitness" of organisms considered by natural selection theory was a one-sided conception of a two-sided relationship. Not all conceivable worlds could have been "fitted to" by living things. So Henderson wrote of the other side, *The Fitness of the Environment* (1913). That idea is, in a sense, a reasonable extension of the niche concept.

Consider beavers. They make their environment fit for beaver living by building dams and lodges. But beavers build dams where there are streams, where the contour of the land is suitable, where there is timber of the right size available as dam material and lodge material and with bark suitable for beaver nutrition. So there is a fitness of some environments for beavers to make those environments more beaver-fit. If the trees beavers use are beaver-symbionts, so then is the stream. For, if water had different properties, that is, if the valences of hydrogen and oxygen were different, a stream would be unfit for beavers.

Thinking somewhat along those lines, then, for Greenstein (1988, p. 28) Henderson's idea meant there is "a gigantic symbiosis at work in the universe." It was, he said, different from the mutual interdependence of two organisms denoted by the word as ordinarily used in biology:

> The first partner in this new relationship is not an organism at all, but rather an inanimate structure: the physical universe as a whole. As for the second, it is alive but it is not any single organism. It is all organisms—life itself.

And between the two, he said, "there is a union."

Greenstein was quite serious. As he insisted (1988, p. 123), "Evolution cannot work in opposition to the laws of physics," and his aim was to elucidate the actual compatibility between the nature of life and the nature of the physical world. For present purposes, I need not attempt even a brief summary of the fascinating list of ways in which, as he explained in detail, life would have been precluded were physical principles, entities, and properties not what they in fact are. Suffice to say that his book provides some cogent examples of Earth system-behavior that lend strong credibility to Lovelock's Gaia concept (e.g., Greenstein 1988, p. 73):

> There is a sense in which the Earth as a whole sweats. After all, the bulk of its surface is covered with water—the oceans. In equatorial regions these oceans evaporate under the blaze of sunlight, and waft into the air as vapor. Thus the tropics are cooled. But the vapor so produced does not remain in the tropics. It drifts away from the equator, northward and southward into cooler regions. There it condenses into rain or snow, and just as energy is spent upon evaporating a liquid, so it is released when vapor condenses. Thus the colder regions of the Earth are warmed.

Clearly this process affects the distribution of life on the planet, and it would not happen if matter had no such property as "latent heat of vaporization."

SPACE AGE SYMBIOSIS: SENSE AND NONSENSE

If calling a book *The Symbiotic Universe* seems like the same sort of semantic inflation that led from "Miss America" beauty pageants to "Miss World" and "Miss Universe" contests, consider this other book title: *Cosmic Ecology* (Seielstad 1983). The fact that it bears a pretentious-sounding title need not preclude our finding in the book some sound statements of serious points,[8] quite pertinent to human ecology. Culture and cultural change are unavoidably important phenomena for human ecologists to consider, and the evolution of culture has never been, as Seielstad (1983, p. 145) reminds us, totally divorced from biological evolution:

> The rewards deriving from skill at exploiting available knowledge were so great that they created a selective pressure toward ever greater encephalization. Over time, *Homo sapiens* evolved into *Homo sapiens sapiens*.
>
> For this, however, a price was paid: specifically, the slowness of development of human children. No other species has such helpless offspring for so long a time. Years, if not decades, are required for the provision of adequate training and education. The other side of this is that the character, skills, and behavior of the adult individual are determined as much, or more, by this directed education as by inborn capabilities.

In this statement, Seielstad has touched on the explanation of how it is possible to have such ramified division of labor in human societies. The trade-off he described—between slowness of maturation and extent of educability—is the basis for the "quasi-speciation" mentioned earlier. Our species has two kinds of inheritance, genes (like other species) and culture (substantially distinctive of our species). A surprising and disturbing implication of this dual inheritance will be discussed later. For now, however, the quoted sentences should be seen by human ecologists as a correct representation of the biology-sociology interface. But Seielstad reverts to the hyperbolic tone of his book's title by saying that, as a result, "the possibilities for flexible behavior are endless." Not literally endless, of course, but the possibilities are indeed enormous.

Seielstad (1983, p. 156) also offers a cautionary statement, warning against anthropocentrism and disregard for where it could take us:

> Man is neither the measure of all things nor the source of all value. Terrestrially, he is not a biological necessity, but a luxury. He is not the end point of evolution but only its most recent product. He dare not dominate life on this planet but rather must coexist with it.

Many have believed otherwise in recent years. With the advent of space exploration, it became easy to suppose humankind was on the threshold of another prodigious evolutionary advance. Earth might be about to become merely our base camp, not our sole habitat. From the standpoint of a human ecologist, it seemed as if the opportunity to look back on the Earth from space might instill a fundamentally changed perspective about the biosphere, enabling people to see it more holistically than ever before. Could that be the experience that would eventually make Gaia theory seem obvious instead of far-fetched? As restated after years of further study by Margulis and Lovelock (1989, p. 1), doesn't it begin to sound almost unquestionable?

> The Gaia hypothesis ... in its most general form, states that the temperature and composition of the Earth's surface are actively regulated by the sum of life on the planet—the biota. Major aspects of the Earth's surface are dynamically maintained in frantic stability. That is, as changes in the gas composition, temperature, or oxidation state are induced by astronomical, biological, or other perterbation, the biota responds to these changes by growth and metabolism. The biological responses, taken together, serve to ameliorate the changes. This regulation of the Earth's surface activities by the biota and for the biota has been in continuous existence since the earliest appearance of widespread life—for at least 3 billion years.

It was probably something like an expectation that this would become a standard "worldview" in the space age that led to Frank White's (1987) book, *The Overview Effect*, whose subtitle announced it was about "Space Exploration and Human Evolution." In the prologue, White (p. xviii) stated the book's thesis as the idea that we space-age humans

> are not simply reaching out into space to use extraterrestrial resources and opportunities here on Earth. Rather, we are laying the foundations for a series of new civilizations that are the next logical steps in the evolution of human society and human consciousness.

That idea is also implicit in the description by Sagan (1990, pp. 31-32) of the unmanned spacecraft that landed on Mars in 1976 and sent back pictures of the Martian surface: the Viking Lander was "a tentacle of the Earth feeling out its environment [another planet] through the agency of one of its most ambitious representatives, humankind." The camera "itself represents the arrival of the life for which [the expedition to Mars was] seeking."

Sagan's book was about "biospheres" (plural)—not the biosphere, but small, self-contained and sealed, partial replicas of it. The expensive glass enclosure in Arizona in which a number of people calling themselves "Biospherians" have been enclosed for a time is an example. These experimental entities are designed to maintain within themselves an ecological balance so as to be self-sustaining with only solar energy as the input continuing after closure. According to Sagan, they are prototypes for enclosed and self-sustaining ecosystems that will someday voyage into space as devices for establishing human colonies on other planets. As such, they would represent a kind of "reproduction" of the Earthly biosphere, signifying, says Sagan (1990, pp. 16-17), "a certain maturity of life." This view sees technology as "natural" and "part of the evolutionary process itself."

Such ideas are being seriously pursued. The president of the Space Studies Institute, Gerard K. O'Neill, wrote the "Foreword" to *The Overview Effect* (White 1987). In it, people working to achieve the establishment of permanent human colonies elsewhere in space—"the breakout from planet Earth"—were said to be hoping for three "vital consequences" (O'Neill 1987, p. xiv):

> First, it will make human life forever unkillable, removing it from the endangered species list, where it now stands on a fragile Earth overarmed with nuclear weapons. Second, the opening of virtually unlimited new land area in space will reduce territorial pressures and therefore diminish warfare on Earth itself. Third, the small scale of space colonies, the largest some tens of thousands of people, will lead to local governments that are simple in form, responsive to the desires of their people, and as reachable and intimate as were the New England town meetings of America's heritage.

What are human ecologists to make of the serious advocacy of space colonization as the means of attaining these three objectives?

Assuming attainment in the reasonable future of technological competence to indulge in extraterrestrial colonization, only the first objective stated by O'Neill even begins to make ecological sense. By dispersing itself into many localities, any species population reduces its vulnerability to extinction (as a species), as any local catastrophe could then not wipe out more than a local subpopulation. Dispersal does not protect individual members of the species population from continuing exposure to whatever risks pertain to the places into which dispersal has taken them. But space colonization is hardly necessary. Barring complete overwhelming of the homeostatic capacities of Gaia, the extent to which *Homo sapiens* has already become dispersed to all continents and major islands of this world suffices to guarantee survival of at least a relict population after any "ordinary" catastrophe, even a nuclear war. The survivors could conceivably be only a very small fraction of the present 5.5 billion, but those who made it through such a demographic bottleneck would proceed to repopulate the planet. The need to adapt by vastly different ways of living to a drastically changed set of environmental conditions they would face after the catastrophe could hardly be greater than the stringent requirements of space travel.

The second hoped-for effect is utterly chimerical. No matter how successful NASA or its Russian counterpart may be in implanting human colonies someday somewhere else in the galaxy, this will not "reduce territorial pressures" on Earth. It is appallingly fanciful to suppose extraterrestrial emigration will ever occur on a scale sufficient to do that. The temptation to think in terms of historical analogy, with European emigration to "the New World" as a model of release from population pressure, is grossly misleading, as even a little indulgence in careful quantitative reasoning would reveal. The current annual increment of Earth's human population is close to 90 million. Assume that we could soon build space ships large enough to accommodate 15 times as many emigrants as the number of astronauts who now go briefly aloft in an American space shuttle. With craft that large—and expensive, both monetarily and in fuel consumption—it would still require a million such launchings a year to export the total natural increase. Human ecologists can safely predict this will not happen.

Assume these spacecraft could be propelled not just into near-Earth orbit like today's space shuttles but could attain escape velocity and never return to Earth—thereby "reducing territorial pressures" for us stay-behind Earthlings. To what destinations would the emigrants be sent? One of the facts of physics cited by Greenstein (1988, p. 255) as having been essential for life to have been possible was the remarkable "emptiness" of the universe, that is, the enormous distances between stars. Only thus was it possible for there to be planetary systems around some stars. But this makes it a totally forlorn hope to relieve population pressure on Earth by emigration to some other (as yet undiscovered) solar system beyond our own. Within our own solar system, Mercury is too close to the sun for realistic consideration as a colony. The large outer planets are either without solid surfaces, too distant from the sun to receive sufficient energy for life, or anyway much too massive (with bone-breaking gravity) for colonization. Suppose, however, the artificial "biospheres" could be transported to the Moon, to Venus, or to Mars, and that by high technology and prodigious efforts the first "pioneers" could begin to transform those inhospitable environments into conditions within which larger numbers of later colonists could actually live. Remember that the Gaia theory does suggest present forms of life could not exist on Earth itself were it not for the way its temperature, its atmospheric composition, and so forth, have already been transformed by past and present biota. Assuming comparably enormous transformations could be wrought on the three reachable planetary bodies soon enough so that the annual population increments-needing-to-be-exported were still under 100 million—a fantastic assumption—how long, then, would it be before that "additional territory" was populated as heavily as the Earth is already?

Apart from the fact that the answer has to be "Not so very long," the per capita energy cost of accelerating human emigrants from Earth to escape velocity, together with their per capita share of a life support system that could survive the acceleration and the airlessness of outer space, together with fuel enough for a soft landing on the hypothetical destination planet—all this energy would far exceed the energy content of a lifetime supply of food here on Earth for that individual. So massive pressure-relieving extraterrestrial emigration will not happen.

None of the above says *Homo sapiens* will never establish colonies on extraterrestrial bodies. What it says, simply, is that any such colonies can never alleviate the condition of overshoot here on Earth. The temptation to believe there can be a space age replication of the relief Europe experienced by sending excess population to "the New World" is based on total failure to do simple arithmetic. Human ecologists should not be guilty of that failure. The distance from Europe to colonizable places in the second hemisphere was only thousands of times greater than the distances familiarly traversed in ordinary daily routines by preindustrial Europeans, and emigration across an ocean did not have to overcome Earth's gravity. The distances to be traversed by extraterrestrial emigrants would be at least millions of times greater than the distances we travel even in our present more frenzied daily routines of industrial living. Europeans emigrating across oceans had to accomplish an "escape velocity" not appreciably different from the speeds of ordinary daily movements; to leave Earth our space-age emigrants would have to accelerate (at prodigious cost in energy expenditure) to seven miles per second!

The third hoped-for effect mentioned by O'Neill, reduction of scale and revival of town-meeting democracy, represents an admirable aspiration that may indeed be a condition congenial to most human ecologists. But it is utterly inconsistent to suppose so massive an undertaking as the launching of a million super-shuttles per year could be mounted by an industrial system and a political regime dedicated to small scale, simple, intimate democracy. Goals 2 and 3 are flatly contradictory with respect to each other.

FALLING OUT AMONG SYMBIONTS

All this aside, the technological optimism at the heart of Sagan's (1990) enthusiasm about Gaian "reproduction" by manmade biospheres begs two vital questions: Can homeostasis fail? Can symbiosis break down? It is important for human ecology to consider the possibility that the answers to both questions may be affirmative.

Various authors already cited have acknowledged past challenges to the biotic homeostasis envisioned in the Gaia theory, challenges enormous enough to have required replacement of the previous biota by evolution of drastically changed biota capable of maintaining a new and very different environmental steady state. But what about the "reproduction" of existing biota through colonization of new habitat not altogether unlike the old? We need not venture into outer space (even by imagination) to find well-studied instances. As already noted, *Homo sapiens* is well dispersed to virtually all regions of the Earth, and people have taken with them many symbionts as they colonized places far from the point of human origin (Crosby 1986). Have past examples of ecosystem replication by human migrants included any failures? More to the point, have any such failures been of a kind that would serve as warning of possible failure of Gaia-like homeostasis?

The answer is clearly affirmative, and Easter Island is a prime example. To the small band of emigrants from some overpopulated Polynesian island elsewhere in the central Pacific Ocean, this forested volcanic island was, together with the immediately adjacent waters, all the world there was for them after they landed with a starter flock of chickens, some plantable kumaras, and so forth. In a thousand years their proliferating descendants completely deforested Easter Island, depleted its other vegetation, presumably causing serious soil erosion as a result, and a deteriorating fresh water supply. From such destruction of the life support system that had enabled them to prosper there followed cultural collapse and a momentous population crash, occurring as aftermath of high cultural florescence (see Bahn and Flenley [1992] for detailed evidence from decades of archaeological research). That this should be a warning to the larger world was explicitly pointed out by Mulloy (1974). For other warning examples, see Tainter (1988).

As to ways symbiosis can break down, the discovery that eukaryotic cells had their origin in microendosymbiosis sheds new light on what had been a mere metaphor, and a pejorative one at that. The human "population explosion" since World War II has been called a "cancer." Calling it that may have seemed at first only a means of casting aspersions on opponents of birth control or of efforts to limit growth. Even sophisticated sources such as Lovelock (1979, p. 139) treated the metaphor as just a metaphor, its implications supposedly overcome by Gaian homeostatic renewal:

> Not so long ago it seemed that mankind was like a cancer on this planet. We had apparently severed the feedback loops of pestilence and famine which regulated our numbers. We were growing unrestrictedly at the expense of the rest of the biosphere and at the same time our industrial pollution and chemically contrived antibiotic agents like DDT were poisoning those few remaining creatures that we had not deprived of their habitats.

Lovelock went on to cite hopeful signs that the problem was beginning to subside. It could still be doubted, however, that the "explosive" growth had started to subside soon enough for the already attained load to be sustainable (Postel 1994), or whether it would subside fast enough to prevent an Easter Island-like collapse as its denoument, or whether rapid subsiding of growth could itself be tolerated by parts of the system (i.e., national economies) adapted to ongoing growth (Daly 1994).

Twenty-four years prior to Lovelock's attempt to dismiss the metaphor, Alan Gregg (1955) had used it seriously, writing about "A Medical Aspect of the Population Problem," and developing some specific details of the ways population growth resembles cancer. His premise was that the differences and interdependencies among the Earth's flora and fauna are analogous to the relations among different types of cells in an organism. Proceeding with this newly invoked "organic analogy," he suggested we "consider the living world as an organism" (p. 681). (Gregg considered the analogy only a "scaffolding" which might serve, but need not be part of, "the final structure of established fact." In this instance, it would call attention to interesting parallels between "growth of the human population of the world and the increase of cells observable in neoplasms.") The parallels can be summarized as follows:

1. Pressure is exerted by the new growths on adjacent structures, which may get displaced.
2. The new growths may be invasive—as reflected on the human population level by deforestation, increased extinctions through loss of habitat, soil erosion.
3. Colonization is like metastasis.
4. "Our rivers run silt," like the bleeding that announces cancer.

Gregg's justification for using the analogy was the conviction that even a bizarre hypothesis can lead to truth, whether true itself or not, depending on how it is used. He was convinced that biology might benefit if this metaphor helped emancipate it from anthropocentrism.

Decades later the "bizarre hypothesis" was again seriously considered by someone in an unusually favorable position to understand its nuances, a man trained in both anthropology and medicine. He has written two remarkable papers that present reasoning in support of the idea that the human species has become *Homo ecophagus* and is devouring the ecosystem. Humanity has taken on the precise characteristics of "a malignant epiecopathologic process engaged in the conversion of all planetary material into human biomass or its support system with coincident terminal derangement of the global ecosystem" (Hern 1990, p. 35; see also Hern 1993). As "malignant characteristics of the human species" Hern (1990, pp. 22-31) discussed detailed comparisons of malignant tumors and human populations. See Table 1.

Table 1. Comparisons Between Malignant Tumors
and Human Populations

Malignant Tumors	Human Species
Rapid, uncontrolled growth	Rapid population growth
Metastasis	Colonization, urbanization
De-differentiation (of cells)	Adaptability through culture (without biological differentiation)
Invasion and destruction of adjacent normal tissues	Ecological destruction by most human societies; now threatens global ecosystems
Grows in spite of host starvation until host dies	?

When I first read Hern's 1990 paper, I felt some misgivings, wondering whether pursuing this version of the organic analogy would really accomplish anything more than to provide a potentially useful way of stigmatizing population growth and environmentally unsound practices. But it is doubtful whether many human reproducers contributing to the 90 million annual global increment would curtail their (our) contributions by internalizing such ideas as "global malignant ecotumor" or "planetary ecopathological process." Even when Hern (1990, p. 33) claimed that his hypothesis "that the human species is a global malignant neoplasm ... does provide a unifying explanation of a wide variety of events and phenomena" I still wondered whether it explained or merely characterized.

Explain *is* the correct term, especially given the additional analogy one could draw between culture and a virus. If human evolution has involved dual inheritance (genetic and cultural), is it inevitably going to have results that resemble what happens to an organism whose DNA gets disrupted by alien DNA from a viral infection? By "the human species," Hern seemed to be referring to that portion of the global biota in which and through which the new form of inheritance (culture) comes into interaction with the old form (DNA). Could that interaction account for humanity displaying the four main characteristics of a malignant neoplasm?

Explanation often means adducing knowledge that makes what was unexpected, without the knowledge, expected with it. Consider a simple example: Things that are dropped fall. The child knows this. But the child's father rubs a balloon on his sweater and holds the balloon over his head and lets it go. The balloon does not fall to the floor; it sticks to the ceiling—much to the child's astonishment (the first time, anyway). The father explains by stating some simple version of principles of electrical attraction, and asserting the fact that rubbing the balloon on his sweater produced a charge of static electricity which sufficed to overcome gravity by attracting the balloon to the nearby ceiling—making expected the otherwise unexpected violation of the familiar principle that things dropped will fall.

If that is what explanation amounts to, and if we find it astonishing that an intelligent species (*Homo sapiens*, intelligent by definition) would destroy the ecosystem on which it depends, perhaps the comparison with cancer does at least *lead to* an explanation. The question to be addressed is this: How did *Homo sapiens* become transformed into *Homo ecophagus*? The short answer might seem to be: By industrializing. A better but subtler answer may be: By fulfilling the potential inherent in being a culture-bearing species.

To explicate the answer, it becomes relevant for human ecologists to consider literature on the biology of cancer, not just to understand modern changes in human mortality rates, but for clues about how symbiosis can break down. Here is one suggestive statement from a chapter titled "The Cellular Basis of Cancer" in Prescott and Flexer (1982, p. 27ff, emphasis added):

> The misfunctions characteristic of cancer cells are fundamentally different from the misfunctions that occur in other diseases. In almost all other diseases, the misfunction stems from the injury or death of normal cells. Bacteria that cause tuberculosis, for example, destroy lung cells, ... polio viruses destroy nerve cells, and hepatitis viruses destroy liver cells.
>
> Cancer cells, by contrast, are not injured, nor are they dying, nor do they directly destroy other cells. They are, by most criteria, remarkably healthy. Cancer cells have two important properties that underlie the nature of the disease. First, cancer cells grow and divide with less restraint, whereas growth and division of normal cells are closely regulated. Second, *cancer cells do not differentiate normally* and therefore do not perform their normal functions in the body. In particular, cancer cells do not die on schedule. Eventually, the resulting overgrowth of misfunctioning cells interferes in some way with the activities of normal cells and tissues.

Elsewhere, Prescott and Flexer (p. 77, emphasis added) make an important statement about the way a normal cell is converted to a cancerous state:

> ... cancer is transmitted from cell to cell through cell division. In particular, the conversion of a normal cell to the cancerous state consists of a heritable defect in the normal controls over a cell's reproduction *and differentiation.*

To have read these statements without having begun to learn about endosymbiosis and eukaryotic cells, they would have had little meaning for human ecology. But Margulis and Sagan give them human ecological meaning (1986, p. 148, emphasis added):

> The body is totalitarian in its regulation of genes. Once a cell becomes a muscle cell, for example, it is so forever. The only exception to this rule of permanent roles within the body is during cancer, when cells seem to revert back to the more primordial condition of reproducing continuously without regard to their place or function in the body. During cancer, chromosomes break apart and *mitochondria reproduce even more rapidly than the cells of which they are a part.* ... It is as if the uneasy alliances of the symbiotic partnerships that maintain cells disintegrate. *The symbionts fall out of line,* once again asserting their independent tendencies, reliving their ancient past.

So, breakdown of symbiosis can be serious. It can happen between the microscopic symbionts that make up eukaryotic cells. It can happen between larger symbionts; it can even happen between large conspecific symbionts— that is, between interdependent human beings. It used to be called social disorganization (Faris 1948), a term that fell into some disfavor when sociologists were perhaps too inclined to be uncritically relativisitic (e.g., see, Martindale 1957). Perhaps a portion of the ecological peril of our time should be understood as a breaking down of symbiosis between humans and our technological symbionts, as well as our fellow human symbionts, and living symbionts of other species.

FROM MUTUALISM TO PREDATION

It is because human beings live interdependently that such precepts as "honesty is the best policy" and "thou shalt not covet, steal, etc." are important cultural norms. But despite (or, in a way, because of) our interdependence, there are pressures that can break down such norms. If division of labor makes us interdependent, it also turns up the pressure to exploit each other.[9] To be interdependent is to be not self-sufficient. It is to cast the incumbents of specialties other than one's own in the role of resources. To the vendor of any product or service, all other humans are potential customers. That is to say, in a society with a highly ramified division of labor, there is pressure on everyone to look upon others as walking billfolds whose "function" is to be available for cash extraction (Blumberg 1989). By no means does everyone in a complex society consciously regard all others that way, but the structure of modern societal life means the pressure to respond that way to others is there.

As one technique of exploitation consider the bearing of false witness. This is not an exclusively human sin. Another word for it is *deception*, and deception occurs elsewhere in the biotic world. Whenever the life of one organism depends on another, the one has reason to manipulate (if possible) the other's actions. The predator has reason to attract prey; the prey organism has reason to escape its predator. If either task can be facilitated by some induced misperception in the other, evolution would tend to result in possession of traits or behavioral tendencies that can deceive. Camouflage may make it harder for the predator to find the protectively colored prey—or the deceptively colored predator may be harder for the prey to discern and avoid. There are human equivalents, and they need to be understood in this ecological perspective, getting past the tendency to view them in moral terms. They are expectable responses to circumstances analogous to those that produce deceptive traits or practices in nonhumans.

The most important conclusion of the nineteenth-century British naturalist, Henry Walter Bates, is said to have been his finding that in the Amazon forests where there lived brightly colored butterflies the birds found unpalatable, unrelated butterflies that were palatable to avian predators were also present and had strikingly similar coloring. As Bates inferred, the similarity of appearance had evolved as a means by which the palatable species could evade predation (Owen 1980, p. 115). Batesian mimicry—a pattern of "saying" to a potential predator "I'm unpalatable" (when it may not be so)—was recognized as evidence supporting Darwin's theory of natural selection. As long as the palatable mimics were not too numerous to spoil the conditioned aversive response by predators to the unpalatable models, mimicry worked. Mimics with less resemblance to models would have a lower rate of survival than mimics with greater resemblance; natural selection occurred.

But recognition of the importance of deception between species goes back at least to the sixth century B.C. We get the image of "a wolf in sheep's clothing" from one of Aesop's fables. In that imaginary case, the disguise was an aid to predation. It was the predator who took on a deceptive appearance. There are actual instances of predatory deception in the animal kingdom that closely resemble this fictitious one. In the United States, two species of firefly afford a striking example. The flashing of the firefly's light ordinarily has to do with mate attraction. Females of one species can imitate the flash code of another so as to attract males of the other species—to be eaten (Owen 1980, p. 123). A female of species A obtains sustenance by appearing to offer sex to male of species B; the so-called "oldest profession" is not exclusively human.[10]

Among humans, the almost explicit exploitation of what sociologists call primary group relationships is symptomatic of the gravitation of American society toward unthinking acceptance of the Coolidge dictum ("The business of America is business"); for example, exploitation (or simulation) of personal relationships in Amway merchandising, the sale of Mary Kay cosmetics by "home beauty consultations" (Sobel and Sicilia 1986, pp. 38-41), and Tupperware-selling parties.

What makes this "pseudo-Gemeinschaft" (Merton 1968, p. 163) of interest to human ecology is the fact that it is a form of human deception practiced for reasons that are broadly equivalent to the reasons for deception in interspecific interactions. Many forms of deceptive communication are endemic in modern society. Some of us remember the delicious irony of the photograph showing President Truman gleefully holding aloft the *Chicago*

Tribune with its banner headline proclaiming "Dewey Defeats Truman" on the morning after his 1948 re-election. To scoff at the *Tribune's* partisan editors for having allowed early returns from Republican precincts to confirm their wishful expectations regarding the election's outcome, however, is to miss the real point. A subtle lie was involved, but one that is deeply institutionalized in the American economy. The date on that issue of the *Tribune* was for the day *after* it was actually printed. That practice of postdating is so customary in the periodical publishing industry that writers of news articles (or headlines) commonly must feign hindsight about events that have not yet happened. This famous false headline was one instance of that. Why are publications postdated? To keep them salable longer, by preventing prospective buyers from concluding, while unsold copies remain, that they contain only "old news" and are not worth buying. Postdating is considered, apparently, a reasonable means of extracting money from those walking billfolds.

If the exigencies of interdependence can exert pressure toward predatory deception among human conspecific symbionts, it is clear that mutualistic symbiosis can break down. If humans can learn to regard other humans as exploitable resources (in many ways far short of, and more subtle than, mere slavery), it is little wonder that a similar attitude toward nonhumans (and hence toward the entire biosphere) has such prevalence. So even the multilateral omnisymbiosis of Gaia is precarious, now that human population has become so great a part of Earth's biota—and especially now that so much of the human population is aided and abetted in its exploitation of the biosphere by powerful technological symbionts. Terminal derangement of a global ecosystem is possible, and there are many signs that such a destiny is ahead on the trajectory our cultural florescence has put us onto. It seems that industrialism and the ecological concept of a homeostatic climax are antithetical.[11]

LIGHT AT THE END OF THE TUNNEL?

Even Herbert Spencer went out of his way to enumerate differences as well as parallels between human society and an organism. It is the principal difference between humans and cancer cells that must give whatever hope there is for Gaia to avoid the terminal derangement Hern foresees as human population goes on growing and further metastasizes. The difference is: humans can think, cancer cells cannot. If humans think clearly enough about all the differences between beneficial mutualism among *Homo sapiens sapiens* and devil-may-care predation among *Homo ecophagus*, and act on that knowledge, we may have a future.

It is up to human ecologists to assist the required clear thinking. There should be carefully designed studies seeking to ascertain the conditions under which mutualistic relations degenerate into parasitic and predatory relations between conspecifics, as well as toward other symbionts. Human ecologists must be prepared to study ecosystems (in which humans are variously involved) of greatly varied magnitude—from intensely local to global. The fact that the various kinds of symbiosis can be highly multilateral needs to be a keynote of human ecological research and theory-building. Insofar as human ecologists hold an evolutionary perspective, it is important to bear in mind that a given species is shaped not only by selection pressures operating directly on it but also by selection pressures operating on other species populations that constitute the organic portion of its environment. We are shaped by the forces that shape our symbionts. Coevolution (as well as symbiosis) is multilateral. If Earth is a self-regulating system, and if each of the constituent species populations in its biosphere has a more or less specifiable carrying capacity, the various carrying capacities for the several species must have some determinable quantitative relation to each other. To ask what is the carrying capacity of the Earth, or some portion of the Earth, for one species (such as *Homo sapiens*) without considering simultaneously the carrying capacities for its various symbiont species is to ask an unanswerable question. That does not render the key concept, carrying capacity, meaningless; it just means it has to be used with more sophistication. What if one population gets "out of control" and overshoots its carrying capacity? What happens then to the various other populations in variously symbiotic relations with the one that "became cancerous?"

The Gaia hypothesis takes the biosphere to be a climax ecosystem, with the various processes characteristic of the biosphere's components being mutually offsetting so as to maintain an approximately steady state (globally). Was Gaia in anything like a Clementsian climax before humans had begun their industrial revolution? Can it be now? If industrialism has taken the biosphere out of climax, what kind of seral stage is it in, and what is the character of the sere along which industrialism is propelling it? What might the next "climax" attained by Gaian homeostasis look like?

Is hubris endemic to the human species? Of all the traits social philosophers have singled out to distinguish humans from other animals, has hubris been given its due? Is it as dangerous as implied in current ecological writing, is it the key to relevance of the "ecophagus" cancer model, and is there an antidote that would be tolerable?

Finally, can consideration of a continuum of symbiosis ranging all the way from microbes to a Gaian planetary biosphere serve as an antidote to a tendency of cautious scholars to undergeneralize? Professional aversion to overgeneralizing is taught in graduate study in many fields. It has doubtless served each of the social sciences, and human ecology, admirably heretofore. But we also undergeneralize, and we seem not to have developed a comparable aversion to that. We undergeneralize when we perceive human problems always as uniquely human, failing to recognize their counterparts occurring among nonhuman populations. It is all too common, for example, to imagine today's human woes are rooted in politics and can be solved politically, or that they have simplistically economic explanations and would yield to economic remedies. Comparative studies should remind us that much of what humans do and much that happens to humans is as it is because we are somewhat like other animals. Like them, our lives happen within ecosystems, our destinies have ecosystemic causes. There is not only no need to separate human ecology from mainstream ecology. There is nothing to be gained by intellectual Balkanization.

NOTES

1. The idea of conspecific symbionts has its most obvious example in human marriage, where the partners, with their more or less differentiated roles, interact mutualistically. Sociologists have dignified the ecological aspect of this relationship with a theory of mate selection based on "complementary needs." But also see Spencer (1844) and Brooks (1970).

2. Two decades before encountering any symbiogenesis literature, I had been teaching sociology in New Zealand, where I became interested in Samuel Butler's ideas on evolution partly because Butler had spent several years in that country raising sheep at the very time Darwin's book was redirecting biological science. Butler had read Darwin's book just after it came out. He commented on it (quite perceptively and favorably) in an early issue of *The Christchurch Press*, the leading South Island newspaper (to which I subscribed more than a century later). The more I subsequently learned about Butler's writings, the more tragic a figure he seemed.

3. Occurrence of that insight in initial vagueness also demonstrates the often-neglected fact that even purposive reading by scholars can sometimes resemble sleepwalking. That is to say, we may follow the right course of reading and make correct use of what we read without knowing the constraints and intuitions that guided us (Catton 1966, pp. 113-115). In my first quick reading of *Microcosmos*, somehow I paid no attention to its citations of Lovelock's *Gaia*, even though I had once skimmed that book, whose previously underappreciated relevance would begin to loom in my thinking afterwards as I pondered implications of the theme put forward by Margulis and Sagan. Anyone's vague notions of Lovelock's theory could be clouded by impressions derived from having heard him talk about it on television a time or two. At any rate, having made a mental association between the Margulis-Sagan idea of microendosymbiosis and the Lovelock idea of Gaian global homeostasis, I was chagrined to find that I was surprised (in rereading) to find these authors citing each other.

4. I, too, deplore the tendency. That was not the way Lovelock's theory appeared to me, and such mysticism has nothing to do with my present effort to discuss a continuum of symbiosis from the microscopic eukaryotic cell to the macroscopic biosphere.

5. According to Golley (1993, p. 75), the ecosystem concept had "become an organizing idea in American, if not international, ecology" by the mid-1960s. Golley also cites a comment (p. 166) by Sheail (1987) to the effect that most recent British Ecological Society presidents, whether or not they had personally done ecosystem research, made reference to the ecosystem perspective in their presidential addresses.

6. Human ecology has to be more than what too many social scientists had been taught to suppose it was—studies of spatial distributions of various social indicators (as plotted on city maps, mainly).

7. Becoming acquainted with Tansley's integral notion of an ecosystem ought to remedy this latter misperception, all too characteristic even now of social science literature.

8. Even the Miss Universe contests, despite their hyperbolous title, do display some genuine examples of female pulchritude.

9. As Durkheim ([1893] 1984, p. 304) said, "...if the division of labour does not produce solidarity it is because the relationships between the organs [of society; i.e., the socioculturally differentiated specialists] are not regulated; it is because they are in a state of anomie."

10. Many of Aesop's fables depicted interactions between individuals of different species. Although anthropomorphised for the stories, which were told to convey some moral principle or bit of folk wisdom, Aesop's animals often reflected real ecological relationships. Often one party to the interaction was a predator and the other was its typical prey. But there was implicit awareness of each species having its specific niche. Aesop told, for example, of a crab "forsaking the seashore" and choosing to forage in a green meadow. The point of the story was the uncrablikeness of this behavior. A hungry fox came along and devoured the crab, but just before being eaten the crab was said to have recognized that its fate was self-inflicted "for what business had I on the land, when by my nature and habits I am only adapted for the sea?" (Townsend 1968, p. 130). If any astrologer ever reads this paper, he or she may enjoy the coincidence of Aesop's use of the crab ("cancer") to represent the hazards of "de-differentiation"—getting out of its assigned niche or role.

11. The modern jargon speaks of "sustainability." Hardin (1993, p. 325) deplores coinage of the phrase "sustainable development" as a device by which "the defenders of the unsteady-state have won a few more years moratorium from the painful process of thinking."

REFERENCES

Allaby, M. 1989. *A Guide to Gaia: A Survey of the New Science of Our Living Earth.* New York: E.P. Dutton.

Allen, F.R. 1971. *Socio-Cultural Dynamics: An Introduction to Social Change.* New York: Macmillan.

Asimov, I. 1989. *Beginnings: The Story of Origins–Of Mankind, Life, the Earth, the Universe.* New York: Berkeley Books.

Bahn, P. and J. Flenley. 1992. *Easter Island, Earth Island.* London: Thames & Hudson.

Barnett, H.G. 1953. *Innovation: The Basis of Cultural Change.* New York: McGraw-Hill.

Bennett, J.W. 1976. *The Ecological Transition: Cultural Anthropology and Human Adaptation.* New York: Pergamon Press.

Benton, T. 1991. "Biology and Social Science: Why the Return of the Repressed Should Be Given a (Cautious) Welcome." *Sociology* 25(February): 1-29.

Beus, C.E. 1993. "Sociology, Human Ecology, and Ecology." Pp. 93-132 in *Advances in Human Ecology*, Vol. 2, edited by L. Freese. Greenwich, CT: JAI Press.

Blumberg, P. 1989. *The Predatory Society: Deception in the American Marketplace.* New York: Oxford University Press.

Brodbeck, M. 1959. "Models, Meaning, and Theories." Pp. 373-403 in *Symposium on Sociological Theory*, edited by L. Gross. Evanston, IL: Row, Peterson.

Brooks, M.A. 1970. "Symbiosis." Pp. 912-914 in *The Encyclopedia of the Biological Sciences*, edited by P. Gray. New York: Van Nostrand Reinhold Co.

Catton, W.R. Jr. 1966. *From Animistic to Naturalistic Sociology.* New York: McGraw-Hill.

————. 1980. *Overshoot: The Ecological Basis of Revolutionary Change.* Urbana: University of Illinois Press.

————. 1987. "The World's Most Polymorphic Species: Carrying Capacity Transgressed Two Ways." *BioScience* 37(June): 413-419.

————. 1992. "Separation versus Unification in Sociological Human Ecology." Pp. 65-99 in *Advances in Human Ecology*, Vol. 1, edited by L. Freese. Greenwich, CT: JAI Press.

Cherrett, J.M. 1989. "Key Concepts: The Results of a Survey of Our Members' Opinions." Pp. 1-6 in *Ecological Concepts: The Contribution of Ecology to an Understanding of the Natural World*, edited by J.M. Cherrett. Oxford: Blackwell Scientific Publications.

Crosby, A.W. 1986. *Ecological Imperialism: The Biological Expansion of Europe, 900-1900*. New York: Cambridge University Press.

Daly, H.E. 1994. "Sustainable Growth: An Impossibility Theorem." *Carrying Capacity Network Clearinghouse Bulletin* 4(April): 1-2,4,7.

deWaal, F.B.M., and A.H. Harcourt. 1992. "Coalitions and Alliances: A History of Ethological Research." Pp. 1-19 in *Coalitions and Alliances in Humans and Other Animals*, edited by A.H. Harcourt and F.B.M. deWaal. New York: Oxford University Press.

Duncan, O.D. 1959. "Human Ecology and Population Studies." Pp. 678-716 in *The Study of Population: An Inventory and Appraisal*, edited by P.M. Hauser and O.D. Duncan. Ann Arbor: University of Michigan Press.

————. 1961. "From Social System to Ecosystem." *Sociological Inquiry* 31(Spring): 140-149.

Durkheim, E. (1893) 1984. *The Division of Labor in Society*. Translated by W.D. Halls. New York: The Free Press.

Elton, C. 1927. *Animal Ecology*. New York: Macmillan.

Espinas, A. 1878. *Des Societes Animales: Etude de Psychologie Comparee*. Paris: Librarie Germer Balliere. (Reprinted in 1924 by Stechert, Hafner, New York.)

Faris, R.E.L. 1948. *Social Disorganization*. New York: The Ronald Press Co.

Fenchel, T. and B.J. Finlay. 1994. "The Evolution of Life Without Oxygen." *American Scientist* 82(January-February): 22-29.

Gates, D.M. 1962. *Energy Exchange in the Biosphere*. New York: Harper & Row.

Golley, F.B. 1993. *A History of the Ecosystem Concept in Ecology*. New Haven, CT: Yale University Press.

Greenstein, G. 1988. *The Symbiotic Universe: Life and Mind in the Cosmos*. New York: William Morrow and Co.

Gregg, A. 1955. "A Medical Aspect of the Population Problem." *Science* 121(13 May): 681-682.

Grene, M. 1987. "Hierarchies in Biology." *American Scientist*, 75(September-October): 504-510.

Harcourt, A.H. and F.B.M. deWaal. 1992. "Cooperation in Conflict: From Ants to Anthropoids." Pp. 493-510 in *Coalitions and Alliances in Humans and Other Animals*, edited by A.H. Harcourt and F.B.M. deWaal. New York: Oxford University Press.

Hardin, G. 1993. *Living Within Limits: Ecology, Economics, and Population Taboos*. New York: Oxford University Press.

Hart, H. 1959. "Social Theory and Social Change." Pp. 196-238 in *Symposium on Sociological Theory*, edited by L. Gross. Evanston, IL: Row, Peterson.

Hawley, A.H. 1944. "Ecology and Human Ecology." *Social Forces* 22(May): 398-405.

Hawley, A.H. 1950. *Human Ecology: A Theory of Community Structure*. New York: The Ronald Press.

Henderson, L.J. 1913. *The Fitness of the Environment*. New York: Macmillan.

Hern, W.M. 1990. "Why Are There So Many of Us? Description and Diagnosis of a Planetary Ecopathological Process." *Population and Environment: A Journal of Interdisciplinary Studies* 12(Fall): 9-39.

————. 1993. "Is Human Culture Carcinogenic for Uncontrolled Population Growth and Ecological Destruction?" *BioScience* 43(December): 768-773.

Hitchcock, D.R. and J.E. Lovelock. 1967. "Life Detection by Atmospheric Analysis." *Icarus* 7(September): 149-159.

House, F.N. 1936. *The Development of Sociology*. New York: McGraw-Hill.

Hutchinson, G.E. 1965. *The Ecological Theater and the Evolutionary Play*. New Haven, CT: Yale University Press.

———— . 1970. "The Biosphere." Pp. 3-11 in *The Biosphere*, edited by Editors of *Scientific American*. San Francisco: W.H. Freeman.

Jones, H.F. 1911. *Charles Darwin and Samuel Butler: A Step Towards Reconciliation*. London: A.C. Fifield.

———— . 1919. *The Note-Books of Samuel Butler*. London: A.C. Fifield.

Koshland, D.E. Jr. 1993. "The Two-Component Pathway Comes to Eukaryotes." *Science* 262(22 October): 532.

Leach, E. 1968. *A Runaway World?* [*The 1967 Reith Lectures*]. London: Oxford University Press.

Lenski, G. and J. Lenski. 1982. *Human Societies: An Introduction to Macrosociology*, 4th ed. New York: McGraw-Hill.

Lovelock, J.E. 1972. "Gaia as Seen Through the Atmosphere." *Atmospheric Environment* 6(August): 579-580.

———— . 1979. *Gaia: A New Look at Life on Earth*. New York: Oxford University Press.

———— . 1987. "Gaia: A Model for Planetary and Cellular Dynamics." Pp. 83-97 in *Gaia: A Way of Knowing: Political Implications of the New Biology*, edited by W.I. Thompson. Great Barrington, MA: Lindisfarne Press.

———— . 1988. "The Gaia Hypothesis." Pp. 35-49 in *Gaia, The Thesis, The Mechanisms and The Implications: Proceedings of the First Annual Camelford Conference on the Implications of the Gaia Hypothesis*, edited by P. Bunyard and E. Goldsmith. Camelford, Cornwall, UK: Wadebridge Ecological Centre.

———— . 1989. "Gaia and the Evolution of Planetary Regulation." Pp. 130-137 in *Gaia and Evolution: Proceedings of the Second Annual Camelford Conference on the Implications of the Gaia Thesis*, edited by P. Bunyard and E. Goldsmith. Camelford, Cornwall, UK: Wadebridge Ecological Centre.

Lovelock, J.E. and L. Margulis. 1974. "Atmospheric Homeostasis by and for the Biosphere: The Gaia Hypothesis." *Tellus* 26(1-2): 1-10.

Margulis, L. 1974a. "Origin and Evolution of the Eukaryotic Cell." *Taxon* 23(May): 225-226.

———— . 1974b. "Five-Kingdom Classification and the Origin and Evolution of Cells." *Evolutionary Biology* 7: 45-78.

———— . 1987. "Early Life: The Microbes Have Priority." Pp. 98-109 in *Gaia: A Way of Knowing: Political Implications of the New Biology*, edited by W.I. Thompson. Great Barrington, MA: Lindisfarne Press.

———— . 1988. "Jim Lovelock's Gaia." Pp. 50-65 in *Gaia, The Thesis, The Mechanisms and The Implications: Proceedings of the First Annual Camelford Conference on the Implications of the Gaia Hypothesis*, edited by P. Bunyard and E. Goldsmith. Camelford, Cornwall, UK: Wadebridge Ecological Centre.

———— . 1991. "Symbiogenesis and Symbionticism." Pp. 1-14 in *Symbiosis as a Source of Evolutionary Innovation*, edited by L. Margulis and R. Fester. Cambridge, MA: MIT Press.

———— . 1992. *Diversity of Life: The Five Kingdoms*. Hillside, NJ: Enslow Publishers, Inc.

Margulis, L. and J.E. Lovelock. 1974. "Biological Modulation of the Earth's Atmosphere." *Icarus* 21(April): 471-489.

———— . 1989. "Gaia and Geognosy." Pp. 1-30 in *Global Ecology: Towards a Science of the Biosphere*, edited by M.B. Rambler, L. Margulis, and R. Fester. Boston: Academic Press, Inc.

Margulis, L. and D. Sagan. 1986. *Microcosmos: Four Billion Years of Evolution from Our Microbial Ancestors*. New York: Summit Books.

Margulis, L. and K.V. Schwartz. 1988. *Five Kingdoms: An Illustrated Guide to the Phyla of Life on Earth*, 2nd ed. New York: W.H. Freeman.

Martindale, D. 1957. "Social Disorganization: The Conflict of Normative and Empirical Approaches." Pp. 340-367 in *Modern Sociological Theory: In Continuity and Change*, edited by H. Becker and A. Boskoff. New York: Dryden.

Merton, R.K. 1968. *Social Theory and Social Structure*, enlarged ed. New York: The Free Press.

Moore, W.E. 1965. "Some Misgivings about Evolutionary Theory: A Comment on Professor Stebbins' Paper." *Pacific Sociological Review* 8(Spring): 10-11.

Mulloy, W. 1974. "Contemplate the Navel of the World." *Americas* 26(April): 25-33.

Nisbet, R.A. 1965. "The Irreducibility of Social Change: A Comment on Professor Stebbins' Paper." *Pacific Sociological Review* 8(Spring): 12-15.

Odum, H.T. 1971. *Environment, Power and Society*. New York: Wiley-Interscience.

O'Neill, G.K. 1987. "Foreword." Pp. xiii-xv in *The Overview Effect: Space Exploration and Human Evolution*, by F. White. Boston: Houghton Mifflin.

Owen, D. 1980. *Camouflage and Mimicry*. Chicago: University of Chicago Press.

Park, R.E. and E.W. Burgess. (1921) 1924. *Introduction to the Science of Sociology*. Chicago: University of Chicago Press.

Postel, S. 1994. "Carrying Capacity: Earth's Bottom Line." Pp. 3-21 in *State of the World 1994: A Worldwatch Institute Report on Progress Toward a Sustainable Society*, edited by L.R. Brown, et al. New York: W.W. Norton.

Prescott, D.M. and A.S. Flexer. 1982. *Cancer: The Misguided Cell*. New York: Charles Scribner's Sons.

Sagan, D. 1990. *Biospheres: Metamorphosis of Planet Earth*. New York: McGraw-Hill.

Sagan, L. 1967. "On the Origin of Mitosing Cells." *Journal of Theoretical Biology* 14(March): 225-274.

Seielstad, G.A. 1983. *Cosmic Ecology: The View From the Outside In*. Berkeley: University of California Press.

Sheail, J. 1987. *Seventy-Five Years in Ecology. The British Ecological Society*. Oxford: Blackwell.

Smith, A. (1776) 1901. *An Inquiry Into the Nature and Causes of the Wealth of Nations*. New York: P.F. Collier and Son.

Sobel, R. and D.B. Sicilia. 1986. *The Entrepreneurs: An American Adventure*. Boston: Houghton Mifflin.

Spencer, H. 1844. "Remarks upon the Theory of Reciprocal Dependence." *The London, Edinburgh, and Dublin Philosophical Magazine and Journal of Science* 24(February): 90-94.

————. [1873] 1961. *The Study of Sociology*. Ann Arbor: University of Michigan Press.

Stebbins, G.L. 1965. "Pitfalls and Guideposts in Comparing Organic and Social Evolution." *Pacific Sociological Review* 8(Spring): 3-10.

Stenseth, N.C. and J. Maynard Smith. 1984. "Coevolution in Ecosystems: Red Queen Evolution or Stasis?" *Evolution* 38(July): 870-880.

Tainter, J.A. 1988. *The Collapse of Complex Societies*. Cambridge UK: Cambridge University Press.

Tansley, A.G. 1935. "The Use and Abuse of Vegetational Concepts." *Ecology* 16(July): 284-307.

————. 1939. "British Ecology During the Past Quarter Century: The Plant Community and the Ecosystem." *Journal of Ecology* 27(August): 513-530.

Taylor, F.J.R. 1974. "Implications and Extensions of the Serial Endosymbiosis Theory of the Origin of Eukaryotes." *Taxon* 23(May): 229-258.

————. 1987. "An Overview of the Status of Evolutionary Cell Symbiosis Theories. Pp. 1-16 in *Endocytobiology III, Annals of the New York Academy of Science*, Vol. 503, edited by J.L. Lee and J.F. Fredrick. New York: The New York Academy of Science.

Timasheff, N.S. 1967. *Sociological Theory: Its Nature and Growth*, 3rd ed. New York: Random House.

Townsend, G.F., Trans. 1968. *Aesop's Fables*. Garden City, NY: International Collectors Library.

Vernadsky, V. (1926) 1986. *The Biosphere*. Oracle, AZ: Synergistic Press.

Vidal, G. 1984. "The Oldest Eukaryotic Cells." *Scientific American* 250(February): 48-57.

Wallin, I.E. 1927. *Symbionticism and the Origin of Species*. Baltimore, MD: Williams and Wilkins.

Warming, E. 1909. *Oecology of Plants*. New York: Oxford University Press.
Wheeler, W.M. 1910. *Ants, Their Structure, Development and Behavior*. New York: Columbia University Press.
White, F. 1987. *The Overview Effect: Space Exploration and Human Evolution*. Boston: Houghton Mifflin.

BASIC DIMENSIONS AND FORMS OF SOCIAL EXPLOITATION:

A COMPARATIVE ANALYSIS

Richard Machalek

ABSTRACT

While social behavior is distributed widely throughout nature and confers numerous benefits to the organisms that express it, these benefits are often accompanied by various costs, one of which is "social parasitism." In biology, social parasitism refers to any form of social interaction whereby an individual (or group) expropriates a resource from another individual or group that produced it. This form of social exploitation is influenced by various aspects of social organization and patterns of interaction characterizing the groups within which it occurs. This article identifies the basic dimensions and forms of social exploitation and proposes the development of a general theory by means of which to explain the evolution of social exploitation across species lines.

INTRODUCTION

From a naturalist's perspective, social behavior is an evolutionary success story. Sociality is distributed widely throughout nature, appearing among a broad

Advances in Human Ecology, Volume 4, pages 35-68.
Copyright © 1995 by JAI Press Inc.
All rights of reproduction in any form reserved.
ISBN: 1-55938-874-9

range of taxa including colonial invertebrates, insects, fish, amphibians, birds, reptiles, and mammals. In fact, at least one biologist even suggests that an appropriately broad definition of social phenomena should encompass chemically mediated, "cooperative" interactions among plants (Trivers 1985, pp. 60-62). According to the utilitarian logic of evolutionary theory, sociality is common in nature because individuals benefit from it.[1] Group living may increase an organism's ability to find food, avoid predators, achieve matings, rear and protect offspring, acquire residences (e.g., nests, burrows, lodges), and so on (Alcock 1984). Among some species (nonhuman as well as human), social behavior may even be intrinsically satisfying, as Fagen (1981) speculates in his book on animal play behavior. Yet, along with these benefits come various costs including increased competition for resources, a higher probability of attracting predators, increased disease transmission, and other threats and risks. Sociologically, one of the most interesting of such liabilities is what biologists call "social parasitism" (Barnard 1984; Wilson 1975). Social parasitism refers to any form of social interaction whereby one individual (or group) expropriates a resource from another individual or group that produced it. Such resources include energy in the form of labor or food, information, or material items such as nests or building materials. By definition, social parasitism describes any pattern of social interaction or any type of social relationship from which one participant derives benefits and the other incurs costs. Specific examples of social parasitism include brood parasitism among birds, labor parasitism (or "slavery")[2] among ants, lactational or nursing parasitism among pinnepeds and ungulates, residence parasitism among insects and birds, prey parasitism among birds and mammals ("kleptoparasitism"), and even reproductive parasitism or "kleptogamy" among a variety of animals such as fish and waterfowl. These and other forms of social parasitism make it clear that exploitative patterns of social interaction are not unique to humans.

Why does social parasitism exist among some species but not others? Does social parasitism signify social "pathology," or is it a pattern of behavior expressed by "normal" individuals living in unexceptional environments? What are the various benefits and who are the beneficiaries of social parasitism? Is social parasitism, in the technical biological sense of the term, present in human societies? Is it legitimate to consider various crimes such as burglary, robbery, embezzlement, fraud, confidence games, and corporate crimes as forms of social parasitism? Can institutionalized, collective forms of social exploitation such as class stratification, racial or ethnic domination, or sexism be characterized as forms of social parasitism? Do these complex, culturally mediated patterns of human social behavior share common features with forms of social parasitism found in nonhuman societies? These and related questions provoke the ideas developed in this paper. The specific phenomenon under investigation is *expropriation*, broadly defined as any behavior by means of which an individual or a group usurps a resource from another individual or group. More specifically, expropriation designates any social interaction in which one participant incurs costs in excess of any benefits received, and another participant receives benefits in excess of any costs incurred. Inasmuch as the "host" of expropriative behavior would be better off not being part of such a relationship, or inasmuch as being in such a relationship prevents the host's entering into another relationship from which she could derive more benefits than costs, the relationship may be said to be "exploitative." Expropriation, then, as defined herein includes most of those behaviors that people commonly regard as exploitative, such as crime.[3] Exploitation, however, is a morally resonant term, and whether a particular form of expropriation is or is not morally exploitative can be determined with finality only politically, in the context of a given value-orientation. Nevertheless, since the idea of exploitation has long been used by social scientists when characterizing various forms of social interaction such as class, gender, and race and ethnic dynamics, the terms expropriation and exploitation will be used here interchangeably.

Since it involves cross-species comparisons, the study of expropriation in this analysis is *comparative* in the broad, biological sense of the term. This represents a distinct departure from the conventional social scientific use of the term comparative, which involves comparisons only among human societies separated by factors such as time, space, culture, or forms of government (e.g., a comparative analysis of class relations in the United States and Japan). In contrast, the perspective developed in this analysis entails a comparison of strategies for expropriating resources among a variety of species such as ants, birds, and humans. As such, this approach subordinates the study of any particular species, human or nonhuman, to the study of social *forms* that may occur among a variety of species.

Cross-species comparisons are rare in sociology. Yet, the logic of putting the study of common social forms ahead of the study of diverse social "contents" is not without precedent in this field. Specifically, the philosopher and pioneer sociologist Georg Simmel championed the development of just such a "formal sociology" (Wolff 1950). For example, instead of focusing primarily on the differences between a spouse-spouse-child triad and a spouse-spouse-lover triad, Simmel's formal sociological analysis is intended to isolate and identify those processes and structures common to both types of triads, and all others as well. In Simmel's view, all triads possess universal features that shape the organization and conduct of the social behaviors expressed by their members, and these universal features can be analyzed theoretically and observed empirically. Comparative sociology shares with formal sociology a primary concern with identifying and explaining elementary or fundamental forms of social organization and conduct. It parts company with this theoretical tradition, however, by expanding the study of social forms to include those found in nonhuman as well as in human societies. The prime objective of the comparative analysis of social forms is an understanding of the constraints involved in the evolution of these forms, whatever the species in which they appear.

If we wish to extend the scope of comparative sociology to include the study of social behavior among nonhumans as well as humans, it may be promising to expand Simmel's argument for studying social forms beyond the scope of human societies alone. Consider the social structural trait that has been a favorite topic of sociological inquiry since Adam Smith and Emile Durkheim: the complex *division of labor* typical of large-scale human societies. As a social form, this organizational trait is not restricted to human societies. Rather, it is common among the social insects (ants, bees, wasps, and termites). In fact, while a complex division of labor organized among members of distinct social categories is relatively new to the evolutionary history of human societies (i.e., about 6000 years before present), it is an archaic trait of social insect societies, dating back about 200 million years. Yet, in fundamental respects, the complex and extensive division of labor commonly found in human societies with large populations is isomorphic in its basic properties to the division of labor present in many social insect societies. That is, a complex division of labor involving large numbers of anonymous individuals who interact cooperatively as members of specialized social groups is a form of social organization that occurs among both human and social insect societies (Machalek 1992).

From their inception, the social sciences (especially sociology, economics, and political science) have devoted extensive attention to the study of various forms of social exploitation. Industrial capitalism's paradoxical production of both vast wealth and extreme poverty was the impetus of the first truly systematic theory of social exploitation: Marx's theory of class and class conflict ([1867] 1967, [1848] 1971). Even today, analyses of various forms of social exploitation based on race and ethnicity, gender, religious identity, nationality, or other social attributes are often but adaptations of Marx's scheme for analyzing class exploitation. Ironically, even sociology, self-defined as the most general and inclusive of the social sciences, lacks a truly general theory of social exploitation. The analysis of social exploitation developed in this paper is rooted both in behavioral biology and the social sciences, and it identifies a new direction to take in order to develop a general (cross-species) theory of social exploitation.

INTERESTS AND SOCIAL LIFE

Despite numerous and often profound differences between their cultures of explanation, both social scientists and evolutionary biologists emphasize that social life is organized largely around the interests of its participants. Members of both of these scientific communities generally concur that, to the extent that individuals share common interests, they are likely to cooperate, but to the extent that their interests diverge, the likelihood of competition and conflict increases. This does not mean that individuals with coincident interests will never compete, sometimes even lethally. Nor does it imply that enemies never cooperate. Instead, this premise simply puts in high relief the wide-spread assumption that common interests, be they based on class, gender, race/ ethnicity, party, status group, religion, cultural kinship, or even genetic kinship, are important determinants of cooperation and conflict.

Biologists commonly interpret social behavior and relationships as "traits" by means of which individuals realize their interests. They distinguish among different types of "intimate" relationships which they call "symbiotic" relationships (Hölldobler and Wilson 1990, pp. 436-529; Wilson 1975, pp. 353-377). The distinctions are made in terms of interests that are realized (or thwarted) for the participants by virtue of their involvement in the relationship. Symbiosis itself is defined as the "prolonged and intimate relationship of organisms belonging to different species" (Wilson 1975, p. 353). We shall modify this definition slightly to include organisms of the same species as well. The simplest way to describe each of these types is with reference to interactions between two participants. Each interactor may be either an individual or a group (such as an organization). There are three basic types of social symbioses: *social mutualism, social commensalism*, and *social parasitism* (Wilson 1975, pp. 353-377). In social mutualism, both parties to the interaction benefit, but not necessarily to the same extent; that is, the exchange of benefits may be more or less symmetrical. Social commensalism describes a situation whereby one party benefits, but the second neither derives a benefit nor suffers a cost. Empirically, social commensalism is difficult to establish with confidence, because it may be virtually impossible to ascertain conclusively that one party is unaffected by the behavior of the other. Finally, social parasitism means that one party benefits at the other's expense.

This tripartite scheme for analyzing social behavior is based on the consequences of behavior for the interests of those involved. Mutualism means that at least some interests of both parties are realized by the interaction. In commensalism, the interests of one participant are realized while those of the second are unaffected. Social parasitism occurs when the interests of one party are realized at the expense of the other. This conceptual distinction leaves open the specific interests at stake in the interaction. While evolutionary biologists, specifically sociobiologists, calculate interests in terms of inclusive fitness, (Hamilton 1964), other types of interests may also be at stake in a social interaction, and they may or may not be relevant to fitness considerations. For example, among humans, interests include material (money, land or other material objects), and symbolic or social concerns (meaning, power, prestige, deference), as well as reproductive success (inclusive fitness). While humans probably rarely, if ever, *conceptualize* inclusive fitness as an "interest" that consciously motivates their behaviors as they do with other types of interests such as power, wealth, or prestige, we shall include reproductive interests among those relevant to human social life so as to be able to incorporate relevant analytical insights from sociobiological theory when appropriate. This allows us to theorize about the possibility that, as with other species, human behavior may be organized and influenced, at least partially, by interests of which actors are entirely unaware.

Here, interests are defined broadly as those factors upon which the well-being of an individual or a group depend. The well-being of individuals and groups is secured typically, but not always of course, by meeting their needs and wants with resources that may be acquired in various ways, including inheritance (transmission from kin), benefaction (gift giving), scavenging/ salvaging (appropriating resources that are incidentally available, perhaps because they have been abandoned by a producer), cooperative exchange (e.g., trade), or expropriation (social parasitism). What determines why individuals will adopt one rather than another of these strategies for acquiring resources? Clearly, numerous factors are involved, but perhaps the fundamental determinant is the degree to which interacting individuals *share* interests (which may or may not be perceived). Thus, we should probably expect overt conflict when the interests of the interactors are mutually exclusive; should expect some mix of cooperation and competition when interests overlap; and should expect cooperation even to the point of sacrifice when interests coincide. As such, it is readily apparent that any analysis of the evolution of social exploitation must take into account the distribution of interests among those involved in the interaction as well as the distribution of resources necessary for realizing their interests.

Behavioral biologists routinely distinguish between two classes of interests: *somatic* interests and *reproductive* interests. Somatic resources are those that contribute to the health and survival of an organism, while reproductive resources contribute more directly toward that individual's reproductive success. This distinction corresponds to the two basic life problems for which natural selection equips organisms with various traits: survival and reproduction (or "fitness," both Darwinian and inclusive). In the calculus of organic evolutionary theory, resources are meaningful only to the extent that they increase an organism's chances of realizing its dual interests of survival and reproductive success. When conceptualizing social behavior as an "adaptation," evolutionary biologists mean that it is a trait that yields consequences which enhance the survival and reproductive chances of the individuals that express it. One of the major evolutionary consequences of social behavior is to make resources available to those who engage in it. In neo-Darwinian theory, somatic resources (such as food and shelter) have evolutionary significance only to the extent that they increase an individual's chances of maximizing its inclusive fitness. Reproductive resources refer to resources that contribute directly to reproductive opportunity, even if they imperil one's personal survival. The most obvious reproductive resource is a mating partner, but other examples include traits that may evolve by sexual selection (as opposed to natural selection) simply because they increase one's chances of being chosen, consciously or otherwise, as a reproductive partner. Or, other individuals who are not reproductive partners may be regarded as reproductive resources if they assist in the care and rearing of offspring (e.g., "helpers at the nest"). The important point in this context is that both somatic and reproductive resources are seen by evolutionary biologists as relevant to the organism only to the extent that they contribute to an individual's inclusive fitness. Therefore, the basic evolutionary significance of sociality is to provide those resources by means of which the realization of an organism's somatic and reproductive interests are realized. Stated more succinctly, sociality is an adaptation—a fitness-enhancing device for those who express it. While this view of social behavior may be seen by most sociologists as unreasonably restrictive, it comprises the foundation of the neo-Darwinian evolutionary theory of society and social behavior.

Ever since the early, raucous days of "the sociobiology debate," many social scientists, especially sociologists, have been unsettled by a view of social behavior that reduces it to the status of a fitness-enhancing device. Part of the antipathy that many social scientists express toward sociobiology is rooted in the difficulty they have envisioning inclusive fitness as a human interest, because social scientists frequently equate interests with consciously held needs or wants. (Who has a *need* or a *want* to maximize inclusive fitness?) Furthermore, it is far from obvious to most sociologists that a great many human interests, especially those of a symbolic nature, exist in service of *either* survival or reproductive success. Although, as noted earlier, behavioral biologists and social scientists tend to share the view that social life is organized around the interests of its participants, they part company over the idea that social organization and interaction evolved in service of a unitary or *master* interest such as fitness maximization. This divergence is most evident when comparing sociobiology and sociology.

Sociobiological theory is built on the premise that social life can be made intelligible in evolutionary terms only when viewed as an adaptation that serves an organism's master interest of maximizing its inclusive fitness. In this view, specific social behaviors such as foraging, protection and defense, courtship and mating, and the rearing of offspring all evolved because they enhance inclusive fitness. However diverse a species' behavioral repertoire, the repertoire is seen as expressing an underlying unity created by the fact that behavioral adaptations evolve in service of the "master interest" of fitness maximization. While sociologists may freely concede this view of the role of interests in nonhuman societies, many remain unconvinced that it explains much about human societies and social behavior. While certain traditions of sociological analysis place great emphasis on the importance of interests in shaping and regulating human social life (e.g., conflict theory, exchange theory, rational choice theory), they are much less likely to describe the full range of diverse interests that humans possess as unified in service of a *master* interest such as fitness maximization. Instead, humans are viewed typically by sociologists as having interests that are much more loosely integrated, or even contradictory, with each other. The realization of symbolic interests, for example, is not seen as necessarily serving the realization of genetic interests. Rather, the realization of some interests, such as occupational attainment, may subvert reproductive activity. By postponing, or even foregoing, parenting in order to realize occupational and economic interests, people in modern industrial societies may very well be reducing their inclusive fitness while they achieve career success (Tiger 1987, pp. 209-256).[4]

While evolutionary theory predisposes biologists to assume that virtually *all* of an organism's interests exist in service of the fundamental interest of fitness maximization, this same premise is alien to many sociologists. Consequently, sociobiological reasoning has failed to capture the imagination of those sociologists seeking to understand the nature and dynamics of cooperation and conflict, including social exploitation, in human societies. The subjugation of one group by another in the name of various ideological interests appears to many social scientists to be wholly unrelated to inclusive fitness, and the sociobiological search for the *possible* adaptive significance of such contests seems ill-advised to these same social scientists. In the absence of theoretically-based empirical studies, sociobiologists, on the other hand, are reluctant to presume the irrelevance to fitness of *any* human behavioral patterns. Instead, they leave open the possibility that social interactions—even if apparently totally removed from reproductive relevance—may be under at least a weak influence of individual behavioral propensities that may have evolved by natural selection.

Such disagreements cannot be settled by argument alone. They are incapable of resolution strictly by theoretical debate, however ingenious or energetic. Instead, their arbitration awaits a judicious combination of creative theoretical reasoning and imaginative empirical inquiry. In the meantime, I submit that it is possible to develop a comparative analysis of expropriative social behaviors that is compatible with both evolutionary biology (à la sociobiology and behavioral ecology) and conventional sociology. As will become apparent, the analysis of expropriation as a class of social *forms* can shed light on behaviors that may be under the influence of genetic processes shaped by natural selection as well as those that are purely the product of culture and the idiosyncracies of biography and history.

Social life is organized on the basis of interests as diverse as inclusive fitness or religious ideologies (which themselves, of course, may be related to inclusive fitness). By mobilizing and making available resources for realizing interests, patterned social behaviors sometimes constitute an opportunity structure for the expropriation of these same resources. In its "elementary forms," expropriation is vividly evident in many nonhuman societies, and such behaviors have been studied extensively by biologists under the rubric of social parasitism. It is to these studies we now turn.

AN OVERVIEW OF THE BIOLOGY OF SOCIAL PARASITISM

What is Social Parasitism?

Because many social scientists are unfamiliar with the details of social parasitism among animals, a few examples will illustrate this fascinating social form. Several species of fishing birds usurp prey from each other, a foraging strategy that biologists call kleptoparasitism. Examples include eagles, pelicans, gulls, and ospreys (Forbes 1991; Tershey, Breese, and Meyer 1990; Daub 1989). Kleptoparasitic behaviors occur among invertebrates such as spiders from whose webs parasites steal prey (Cangialosi 1990; Elgar 1989). Among birds, cuckoos and cowbirds have become notorious as "brood parasites" (Lack 1968; Meyerriecks 1972). Brood parasites are birds (but sometimes insects as well) that deposit their eggs in the nests of birds of other species. When the alien chick hatches, it is fed and cared for by the "foster" mother as if it were her own offspring. Occasionally, the mother's own offspring die as a result of her neglect of her own offspring, due to her care for the alien brood parasite chick. In fact, in some cases the newly hatched chick will kill the host species' nestlings. Numerous recent studies document the extensiveness of brood parasitism among birds (e.g., Birkhead, Burke, Zann, Hunter, and Krupa 1990; Roeskaft, Braa, Kursnes, Lampe, and Pedersen 1991; Brown and Sherman 1989; Sealy, Hobson, and Briskie 1989; Brown and Brown 1989). Fish also practice brood parasitism, but in their case, it is often the parental investment of the male that is exploited when he is deceived into guarding eggs that were fertilized by another male (Dominey 1980). Both birds and insects that construct burrows or nests in which they live and rear young are vulnerable to nest parasitism. It is not uncommon for birds (such as swallows, juncos, or geese) or insects (such as wasps) to construct nests or burrows from which they are then displaced by other individuals (Brockmann, Grafen, and Dawkins 1979; Sullivan, Cole, and Villalobos 1989; Cervo, Lorenzi, and Turillazzi 1990; Brown and Brown 1991).

One of the most highly evolved forms of social parasitism yet discovered by behavioral biologists is slave-making among ants (Wilson 1971; Hölldobler and Wilson 1990). While numerous animal species routinely expropriate food produced by others, the so-called "slave-making" ants have carried social parasitism to extreme levels. For example, *Teleutomyrmex schneideri* has evolved a society that lacks a worker caste and, therefore, must raid the colonies of other ant species in order to capture and enslave a labor force on which it must depend (Hölldobler and Wilson 1990, pp. 436-437). Furthermore, *T. schneideri* has evolved to become so thoroughly dependent on its "enslaved" worker caste hosts that it has undergone morphological changes that represent a loss of those very behavioral capabilities required of self-sustaining adult insects. For example, the mandibles of this ant are "so degenerate that the parasites are probably unable to secure food on their own" (Hölldobler and Wilson 1990, p. 437). Not only are these animals food-dependent, "they are unique among all known social insects in being ectoparasitic," because they actually ride the backs of their hosts for transportation (Hölldobler and Wilson 1990, p. 436).

"Slavery," or labor parasitism, is not the only type of expropriation to which ant societies fall victim. In addition, some ant societies harbor food parasites (trophic parasites) as do some other social species, such as bees and termites. In fact, even some vertebrate species, such as wild dogs or cheetahs, suffer food parasitism by others, such as hyenas (Wilson 1975, pp. 361-362). Occasionally, social parasitism involves the usurpation of information rather than labor or material items. "Satellite" male frogs, for example, will wait at the edges of a dominant male's calling territory and attempt to copulate with females who are attracted to the dominant male's call. This example illustrates parasitism of both information and energy (and perhaps even territory as a material resource) from the host. While this list of expropriative forms is far from exhaustive, it illustrates the wide range of expropriative activities and the diversity of species in which this social form can be found.

Varieties of Social Parasitism

While biologists have yet to produce a comprehensive, systematic taxonomy of the varieties of social parasitism, they have introduced a number of concepts for describing this phenomenon that have become common in the behavioral biological literature. Among the most widely discussed forms of social parasitism are kleptoparasitism (or "piracy"), brood parasitism, nest parasitism, "slavery," trophic parasitism, and "satellites." The most extensive efforts by biologists at developing a typology of forms of social parasitism are those proposed by entomologists, most of whom are interested in explaining how social parasitism among the social insects evolved (Wilson 1971, 1975; Hölldobler and Wilson 1990). Yet, these classification schemes fail to specify and analyze the fundamental *sociological* dimensions implicated in this social form. A comparative sociological analysis of expropriation requires attention to the descriptive detail reported in observations of this phenomenon. By way of example, the remainder of this section consists of brief descriptions of the various forms of expropriation listed above.

Kleptoparasitism

Kleptoparasites have been described as thieves, but for some, this is too anthropomorphic a characterization. In everyday vernacular, the notion of theft implies some idea of property as a right. Since "theft", "property," and "right" are categories of cognitive and normative culture used to describe relations among humans, it is hard to defend the direct application of such concepts to the description of nonhuman animal behavior patterns. The same can be said for the notion of "slavery" among ants. A simple solution to this problem is to use the term expropriation where one might otherwise use words such as steal or enslave. Expropriation has the advantage of being more purely descriptive and generally free of the cultural connotations of terms associated with the human practice of theft. All the same, with these cautionary injunctions firmly in mind, I believe that the occasional, judicious use of terms such as "theft" and "piracy" can be helpful in describing the social nature of nonhuman expropriative behaviors.

Kleptoparasitism is a potentially less expensive way of acquiring a resource than having to produce it. Biologists conceptualize resource production "costs" in terms such as risk of injury or death, caloric investment, time spent in a productive act, time and energy invested in learning productive behavior, and so on (Krebs and Davies 1981, pp. 49-91). Kleptoparasitism provides a short-cut alternative to producing a resource. When, for example, an American bald eagle searches for and locates a fish, dives to catch it, seizes it, and expends energy flying the fish to its nest, it has engaged in a productive activity that involves the sorts of costs named above. A potentially less costly, though not cost-free, alternative is to expropriate a fish from another eagle that is already transporting its prey to its nest. In a study of kleptoparasitism among American bald eagles, Hansen observed that a ratio of 42% fishing and 58% stealing appears to be an "evolutionary stable state" (1986, p. 791). Such behaviors are particularly easy to observe among birds, such as gulls, which forage in close proximity to each other and have numerous and reliable opportunities to usurp food items collected by others.

Besides birds, spiders are also vulnerable to kleptoparasitism. Spinning webs that trap prey is a food production strategy among spiders. Their webs immobilize and trap prey, and this invites opportunistic expropriative behavior. The phenomenon is sufficiently common that it has occasioned biological studies of strategies by means of which spiders are able to defend against such expropriative threats (Cangialosi 1990; Elgar 1989).

While apparently rarer than among birds and arthropods, kleptoparasitic expropriative strategies do occur among mammals. For example, hyenas will expropriate animals killed by other predators and even follow these predators as they hunt, should an expropriative opportunity arise (Estes and Goddard 1967). It is not unreasonable to expect that this sort of expropriative activity may occur among other predators, such as bears, when they encounter a prey item killed by a smaller animal, such as a coyote. In fact, inasmuch as male lions often contribute little to a pride's actual hunting efforts, most of which are expended by cooperative groups of lionesses, but help themselves to the prey killed by the females, one wonders whether these males should not be regarded, at least sociologically, as intraspecific food parasites.

Kleptoparasitic strategies are not always executed by force. The behavior of a staphylinid beetle (*Atmeles pubicollis*) enables it to insinuate itself into ant colonies from which it solicits food regurgitations. Unlike the kleptoparasites discussed above, it does not use force to wrest food from its host but, rather, employs a combination of chemical and tactile signals to induce its host into providing it with food (Hölldobler 1970; Wilson 1975, pp. 375-377). Thus, deception is used even in nonhuman societies to expropriate resources from their producers.

Brood Parasitism

While kleptoparasites typically expropriate resources such as prey or perhaps nesting materials, brood parasites expropriate labor, namely, parental investment (Trivers 1972), from unwitting parents. A variety of birds has evolved as brood parasites. These include cuckoos, cowbirds, zebra finches, and black-headed ducks (e.g., Mueller, Eggert, and Dressel 1990; Birkhead et al. 1990; Wilson 1975; Meyerriecks 1972; Lack 1968). Even insects, such as beetles, occasionally evolve brood parasitic strategies (Mueller et al. 1990). Among the most widely researched brood parasites are the cuckoos. Cuckoos have evolved physical adaptations that serve their strategy of dumping their eggs into the nests of other species, such as warblers, to be raised by these unwitting "foster parents." For example, cuckoo eggs mimic in their appearance those of their hosts; cuckoo females have ovipositor-like cloacae that allow them to insert their eggs into host nests that would otherwise be inaccessible; cuckoo eggs have tough shells to prevent their breaking when they are "dumped"; and some of the parasitic young even resemble their hosts (Wilson 1975, pp. 365-366). Host mothers, such as warblers, erroneously feed and care for the parasitic cuckoo chicks that have hatched in their own nests, sometimes at the expense of neglecting their own young. These parasitic behaviors reach extremes among both European cuckoo and honeyguide chicks which have evolved behavioral strategies by means of which they evict or kill the offspring of their hosts.

Not surprisingly, brood parasitism is of great interest to sociobiologists since it bears on competition directly relevant to reproductive success. Not only are brood parasites able to increase their fitness by foisting off their young on unrelated parents, they also subvert the reproductive success of their hosts, perhaps thereby reducing competition for somatic resources. Brood parasites expropriate labor from others both directly and indirectly. By being deceived into feeding and caring for parasitic young, hosts suffer direct labor exploitation. By harboring alien chicks in nests that were constructed for rearing their own offspring, hosts suffer indirect labor exploitation. From the point of view of the parasite, however, brood parasitism is a very successful strategy for producing more young than would otherwise be possible when offspring require intense and prolonged parental care. In fact, brood parasitism is an obligatory form of reproduction among "at least 50 species of cuckoos" (Wilson 1975, p. 364).

Nest (or Burrow) Parasitism

Nest parasitism can be distinguished from brood parasitism in that nest parasites usurp the burrows or nests of others, but their offspring are not cared for by the host species. Among insects, some species such as digger wasps excavate burrows in which.they lay eggs. Occasionally, the burrow is usurped by another individual (Brockmann et al. 1979). Similar nest usurpation occurs among other wasp species (Cervo et al 1990), birds such as juncos (Sullivan et al. 1989), snow geese (Lank, Mineau, Rockwell, and Cooke 1990), cliff swallows (Brown and Brown 1991), and others (Rowhwer and Freeman 1989). Like kleptoparasitism, nest parasitism is a form of "product" parasitism whereby individuals usurp material resources from their producers. Again, since residences (nests, burrows) are presumably costly to construct, and since they function largely to house young, residence parasitism has a direct impact on an organism's prospects for reproductive success and, thus, is of central interest to sociobiologists. A form of social parasitism called *xenobiosis* describes nest parasitism among ants. Xenobionts are ants that live in the nest walls of other ant species. Xenobionts often enter the living spaces of their hosts to usurp food. Finally, xenobiotic ants sometimes even exploit their hosts as food sources, preying upon them. As such, they are both parasites and predators of their hosts.

Slavery (Dulosis)

As discussed earlier, *slavery* among ants has received considerable attention from myrmecologists. One of the most recent and comprehensive summaries of social parasitism among ants is available in Hölldobler and Wilson (1990, pp. 436-470). The following discussion of social parasitism among ants draws liberally from their work and from Wilson (1971, 1975). While the biological details of social parasitism among ants are intrinsically fascinating, a relatively brief overview of key features of this phenomenon is adequate for the purposes at hand. Social parasitism among ants is very complicated, and Hölldobler and Wilson note that "its study has become virtually a little discipline of entomology in itself" (1990, p. 437).

Social parasitism in ants is associated with nesting patterns, and two forms can be identified: compound nests and mixed colonies. Compound nests are composed of two species that live close together, or even intermingle, but keep their broods apart. Social parasitism may or may not be present in this form. In mixed nests, the two species live among each other and their broods are mixed together and cared for communally. Hölldobler and Wilson note that mixed colonies almost always signify social parasitism. Biologists use several technical terms to distinguish among forms of social parasitism associated with compound nests (e.g., cleptobiosis, lestobiosis, parabiosis, and xenobiosis). In mixed colonies, three basic types of social parasitism can be distinguished: temporary social parasitism, slavery (dulosis), and permanent social parasitism (inquilinism) (Hölldobler and Wilson 1990, pp. 445-446). For some species, the parasitic strategy is optional or opportunistic (facultative), and the parasite is capable of providing for itself. For other species, parasitism is necessary (obligatory), inasmuch as the species has evolved to be workerless. Basically, socially parasitic ants expropriate three resources from others: nest space, food, and labor.

A brief description of select aspects of behaviors involved in social parasitism among ants will highlight interesting and sociologically suggestive features of this phenomenon. In the case of temporary social parasitism, a queen may use a variety of techniques to insinuate herself into a host colony. These techniques include threat displays, submission displays, allowing herself to be brought into the nest by host workers, stealth, or "freezing" and "playing dead" when her intrusion is detected. Queens of one genus, *Protomognathus*, forcibly evict *Leptothorax* adults from their nest until the *Leptothorax* workers and queens flee and leave their brood to the intruder. One parasite, *Harpagoxenus sublaevis*, emits a "propaganda" pheromone when she enters a host nest, and the host workers then begin to attack each other. The parasite queen then typically kills the host queen or queens and usurps the labor of the host workers until she raises her own worker caste.

"Slavery," or dulosis, is a form of social parasitism whereby the host worker caste becomes a work force for the parasite species. Typically, slavery involves a raid on the host's nest and the forcible extraction of brood (more often than not, pupae). These pupae are then transported back to the parasite's nest where they eclose, mistakenly "recognize" their captors as members of their own species, and become an "enslaved" worker caste for an alien species. Some parasitic species (e.g., *Strongylognathus testaces*) even keep slave queens alive so that they continue to reproduce a captive labor force. Slave ants perform multiple tasks for their captors, including feeding them with liquid food regurgitations. It is common for workers in slave-making species to undergo a sort of behavioral "degeneration" or "decay" whereby they lose the capacity to work competently. In fact,

Hölldobler and Wilson (1990, p. 455) describe the "amazon ant," *Polyergus*, as the evolutionary pinnacle of the dulotic ants, because it is entirely dependent on its slaves for labor.

Finally, inquiline, or permanently socially parasitic, ants spend their entire life cycle in the presence of their hosts/slaves. Permanent social parasites are so totally dependent on their hosts that they are said to exhibit an "inquiline syndrome" (Hölldobler and Wilson 1990, p. 467). This syndrome involves the complete loss of a worker caste and even the acquisition of distinct morphological traits. They lose the capacity to forage, to care for brood, to repair nests, and so on. The morphological changes they undergo signify the loss of behavioral capacities required for self-sufficiency. In fact, as noted earlier, inquiline queens of the species *Teleutomyrmex schneideri* depend on host queens even for transportation. This parallels an irony associated with human slavery, the fact that the subjugators become dependent on the subjugated.

Most of the time, social parasitism among ants involves the expropriation of food, labor, or nests. However, some species of ants apparently expropriate information as well. For example, both *Camponotus lateralis* and *Formica pratensis* follow other ants (*Crematogaster scutellaris* and *Formica cunicularia* respectively) on odor trails to food sources, then expropriate the food. While the ultimate resource expropriated is food, it is interesting to note that the food parasitism is enabled by information parasitism. When the food parasitism involves the parasite's intrusion into the host's social system only enough to expropriate food, myrmecologists call it *trophic parasitism* in order to distinguish it from xenobiosis, whereby the parasites and hosts live in close proximity. Technically, trophic parasitism is a form of kleptoparasitism.

Satellites

The satellite represents the final type of expropriator that will be described in this brief overview of social parasitism among animals. Male crickets, frogs, and toads use loud acoustical signals to attract female mates (Alcock 1984; Krebs and Davies 1981). Biologists use the term satellite to describe other noncalling males that position themselves close to the signalling male. When females are attracted to the caller, the satellite intercepts the females and attempts to mate with them. Thus, the satellite male is parasitizing the efforts (energy and information) expended by the calling male that is attempting to attract mates. Among some species, such as bullfrogs, the satellite has a very poor success rate at mating (Howard 1978), but among others, such as treefrogs, the satellite males have mating success rates that are competitive with the callers (Perrill, Gerhardt, and Daniel 1978).

As an expropriative strategy, satellite behavior may enable an individual to avoid certain risks associated with production, even though callers may have, on average, more mating success than satellites. For example, Howard (1978) found that bullfrog callers incur a greater risk of predation than satellites, because their calls attract not only female frogs, but snapping turtles as well. Similarly, Cade (1979) showed that calling crickets also incur the cost of attracting a parasitic fly that can kill the cricket. Thus, even though the socially parasitic satellite males may not be as successful in securing matings as callers, they may not incur as many risks and costs either.

This brief overview of various forms of social parasitism is intended to illustrate the sorts of expropriative behaviors that occur in nonhuman societies. It is far from exhaustive. In fact, Hölldobler and Wilson (1990), in discussing social parasitism among ants, suggest that social parasitism may be much more pervasive than previously recognized: "A rich variety of new parasitic species... continue to be discovered at such a consistently high rate as to suggest that at this moment only a small fraction of the total world fauna of social parasites is known" (p. 446). This suggests that nonhuman societies may very well represent a rich data source for comparative sociologists interested in studying the nature, causes, and consequences of expropriation.

THE DIMENSIONS AND FORMS OF EXPROPRIATION

Whether it occurs among invertebrates or vertebrates, nonhumans or humans, social parasitism is not reducible to purely biological (morphological and physiological) terms. Rather, it is the product of a confluence of ecological, social *and* biological factors. Since various forms of social parasitism are distributed widely across species lines, this creates an opportunity to try to specify general ecological, social organizational, and social interactive conditions under which social parasitism is likely to occur. The analysis presented here focuses primarily on properties of social organization and interaction that are implicated in the evolution of social parasitism. By identifying key sociological dimensions of social parasitism, we take an important step forward toward the development a general theory of social exploitation.

Social Parasitism or Asymmetric Mutualism?

Technically, social parasitism refers to an interaction or relationship from which one participant derives benefits and the other suffers costs. As such, parasitism must be distinguished from *asymmetric mutualism*. In "social mutualism," both participants benefit, but not necessarily in the same way or to the same degree. A classic example of asymmetric mutualism among humans is the relationship between capital and labor as characterized by Marxist theorists. While labor derives benefits (receiving, at minimum, a wage) from this relationship, capital enjoys a disproportionately larger benefit because of its ability to control surplus value and extract profit. Accordingly, the relationship has been characterized as exploitative by Marxist thinkers. Asymmetric mutualism also raises questions of equity and fair exchange, considerations that are central to the exchange theory tradition in sociology (Blau 1964, 1971)—that is, while a certain degree of asymmetry in a mutualistic relationship may not be problematic for either participant, if the asymmetry becomes too great, then the relationship may come to be regarded (by a detached observer, by one participant, or by both) as exploitative. Asymmetric mutualism among humans may be legitimated in a variety of ways. For example, it may be that participant A provides more resource value to participant B than vice versa, but A's "wealth" (resource holding potential) may be such that the cost incurred is negligible. On the other hand, even a slight tax may be exploitative when it is levied on an individual struggling to meet subsistence requirements.

The distinction between asymmetric mutualism and social parasitism is familiar to evolutionary theorists in the context of game theoretic explanations of cooperation and conflict. In the Prisoner's Dilemma model commonly employed by game theorists, an individual who "cheats" while the other player "cooperates" is behaving exploitatively by having violated the norm of reciprocity that calls for cooperation to be reciprocated. In this context, Robert Trivers' classic paper, "The Evolution of Reciprocal Altruism" (1971), contains a discussion of two forms of cheating: "In *gross cheating* the cheater fails to reciprocate at all, and the altruist suffers the costs of whatever altruism he has dispensed without any compensating benefits... *Subtle cheating*, by contrast, involves reciprocating, but always attempting to give less than one was given, or more precisely, to give less than the partner would give if the situation were reversed" (pp. 46-47). Trivers' distinction between gross and subtle cheating allows us to broaden the conventional biological conception of social parasitism to include asymmetric mutualistic interactions as well as truly parasitic interactions. Thus, we regard both gross and subtle cheating as forms of social parasitism.

Asymmetric mutualism (subtle cheating) is important in this theoretical context for two reasons. First, it is often difficult to determine with confidence, especially among humans, if a particular relationship or interaction is truly parasitic. That is, it is hard (if not impossible) to know that a host is *not* receiving some benefit. If the host receives some benefit from the interaction, then the relationship must be classified as mutualistic, however imbalanced, rather than truly parasitic. This problem is especially vexing with reference to humans, because an apparent victim may actually be receiving some sort of subtle, cryptic, perhaps entirely psychological but nevertheless real, benefit from an interaction that looks purely parasitic to the less perceptive eye. The second reason it is important to expand the scope of a general theory of social exploitation to include asymmetric mutualism is that it is probably more common among humans than is true social parasitism (gross cheating). And, ironically, asymmetric mutualism may be far more costly to its hosts than is true social parasitism.

How could asymmetric mutualism represent a greater threat to hosts than true social parasitism? Evolutionary studies of parasite-host relationships have revealed fascinating and paradoxical dynamics. From an evolutionary perspective, parasites (be they somatic or social parasites) are confronted with an optimality problem. That is, any parasite should be expected to evolve so as to extract as great a volume of resources as it can from its host in order to maximize its survival and reproductive chances, but not so great a volume as to incapacitate or destroy the host before it has been exploited as fully as possible by the parasite. Put differently, a successful parasitic strategy is one in which the parasite exercises appropriate restraint so as to maximize its long-term use of its host's ability to provide resources from which the parasite can benefit in fitness terms. If the parasite taxes its host too severely, it may kill or incapacitate the host and thereby fail to extract maximum value from the host's productive capacities. On the other hand, if the parasite does not tax the host sufficiently, it may fail to compete with other parasites that are more successful at extracting value from their hosts. In principle, there should be an optimality point (or range) at which parasites evolve to extract maximum resources from their hosts over the course of the entire host-parasite relationship. In such a scenario, we would expect parasite strategies to evolve so as resist detection by the host or to inhibit the host from "recognizing" (consciously or otherwise) the true costs of harboring the parasite.

In fact, among humans perhaps the most successful parasitic strategy is that which misrepresents itself as beneficial to its host. Endowed with consciousness, humans are able to attempt to assess the costs and benefits that derive from their associations with others. Thus, humans do not depend exclusively on the forces of natural selection to acquire defensive responses against threats of social parasitism. Instead, they may learn to recognize social parasitism for what it is and take steps to avoid or deter it. As a result, deceptive communication has evolved to assume an extremely important role in patterns of social parasitism among humans. This has long been acknowledged by social thinkers devoted to the analysis of the role of deception in human affairs. Ideologies, for example, represent cultural deception systems that obscure the interests of one group to the advantage of another. In Marxist theory, the dominant ideology of the capitalist class generates false consciousness among workers, thereby preventing them from realizing that their class interests do not coincide with those of the bourgeoisie. As a result, the proletariat class is complicit in its own victimization by subtle cheating on the part of the bourgeoisie.

Gross cheating, on the other hand, involves a blatant violation of the norm of reciprocity and, as a result, is more likely to be detected and reacted against by its victims. From an evolutionary perspective, gross cheating is likely to create more immediate and severe selection pressures than does subtle cheating and may thereby favor the more rapid evolution of counter parasitic strategies among hosts. In either case, the effects of subtle cheating (asymmetric mutualism) may be more insidious over the life course of a host, and thus represent a more serious threat than overt, gross cheating. By taking without reciprocating, a true social parasite is more likely to be recognized (via either consciousness or natural selection) as an "enemy." The victim in an asymmetric mutualistic relationship, on the other hand, may be slower and less effective in mounting a self-defense against an exploiter from whom she is deriving at least *some* benefits.

One of the important lessons of evolutionary game theory (Axelrod 1984) is that gross cheating is a difficult strategy to employ in a social situation involving iterated interactions, because repeated encounters give victims of cheating the opportunity to retaliate. For this reason, we would expect subtle cheating to be more common in patterns of social interaction involving the same individuals over long periods of time. In marriages, families, and communities, for example, subtle cheating is likely to be a greater problem than gross cheating. A good example can be found in studies of inequities between husbands and wives in terms of sharing domestic labor and child rearing responsibilities (Hochschild 1989). These studies routinely report husbands adopting, consciously or otherwise, behavioral strategies that enable them to avoid their fair share of domestic labor, even when their wives are fully employed in the paid labor force.

The confidence artist, on the other hand, behaves as a gross cheater precisely because she does not expect to encounter her host in subsequent interactive situations. Instead, con artists are well known for their habits of working quickly and moving on before their victims can retaliate. For this reason, Mayer (1974) has observed "The great enforcer of morality in commerce is the continuing relationship, the belief that one will have to do business again with this customer, or this supplier, and when a failing company loses this automatic enforcer, not even a strong-arm factor is likely to find a substitute" (p. 280).

The Basic Dimensions of Expropriation

As noted earlier, biological studies of social parasitism reveal that this social form is distributed widely among taxa ranging from invertebrates to vertebrates. The behaviors themselves may involve relatively simple and short-lived events (such as acts of food theft) or long-term, complex interactions among populations of individuals (such as slavery). However simple or complex, the basic dimensions of any expropriative event or relationship always include resources, the activities of a producer, and the activities of an expropriator. The producer may be an individual or a group, as may be the expropriator. The resources that are expropriated may include those that are used in production activity or the product itself. Organisms expropriate three basic classes of resources from each other: energy, information, or material items. Expropriative activity may involve any or all of these types of resources.

Examples of energy exploitation include slavery among ants, brood parasitism among birds, and labor exploitation among humans. In each of these cases, some individuals exploit others, extracting from them energy in the form of labor. Information exploitation transpires when satellite male frogs copulate with females who have been attracted by the mating calls of another male or when a forager, who has located a food source, is followed by others with whom it then must compete. Information expropriation is undoubtedly most fully evolved among humans, where it assumes complex forms such as corporate espionage, copyright infringements, and the pirating of computer software. Finally, material items, such as food, nests, and virtually all human artifacts, represent the class of resources that is probably most commonly expropriated in social systems. The cursory overview of social parasitism presented earlier suggests that food parasitism may be the most common form of expropriation in nonhuman societies.

In both human and nonhuman societies, the basic means of expropriation include *crypsis, deception*, and *coercion*. Cryptic forms of expropriation are those that are not detected by their hosts. An example is found in the behavior of "thief ants" belonging to the subgenus *Diplorhoptrum* of *Solenopsis*, which burrow next to the nests of much larger ant species, stealthily enter their chambers, and prey on the brood (Wilson 1975, p. 361). In human societies, crimes such as embezzlement or shoplifting illustrate cryptic expropriative behaviors.

In contrast to crypsis, deceptive expropriative behaviors are detected by their hosts, but they are not recognized and reacted to defensively. For example, birds that behave as brood parasites use deception by laying eggs that mimic their host's eggs, thereby deceiving the host into hatching and feeding the parasite's chicks. In ant societies, other arthropods such as beetles mimic ant communication codes and solicit food from their ant hosts. Among fish, small male sunfish (described as "transvestite" strategists by biologists) misrepresent themselves as females, "court" large males guarding nests containing eggs, and then fertilize the eggs being guarded by the larger males. Because of the complexities associated with culture and consciousness, however, humans seem most vulnerable to expropriation based on deception (Cronk 1991; Lopreato 1984). By obscuring conflicts of interest or even misrepresenting opposed interests as coincident, humans routinely mislead each other into complying with and even providing resources to their competitors and enemies. As discussed earlier, the complexity and subtlety of human interest systems often make it very difficult for humans even to identify, much less pursue rationally, their "true" interests. As a result, humans are highly vulnerable to expropriative strategies that effectively deceive hosts about whose interests are really being served by a social interaction or relationship. In fact, social activists have assigned themselves the task of "consciousness-raising" in order to help hosts realize how they subsidize expropriators and what they must do to liberate themselves of these social parasites.

As with deception, coercive expropriative behavior is detected and recognized by its host, but the expropriator makes no effort to conceal the nature of her activity. Instead, coercive expropriative activity is commonly displayed openly as a threat of force. The possession of coercive power enables both hyenas and organized crime figures, for example, to extort resources from hosts who are capable of producing usurpable resources but incapable of defending them. Biologists use the concept of "resource holding potential" (RHP) to describe those traits possessed by individuals that enable them to acquire and control a valued resource (Barash 1982; Parker 1974). RHP traits include attributes such as size, strength, age, and experience. Among humans, various social status attributes such as education, income, and occupation help comprise a person's "RHP profile." In a contest over resources, the individual or group with the RHP advantage is often in a position to use RHP superiority to adopt a coercive expropriative strategy. Coercion, however, entails risks and costs that may be avoidable when using deception and crypsis. In addition, because of the costs it imposes on hosts, coercion may represent, ironically, a strong selection force favoring the evolution of effective counter-coercive strategies in the host population. Thus, coercive strategies tend to limit their own persistence and proliferation. For these reasons, coercion may be less stable and productive as a form of long-term expropriation than are either crypsis or deception. This observation is consistent with the more conventional sociological claim that the exercise of raw power is an expensive and risky means of extracting resources over a long period of time from a subjugated population.

Whatever the species in which they are found, expropriative social forms involve, at minimum, a producer, contested resources, and an expropriator who uses crypsis, deception, or force in order to extract energy, information or a material item from a producer. The diversity of patterns of expropriation found among various species is evident in the overview of social parasitism presented earlier. It is possible, however, to identify several fundamental forms of expropriation amidst this diversity. Specifying these forms will bring us another step closer to the development of a general, interspecific theory of social exploitation.

The Basic Forms of Social Exploitation

While patterns of expropriation vary widely within and among social species, we can identify at least five dimensions in terms of which basic forms of expropriative behavioral strategies can be specified: (1) individual versus group expropriation; (2) opportunistic versus manipulative expropriation; (3) facultative versus obligatory expropriation; (4) temporary versus permanent expropriation; and (5) subtle versus gross expropriation. These forms are distributed widely, and unevenly, among social species. Each will be described briefly in turn.

Individual versus Group Expropriation

Simple forms of expropriation, such as food theft, are occasionally adopted by individual organisms such as many large carnivores, which will drive smaller predators from their prey and usurp it for themselves. Individual expropriators may also use deception or crypsis to extract a resource from an unwitting host. Expropriative strategies adopted by groups tend to occur in more complex social systems, such as those displayed by the social insects and modern humans. Slavery among ants illustrates a highly-evolved form of social parasitism wherein an entire caste or species may extract labor or food from other ants. Among humans, the domination and exploitation of one social class by another illustrates a form of group expropriation that is at least as old as the era in which horticultural societies began to become prevalent (about 9,000-10,000 years ago). In addition to social class, gender, religion, race and ethnicity, and occupation also have helped to define the bases on which humans have expropriated resources from each other. Unlike many other species, humans appear to have been equally deft in executing both individual and group strategies of social exploitation.

Opportunistic versus Manipulative Expropriation[5]

When an expropriator adopts an opportunistic strategy, she is simply usurping a resource that has been produced by another organism. Here, the expropriator does not actively manipulate the behavior of the producer in order to get the resource. Manipulation, on the other hand, occurs when the expropriator actively alters the behavior of the host so as to make a resource available to the expropriator. An eagle that seizes a fish which it has forced another eagle to drop is using an opportunistic expropriative strategy. A European cuckoo chick which opens its beak to solicit food from a warbler female is actively manipulating the warbler's behavior to provide it with food. In fact, Hölldobler conducted a series of experiments in which he was able to demonstrate that the staphylinid beetle has evolved the capacity to manipulate the behavior of its ant hosts so as to deceive them into carrying the beetle itself into their nests where it then induces its ant hosts into regurgitating food to it (in Wilson 1975, pp. 375-377). It is doubtful, however, if any other species is able to match humans for their ability to manipulate each other into producing and providing resources to nonreciprocators.

Facultative versus Obligatory Expropriation

Among some species, acquiring resources by expropriating them from others is not optional, it is obligatory. Obligatory social parasites must, at some stage in their life cycle or under certain circumstances, depend on hosts. The "ultimate" parasitic ant, *Teleutomyrmex schneideri*, practices inquilinism, an extreme form of dependence on its hosts. *Teleutomyrmex's* dependence is so complete that it has undergone what some biologists describe as a "degeneration" of its capacity to work at all. Instead, it must capture and "enslave" laborers from a host species (such as *Tetramorium caespitum*) to provide labor for its own survival. Alternatively, other species may adopt expropriative behaviors only under certain conditions. In fact, social parasitism is often a conditional strategy that is used to get resources under some circumstances but not others (Dawkins 1980, pp. 343-435). This form of expropriation is said to be facultative. Many kleptoparasites are facultative expropriators, and most forms of expropriation among humans are facultative rather than obligatory. As a conditional strategy, facultative expropriation may be adopted when an individual is incapable of producing resources for itself, perhaps because it has a deficient RHP profile. Or, an individual can take advantage of superior RHP traits and use this superiority to usurp resources from vulnerable producers incapable of defending themselves. In either case, expropriation represents a conditional, facultative behavioral strategy.[6] That is, it will be adopted in some circumstances but not others.

Temporary versus Permanent Expropriation

Facultative or obligatory expropriative strategies may be either temporary or permanent. As with some somatic parasites, such as the parasitoid wasps, expropriative strategists may depend on a host at some stages in their life cycle but not at other stages. Brood parasitic birds are a good example. As chicks, brood parasitic birds depend on their host ("foster") parents for food until they fledge, then they become self-sufficient foragers. Thus, their parasitism is obligatory but temporary. On the other hand, the inquiline syndrome among ants signifies a state of permanent parasitism among the "slave-makers." Because of the degeneration of the morphological traits required for productive activity, they are permanently dependent on productively competent hosts. Specifically, their mouthparts have evolved to become so small that they "lose the ability to feed themselves and must be sustained by liquid food regurgitated to them by the host workers" (Hölldobler and Wilson 1990, p. 467).

Sociologists may recall that the classical social theorist Vilfredo Pareto ([1916] 1963) discussed an analogous phenomenon in human societies. Studying social inequality among humans, Pareto observed a tendency for elites who inherit their dominant social positions to experience, over generations, a deterioration of the very sorts of skills and talents that helped to place and maintain them in their dominant positions. By describing a deterioration of elite qualities in the governing class, Pareto was noting something approaching an inquiline syndrome among humans and explaining how those elites who become excessively dependent on their subordinates make themselves vulnerable to revolutionary overthrow.

Subtle versus Gross Expropriation

Finally, systems of social exchange are vulnerable to two forms of expropriation discussed earlier, gross and subtle cheating (where, recall, gross cheating refers to a failure to reciprocate at all, while subtle cheating describes a situation where the reciprocator attempts to return less in quantity, in value, or both, than was received from a partner). As also noted earlier, Trivers distinguished these two types of expropriative behavior for analysis of systems of social interaction based on reciprocity or exchange. Both gross and subtle cheating presuppose the existence of a system of cooperative exchange, something that is not necessary for the evolution of the other forms of social exploitation discussed above. Accordingly, both gross and subtle cheating are most likely to be found in prolonged social relationships involving recurrent acts of reciprocity.

Pair-bonded species, such as some birds, provide a good example of a social opportunity for subtle cheating. Altricial species of birds face a situation wherein the survival of offspring depends on both parents' foraging in order to feed the offspring. This creates an opportunity for one parent to shirk its food collecting activities and, instead, seek additional mating opportunities, leaving the other parent with disproportionate responsibility for feeding its chicks. In such a case, either gross or subtle cheating could occur. If, however, the young require intense parental investment from both parents, then it is likely that natural selection will penalize efforts at expropriation between mates. In short, either gross or subtle cheating is likely to prove maladaptive in pair-bonded species with offspring requiring a high degree of parental investment from both parents.

Humans, too, are vulnerable to gross and subtle cheating among individuals and between groups. The literature on industrial workers has long documented how they develop norms which sanction workers who violate norms of cooperative behavior by producing either too little or too much, thereby threatening some optimal state of the expenditure of work effort. Similarly, literature on family and intimate relations records a high incidence of conflict in families based on perceptions of inequity in domestic work responsibilities. Finally, a great deal of research on social conflict focuses on the struggles between entire collectivities, such as social classes, that are at odds with each other in disputes involving long-standing histories of gross and/or subtle cheating. To be sure, Marx hinged nothing less than the fate of industrial capitalism on the prediction that the host proletariat class eventually would mobilize against the parasitic bourgeoisie in a revolutionary rejection of relations organized around institutionalized patterns of subtle cheating.

Summary

The five sets of social forms identified and described in this section represent but a first approximation of the sort of effort that is required to isolate and classify fundamental forms of expropriation that can be found among a variety of social species. The utility of these conceptual distinctions will be borne out only by efforts to apply them, and I hope and expect this list of fundamental social forms will be modified and expanded by comparative research on the evolution of social exploitation.

IS SOCIAL EXPLOITATION PATHOLOGICAL?

If expropriative behavior is exploitative in the sense discussed here, is it also pathological? When individuals or groups usurp information, energy, or material resources from each other, is this behavior symptomatic of some sort of pathology at the biological, psychological, social or cultural level? While expropriation *may* be rooted in pathological conditions located at some level of a living system, we need not *assume* pathology in order to develop a coherent theoretical understanding of social exploitation. Instead, expropriative behavior may be understood more parsimoniously as an expression of competition among individuals (or groups) whose interests do not coincide.

Intuitively, it is very appealing at the outset to view social exploitation as rooted in pathology, especially social pathology. In sociology, pathology has often been characterized as some sort of flaw in the organization or processes of society. Thus, the roots of social problems are sought in stratification systems, cultures of poverty, sexist socialization programs, role conflicts, disjunctions between culture and social structure that yield anomic circumstances, or other such presumed flaws in what otherwise could be robust and just social systems. The most influential system of social thought to favor the view of social exploitation as springing from a form of social organization that is fundamentally flawed is Marxism. The flaw, of course, is characterized as a contradiction deriving from the fundamental nature of the relation between capital and labor. From this fundamental contradiction arises many others, all of which are exacerbated by the very structure of the capitalist mode of production. The traditional Marxist view of a less flawed, even utopian, society is one that eradicates the fundamental contradiction inherent in the relation between capital and labor by destroying the institution of private property, thereby removing the structural basis of social exploitation. This results in the emergence of a social system organized to maximize the benefit of the (classless) society as a whole. A utopian socialist society is a society that exists for the good of the entire group.

Somewhat ironically, structural-functionalism, the theoretical perspective in sociology routinely regarded as the antithesis of Marxism (or of conflict theory in general), is also based on an underlying assumption that normal or "healthy" social systems are organized so as to maximize the well-being of the social system as a whole. The entire conceptual apparatus of structural-functionalism, especially its most influential variant—that produced by Talcott Parsons— reflects the assumption that social structures and processes are organized for the benefit of society as a whole. This is illustrated vividly by several of Parsons' famous constructs, such as those referring to the system requisites or functional prerequisites of society (Parsons, Bales, and Shils 1953). Actually, most sociological thought is based largely on the assumption that the structures and processes of societies exist for the benefit of society as a whole or for certain groups, such as dominant classes, within society.

In evolutionary biology, this logic is called "group benefit" or "group selection" reasoning, and today it has few subscribers. In 1966, the evolutionary biologist G.C. Williams wrote an influential treatise challenging the idea that social traits evolve for the benefit of groups themselves, thereby ushering in an era of evolutionary thought dominated by the alternative perspective that group life represents a complex of adaptations favoring the interests predominantly of the individuals involved in it. In fact, with a few exceptions (see Wynne-Edwards 1962; Wilson in press), most evolutionary scientists have come to eschew group-benefit reasoning in favor of an alternative view that social life evolved in service of the reproductive success of individuals and their close kin, or, stated differently, the replicative success of the genetic material "housed in" and conveyed by individuals (Dawkins 1982, 1989).

Although group-benefit reasoning still typifies much contemporary sociological work, the version represented by Parsons' structural-functional thinking has come under severe criticism for almost three decades. The radical critique mounted against structural-functionalism has been largely successful in dissuading most sociologists from continuing to view society as a reified system organized by mechanisms designed to assure its survival as an autonomous entity. Instead, Parsons' version of "group-benefit reasoning" has been replaced by another that seeks to place primary emphasis on conflicts of interests *among groups* within societies, or within larger social system units such as the "world system." Yet, the basic logic of what evolutionary biologists call "group-benefit reasoning" remains in tact even here, in conflict theory. Instead of interpreting patterns of social organization and social process as regulated by some sort of mechanisms designed to assure the survival and functional integrity of society as a whole, conflict theorists emphasize that social structures and processes are an expression of the struggles among various collectivities that are described as conflict groups or interest groups. Originally developed in order to analyze the struggle between classes, conflict theory has been expanded to accommodate other group struggles organized along lines of race/ethnicity, gender, occupation, religion, or more abstractly, "imperatively coordinated associations" of any sort (Dahrendorf 1959). In this view, membership in a particular conflict group means sharing common interests with other members of the group, an outcome based on a shared position in the social relations of production, common gender, or other shared social attributes, such as race, ethnicity, or religion. Thus, patterns of social exploitation *within* a conflict group (such as a class) are likely to be seen as pathological, because the group itself is understood to exist on the foundation of some shared interest created by a commonly held social attribute. While the logic of conflict theory shares much more in common with modern biological evolutionary theory than does its archrival structural-functionalism (despite the interpretation of some social theorists such as Maryanski and Turner [1991]), both perspectives are based ultimately on group-benefit reasoning, albeit the "group" in one instance is conceptualized as an interest group *within* society as a whole (e.g., a "class"), while in the second instance the "group" is conceptualized *as* "society as a whole."

Building an explanation of social behavior on the basis of group-benefit reasoning may impose an unnecessary burden on the social analyst. While it may be possible in some instances to employ group-benefit reasoning in order to explain social patterns, it is unnecessary to reify the group as an integrated, autonomous entity as have generations of sociologists. That is, by trying first to see how much of group life we can explain as having derived from the efforts of individuals to realize their interests, we may be able to avoid many of the problems (e.g., reification of the group) associated with group-benefit reasoning. Only when it becomes implausibly difficult to explain a social pattern in terms of the benefits it bestows upon individuals might it become necessary to begin exploring the possibility that it evolved because of the benefits it yields to "the group." In criticizing group-benefit reasoning in social theory, Trivers (1985) describes rather vividly his struggles with overcoming the appeal of this form of thinking, especially in the social sciences:

> This fallacy has been so wide-spread and so powerful in its repercussions that it deserves special treatment. Indeed, I remember well the grip it had on my own mind—and the confusion it generated—while I was still an undergraduate. So many disciplines conceptualized the human condition in terms of individual versus society. Sociology and anthropology seemed to claim that the larger unit was the key to understanding the smaller one. Societies, groups, species—all evolved mechanisms by which individuals are merely the unconscious tools in their larger designs. In the extreme position, the larger groups were imagined to have the cohesiveness and interconnectedness usually associated with individual organisms (p. 67).

And, when Trivers (1985) finally confronted head-on the implications of reliance on group-benefit reasoning, "whole worlds of sociology, anthropology, and political science came crashing to the ground" (p. 81). While we are not guaranteed the sort of epiphany reported by Trivers when he realized the fallacy of naive group-benefit reasoning, it is worth seeing what might be gained by abandoning, at least temporarily, the long-standing sociological reliance on this logic.

By reframing the analysis of expropriative social behavior in evolutionary terms, we gain the analytical advantage of not having to *assume*, at the outset, that expropriation signifies pathology (biological, psychological, social, or cultural), yet we reserve the right to *discover* that a particular expression of social exploitation may be diagnostic of some underlying pathological condition. In other words, modern evolutionary theory gives us an opportunity first to try to determine whether a particular form of expropriative social behavior is expressive of competitive relations among individuals whose interests diverge before we are compelled to search for evidence of some sort of pathological ("dysfunctional," "contradictory") arrangement from which expropriation arises.[7]

By relaxing the assumption of group-benefit reasoning, we can look anew at the evolution of social exploitation among diverse social species, both human and nonhuman. Instead of having to resort to the notion that expropriation is caused by traits of "abnormal" individuals or by the features of exceptional social environments, we can see how much expropriative behavior can be explained as competition among individuals whose interests fail to coincide. It is important to interject that this does not imply an ethical or moral endorsement of competition. The consequences of competition in the form of "normal" patterns of expropriation may be abhorrent, and worthy of condemnation and concerted efforts toward eradication. To interpret expropriation as competition but as not necessarily "pathological" does not imply an acceptance of social exploitation as biological destiny.

CONCLUSIONS

No other scientific discipline has devoted as much scholarly attention to the study of various forms of social exploitation as has sociology. Many of the specialty areas within sociology focus extensively on the study of one or another variety of social exploitation, including social stratification, race and ethnic relations, gender studies, criminology, collective behavior and social movements, political sociology, social problems, and several entire theoretical perspectives such as Marxism, critical theory, and a variety of other strains of "conflict theory." To a naturalist, it might seem puzzling that virtually none of these specialties has expanded its scope of inquiry to include social exploitation (when defined as expropriative behavior) in nonhuman societies as well. Essentially, the study of social exploitation by sociologists remains restricted to one species—humans. To a large extent this is probably due to an assumption shared, consciously or otherwise, by most sociologists that human and nonhuman animal behaviors are incommensurable. In a sense, few naturalists would disagree. If one wants to learn about flying foxes, one should study flying foxes. If one wants to learn about humans, one should study humans. If, on the other hand, we want to learn about fundamental properties of social organization and interaction in general, it is not clear that we are well-advised to restrict our attention to but one social species. Should we be interested in trying to identify those basic aspects of social organization and social interaction that inhibit or promote the incidence of expropriation within a society, we may be well-served by adopting a broad, truly comparative, interspecific approach. Having determined the generic features of social exploitation, we may then be in a better position to identify unique, species-typical forms of social exploitation and explain how they work. Thus, the perspective introduced in this essay is marked by an enthusiasm for a more naturalistic, cross-species mode of social analysis that is informed by insights from behavioral biology, especially behavioral ecology, ethology, and sociobiology. Such an approach affords the promise of being able to lead us closer to an understanding of aspects of social exploitation that are basic to the social lives of any social species, human or nonhuman. And, instead of culminating in a vulgar reductionism in which the species-typical features of behavior (such as culture and consciousness) are neglected or obscured, comparative analysis can highlight how diverse phylogenies yield diverse species, each of which can be understood only by analyzing these phylogenies and the unique, evolved behavioral capacities that each species exhibits. An evolutionary and ecological analysis of social behavior written in this key can only enrich our understanding of and appreciation for the behavioral diversity that exists among various social species.

According to evolutionary theory, group life is based on at least one of two foundations: genetic kinship or reciprocity. In some species and in some circumstances, both factors undergird the establishment and regulation of social behavior. Kin selection theory explains cooperation among related participants as a form of self-interested behavior. The behavior is self-interested, because the participants share genetic material and thus benefit mutually by contributing to each other's advantage. Reciprocity theory, on the other hand, sees group life as deriving from the exchange of various resources from which those involved benefit, related or not. Both perspectives reduce cooperation to an interest-serving device. Still, both perspectives may appear too narrow to many sociologists who would contend that at least some aspects of group life and social behavior cannot be reduced to such utilitarian, interest-serving mechanisms. With reference to humans at least, the objection is probably legitimate. There may very well be features of human societies that do not derive from the interests (either material or symbolic) of their members. When this is true, evolutionary theory may have little to offer by way of explanatory power. In such cases, an alternative approach must be taken.

Yet, at least several decades of research in behavioral biology and one and one-half to two centuries of social scientific inquiry converge to lead us to conclude that a great deal of group life appears organized primarily on the basis of the interests of those engaged in it. Accordingly, it seems only prudent first to try to explain as much of social behavior as possible in terms of the interests at stake in the interaction before pursuing alternative explanatory avenues. Nowhere does this seem more appropriate than with the study of expropriative social behavior. To a large extent, evolutionary biology and sociology converge in their emphasis on the role of interests in shaping social life. They differ, as discussed earlier, with regard to the specific interests they see as relevant to organizing social behavior, with biology placing primary emphasis on genetic interests and sociology emphasizing nongenetic (e.g., economic, political, symbolic) interests.

While the type of analysis proposed in this essay leaves open the specific types of interests at stake in conflicts between producers and expropriators, evolutionary and ecological reasoning suggest that the role of genetic interests in shaping patterns of production and expropriation should be considered in all studies, even those involving human societies. This need not be done at the expense of failing to acknowledge the influence of other classes of interests as well. Instead, it provides the researcher with a sufficiently broad analytical framework that admits the possible influence of multiple factors in human social behavior. At minimum, the assumption of a broadly comparative, cross-species stance toward the study of social exploitation expands the scope of social science inquiry and presents otherwise "hominid bound" social scientists with new research opportunities. More promising still is the prospect of identifying features of social organization and aspects of social interaction that influence expropriative behavior in any society, human or nonhuman. And finally, most ambitiously, the mode of analysis proposed here could help promote cooperation between social scientists and behavioral biologists and thereby enable us to develop a more complete scientific understanding of the evolution of social exploitation in nature.

ACKNOWLEDGMENTS

At an early stage in the development of these ideas, I received valuable guidance from several people including Norman Carlin, Ivan Chase, Mark Moffett, Robin Stuart, and Edward O. Wilson. I am very appreciative of their assistance. Special thanks are due my colleague Larry Cohen, for helping to clarify my thinking about expropriation as we developed an evolutionary approach to the study of expropriative crime. This work has been supported by a sabbatical leave granted by the University of Wyoming.

NOTES

1.   Despite the beliefs of more than a few social scientists, the utilitarian logic of contemporary evolutionary theory in biology bears little resemblance to classic utilitarian thinking in sociology and economics. While, historically, sociological utilitarianism entailed a view of "actors" as "unregulated and atomistic...in a free and competitive marketplace rationally attempting to choose those behaviors that will maximize their profits in their transactions with others," biological evolutionary theory does not share the "concern with actors...seeking goals and the emphasis on ...choice-making capacities of human beings"(or any other organism) that helped define classical utilitarian theory in the social sciences (Turner 1991, p. 53). Yet, sociologists commonly err by trying to reduce the rather more subtle logic of organic evolutionary theory to no more than a warmed-over version of classic utilitarian social theory (e.g., Maryanski and Turner 1991, pp. 166-167). The difficulty resides with social scientists' misunderstandings of the theory of natural selection. For example, they commonly misrepresent evolutionary theory as imputing teleological properties to genes and contend erroneously that evolutionists posit a "need for fitness" on the part "goal-directed genes [which] are seen as trying to maximize their fitness"(Maryanski and Turner 1991, pp. 165-167). Instead, what is utilitarian about modern evolutionary theory is the focus on adaptations, traits that are "useful" to the organisms which acquire them (and not by any teleological or "goal-directed" processes). Basically, evolution is a theory about alternative versions of information (alleles) that become more or less numerous in populations across generations because of their consequences for the individuals that bear and transmit them. While the processes whereby these alleles appear and disappear and become more or less numerous in populations may *appear* teleological to someone less than fully-informed about the mechanisms of evolution by natural selection, there is nothing whatsoever teleological about "evolutionary utilitarianism."

2.   See Robin Stuart's (1983) note on the use of anthropocentric terminology in the animal behavior studies for an excellent discussion of this issue. Hölldobler and Wilson (1990, p. 453) suggest that true slavery, as in humans, involves intraspecific exploitation. Ant slavery typically involves two different species and may be better compared to forced domestication.

3.   An application of the idea of crime as expropriative behavior can be found in Cohen and Machalek (1988, 1994) and Machalek and Cohen (1991).

4.   This example has to be forwarded with caution, because it is not clear that reducing fertility, per se, always translates into reduced fitness, especially among socially advantaged people living in industrial societies. Instead, such behavior may represent a K-selected strategy for producing fewer offspring in whom one is able to invest more resources, thereby increasing their chances of survival and reproductive success. A K-selected reproductive strategy means that a parent has ample resources to invest in a relatively small number of offspring, thereby maximizing the offspring's health, survival chances, and thus reproductive opportunities. Thus, postponing reproduction until one has enough resources to adopt a K-selected strategy may actually turn out to yield greater fitness than if one produced as many offspring as possible as early in life as possible, regardless of one's economic circumstance.

5.   This distinction is essentially the same as Barnard's (1984) distinction between "usurpation" and "manipulation," except that I prefer to use the term opportunism rather than usurpation, which I reserve for more general usage throughout this essay.

6. Cohen and Machalek (1988) discuss certain forms of crime as conditional, facultative strategies that are adopted by individuals who may be either advantaged or disadvantaged in terms of RHP traits relevant to resource acquisition.

7. Of course, one can salvage the position that social exploitation is always diagnostic of pathology by defining all competition as pathological. This sort of ideological sleight of hand gives us desperately little purchase on trying to develop a causal understanding of social exploitation, however. Instead, it effectively redefines almost all relationships in nature as "exploitative" or expropriative, a position affording virtually no explanatory power within the explanatory paradigms of either modern evolutionary biology or social science.

REFERENCES

Alcock, J. 1984. *Animal Behavior: An Evolutionary Approach*, 3rd ed. Sunderland, MA: Sinauer Associates, Inc.

Axelrod, R. 1984. *The Evolution of Cooperation*. New York: Basic Books.

Barash, D.P. 1982. *Sociobiology and Behavior*, 2nd ed. New York: Elsevier.

Barnard, C.J., ed. 1984. *Producers and Scroungers: Strategies of Exploitation and Parasitism*. New York: Chapman and Hall.

Birkhead, T.R., T. Burke, R. Zann, F.M. Hunter, and A.P. Krupa. 1990. "Extra-pair Paternity and Intraspecific Brood Parasitism in Wild Zebra Finches *Taeniopygia guttata*, Revealed by DNA Fingerprinting." *Behavioral Ecology and Sociobiology* 27: 315-324.

Blau, P.M. 1964. *Exchange and Power in Social Life*. New York: Free Press.

_____ . 1971. "Justice in Social Exchange." Pp. 56-68 in *Institutions and Social Exchange: The Sociologies of Talcott Parsons and George C. Homans*, edited by H. Turk and R.L. Simpson. Indianapolis, IN: Bobbs-Merrill.

Brockmann, H.J., A. Grafen, and R. Dawkins. 1979. "Evolutionary Stable Nesting Strategy in a Digger Wasp." *Journal of Theoretical Biology* 77: 473-496.

Brown, C.R. and M.B. Brown. 1989. "Behavioral Dynamics of Intraspecific Brood Parasitism in Colonial Cliff Swallows." *Animal Behavior* 37: 777-796.

_____ . 1991. "Selection of High-Quality Host Nests by Parasitic Cliff Swallows." *Animal Behavior* 41: 457-465.

Brown, C.R. and L.L. Sherman. 1989. "Variation in the Appearance of Swallow Eggs and the Detection of Interspecific Brood Parasitism." *The Condor* 91: 620-627.

Cade, W. 1979. "The Evolution of Alternative Male Reproductive Strategies in Field Crickets." Pp. 343-379 in *Sexual Selection and Reproductive Competition in Insects*, edited by M. Blum and N.A. Blum. London: Academic Press.

Cangialosi, K.R. 1990. "Social Spider Defense Against Kleptoparasitism." *Behavioral Ecology and Sociobiology* 27: 49-54.

Cervo, R., M.C. Lorenzi, and S. Turillazzi. 1990. "Nonaggressive Usurpation of the Nest of *Polistes bigulmis bimaculatus* by the Social Parasite *Sulcopolistes atrimandibularis* (Hymenoptera Vespidae)." *Insectes Sociaux/Social Insects* 37: 333-347.

Cohen, L.E. and R. Machalek. 1988. "A General Theory of Expropriative Crime: An Evolutionary Ecological Approach." *American Journal of Sociology* 94: 465-501.

_____ . 1994. "The Normalcy of Crime: From Durkheim to Evolutionary Ecology." *Rationality and Society* 6(April): 286-308.

Cronk, L. 1991. "Communication as Manipulation: Implications for Biosociological Research." Paper presented at the Annual Meetings of the American Sociological Association, Cincinnati.

Dahrendorf, R. 1959. *Class and Class Conflict in Industrial Society*. Stanford, CA: Stanford Univeristy Press.

Daub, B.C. 1989. "Behavior of Common Loons in Winter." *Journal of Field Ornithology* 60: 305-311.

Dawkins, R. 1980. "Good Strategy or Evolutionary Stable Strategy?" Pp. 331-367 in *Sociobiology: Beyond Nature/Nurture? Reports, Definitions and Debate*, edited by G.W. Barlow and J. Silverberg. Boulder, CO: Westview.

————. 1982. *The Extended Phenotype: The Gene as the Unit of Selection*. Oxford: W.H. Freeman.

————. 1989. *The Selfish Gene*, 2nd ed. Oxford: Oxford University Press.

Dominey, W. 1980. "Female Mimicry in Male Bluegill Sunfish—A Genetic Polymorphism?" *Nature* 284: 546-548.

Elgar, M.A. 1989. "Kleptoparasitism: A Cost of Aggregating for an Orb-Weaving Spider." *Animal Behavior* 37: 1052-1055.

Estes, R.D. and J. Goddard 1967. "Prey Selection and Hunting Behavior of the African Wild Dog." *Journal of Wildlife Management* 31: 52-70.

Fagen, R. 1981. *Animal Play Behavior*. Oxford: Oxford University Press.

Forbes, C.S. 1991. "Intraspecific Piracy in Ospreys." *The Wilson Bulletin* 103: 111-112.

Hamilton, W.D. 1964. "The Genetical Evolution of Social Behavior." *Journal of Theoretical Biology* 7: 1-52.

Hansen, A.J. 1986. "Fighting Behavior in Bald Eagles: A Test of Game Theory." *Ecology* 67: 787-797.

Hochschild, A. 1989. *The Second Shift: Working Parents and the Revolution at Home*. New York: Viking.

Hölldobler, B. 1970. "Zur Physiologie der Gast-Wirt-Beziehungen (Myrmecophilie) bei Ameisen: II, das Gastverhältnis des imaginalen *Atemeles pubicollis* Bris.(Col. Staphylinidae) zu *Myrmica* und *Formica* (Hym. Formicidae)." *Zeitschrift für Vergleichende Physiologie* 66: 215-250.

Hölldobler, B. and E.O. Wilson 1990. *The Ants*. Cambridge, MA: The Belknap Press of Harvard University Press.

Howard, R.D. 1978. "The Evolution of Mating Strategies in Bullfrogs, *Rana catesbiana*." *Evolution* 32: 850-871.

Krebs, J.R. and N.B. Davies 1981. *An Introduction to Behavioural Ecology*. Sunderland, MA: Sinauer Associates, Inc.

Lack, D. 1968. *Ecological Adaptations for Breeding in Birds*. Oxford: Oxford University Press.

Lank, D.B., P. Mineau, R.F. Rockwell, and F. Cooke. 1990. "Frequency-dependent Fitness Consequences of Intraspecific Nest Parasitism in Snow Geese." *Evolution* 44: 1436-1453.

Lopreato, J. 1984. *Human Nature and Biocultural Evolution*. Winchester, MA: Allen & Unwin.

Machalek, R. 1992. "The Evolution of Macrosociety: Why Are Large Societies Rare?" Pp. 33-64 in *Advances in Human Ecology*, Vol. 1, edited by L. Freese. Greenwich, CT: JAI Press.

Machalek, R. and Lawrence E. Cohen. 1991. "The Nature of Crime: Is Cheating Necessary for Cooperation?" *Human Nature* 2: 215-233.

Marx, K. (1867) 1967. *Capital: A Critical Analysis of Capitalist Production*. New York: International Publishers.

————. (1848) 1971. *The Communist Manifesto*. New York: International Publishers.

Maryanski, A. and J.H. Turner. 1991. "Biological Functionalism." Pp. 152-177 in *The Structure of Sociological Theory*, 5th ed., edited by J.H. Turner. Belmont, CA: Wadsworth.

Mayer, M. 1974. *The Bankers*. New York: Ballantine Books.

Meyerriecks, A.J. 1972. *Man and Birds: Evolution and Behavior*. Indianapolis, IN: Pegasus, Bobbs-Merrill.

Mueller, J.K., A.K. Eggert, and J. Dressel. 1990. "Intraspecific Brood Parasitism in the Burying Beetle, *Necrophorus vespilloides* (Coleoptera: Silphidae)." *Animal Behavior* 40: 491-499.

Pareto, V. (1916) 1963. *A Treatise on General Sociology*, 4 vols. New York: Dover Publications. (Also known as *The Mind and Society*)

Parker, G.A. 1974. "Assessment Strategy and the Evolution of Animal Conflicts." *Journal of Theoretical Biology* 47: 223-243.

Parsons, T., R.F. Bales, and E.A. Shils. 1953. *Working Papers in the Theory of Action*. Glencoe, IL: Free Press of Glencoe.

Perrill, S.A., H.C. Gerhardt, and R. Daniel. 1978. "Sexual Parasitism in the Green Tree Frog, *Hyla cinerea*." *Science* 200: 1179-1180.

Roeskaft, E., A.T. Braa, L. Kursnes, H.M Lampe, and H.C. Pedersen. 1991. "Behavioral Responses of Potential Hosts Towards Artificial Cuckoo Eggs and Dummies." *Behavior* 116: 64-85.

Rowher, F.C. and S. Freeman. 1989. "The Distribution of Conspecific Nest Parasitism in Birds." *Canadian Journal of Zoology* 67: 239-253.

Sealy, S.G., K.A. Hobson, and J.V. Briskie. 1989. "Responses of Yellow Warblers to Experimental Intraspecific Brood Parasitism." *Journal of Field Ornithology* 60: 224-229.

Stuart, R. 1983. "A Note on Terminology in Animal Behavior, with Special Reference to Slavery in Ants." *Animal Behavior* 31: 1259-1260.

Sullivan, K.A., J. Cole, and E.M. Villalobos. 1989. "Intraspecific Nest Usurpation by a Yellow-eyed Junco." *The Wilson Bulletin* 101: 654-655.

Tershey, B.R., D. Breese, and G.M. Meyer. 1990. "Kleptoparasitism of Adult and Immature Brown Pelicans by Heermann's Gulls." *The Condor* 92: 1076-1077.

Tiger, L. 1987. *The Manufacture of Evil: Ethics, Evolution and the Industrial System*. New York: Marion Boyars.

Trivers, R.L. 1971. "The Evolution of Reciprocal Altruism." *Quarterly Review of Biology* 46: 35-57.

————— . 1972. "Parental Investment and Sexual Selection." Pp. 136-179 in *Sexual Selection and the Descent of Man 1871-1971*, edited by B Campbell. Chicago: Aldine.

————— . 1985. *Social Evolution*. Menlo Park, CA: Benjamin/Cummings.

Turner, J.H. 1991. *The Structure of Sociological Theory*, 5th ed. Belmont, CA: Wadsworth.

Williams, G.C. 1966. *Adaptation and Natural Selection*. Princeton, NJ: Princeton University Press.

Wilson, D.S. In press. "Reintroducing Group Selection to the Human Behavioral Sciences." *Behavioral and Brain Sciences*.

Wilson, E.O. 1971. *The Insect Societies*. Cambridge, MA: The Belknap Press of Harvard University Press.

————— . 1975. *Sociobiology: The New Synthesis*. Cambridge, MA: The Belknap Press of Harvard University Press.

Wolff, K.H., Trans. and ed. 1950. *The Sociology of Georg Simmel*. Glencoe, IL: Free Press of Glencoe.

Wynne-Edwards, V.C. 1962. *Animal Dispersion in Relation to Social Behavior*. Edinburgh: Oliver and Boyd.

ARE THE DILEMMAS POSED BY PUBLIC GOODS AND COMMON POOL RESOURCES THE SAME?

Yeongi Son and Jane Sell

ABSTRACT

We compare the dilemmas of public goods with those of resource goods by examining the theoretical issues associated with expected utility formulations and with prospect theory. If prospect theory is correct, it seems to imply that resource dilemmas should be easier to solve than public goods dilemmas. The reasoning behind such a conclusion rests with the concepts of risk aversion and the endowment effect. Few studies have directly compared the two kinds of dilemmas, however, and those that do, do not find consistent results. We discuss what might be theoretically and empirically necessary for a direct comparison.

INTRODUCTION

Large or small scale resource development and maintenance issues are often referred to as social dilemmas if they are characterized by conflict between short-run individual interests and long-run group interests (see Dawes 1980).

Advances in Human Ecology, Volume 4, pages 69-88.
Copyright © 1995 by JAI Press Inc.
All rights of reproduction in any form reserved.
ISBN: 1-55938-874-9

Cases of such dilemmas may range from the protection of the Coachella Valley fringe-toed lizard to establishment of international alliances such as NATO. These two cases represent different versions of a conflict in interests. The fringe-toed lizard thrives in a particular desert environment in which the sand is fine and wind-blown. Human development and settlement has encroached upon the environment of the lizard, threatening its existence. Here the social dilemma revolves around the interests of the developers and land-dwellers in the short-run, versus the existence of an entire species and the benefit such biodiversity brings. In the political alliance case, all nations must agree to give up some of their resources (money, autonomy) for the long-term expected benefit of protection against common enemies. The interest conflict then is the reluctance to "give up" individual resources for the long-term benefits of collective defense.

There is a thriving literature in social dilemmas which spans disciplines and methodologies. Social dilemmas are generally characterized by two subsets or types: public goods, as exemplified by NATO and resource goods as illustrated by the fringe-toed lizard. Each of these subsets has its own "classic" statement; for public goods it is Mancur Olson's (1965) *The Logic of Collective Action;* for resource dilemmas it is Garrett Hardin's (1968) "The Tragedy of the Commons." There is some controversy whether these two types of dilemmas are, in fact, theoretically the same: Some have maintained that they are equivalent (e.g., Ledyard forthcoming), some have argued that they are different (e.g., Kramer and Brewer 1986), and others have tried to remain agnostic about the issue (Sell 1988).

We address this controversy. In doing so, we are required to address some fundamental issues often represented as pitting expected utility theory against prospect theory. We first describe these two theories as they relate to the social dilemma issue. We then examine the properties that might drive possible differences, and examine evidence regarding these differences. We argue that the competition between the two theories is not zero-sum; but, we also argue that it is important to distinguish the two dilemmas.

In discussions of social dilemmas and sometimes in definitions of social dilemmas, "incentive problems" are invoked (e.g., the Dawes [1980] definition is based on such problems). These "incentive problems" actually derive from some assumptions regarding utility functions—the starting point of so much economic theory. As it turns out, there is some disagreement about the form and structure of utility functions, which affects any predictions and explanations that incorporate these functions. As this is the case, let us first consider the relatively noncontroversial issue of how public goods and public resources are defined, irrespective of consideration of utility functions.

THE NONEXCLUDABILITY PROPERTY

The defining property of both public goods and public resources is nonexcludability: Ownership or rights of access to the good or resource do not hinge on individual contribution to the acquisition of the good or resource. This separates public goods and resources from private goods (and resources) because private goods are necessarily tied to an actor's payment. For example, if the Grusak family goes to a store and buys a swing set, the Grusaks own the swing set—it is their private good. They can choose to exclude access to neighbors and others based on their own preferences. If the community buys a swing set for a public park, access is not just limited to those who pay the highest taxes, or those who pay taxes at all. In fact, those who are most likely to use the swings—children who don't have swings at home—are probably those who are least likely to have paid for the good.

When a resource already exists and all can partake of it (that is, again, it is nonexcludable), the resource is public. The oceans are resource goods and, while there are rules about rights to oceans, no one nation or one group of people *own* the oceans. Examples of such goods are usually of a biological nature, but it is theoretically possible that the resource might not involve living organisms.[1]

For economists, the property of nonexcludability creates a whole context that must be considered apart from market contexts. In market situations supply and demand can operate, and competition can emerge. Further, the valuation of a good or resource is easily determined by examining what an actor, be it an individual or a firm, is willing to pay. For public goods or resources, the market cannot operate: The community is not asking each community member to buy an inch of bar for the swing set that could be used only by their family; the community is attempting to provide the good for the consumption of all members.

Based on this nonexcludability property and some assumptions about utility functions, economists argue that public goods create two related problems. First, because benefits are provided regardless of individuals' payment, individuals have an incentive to "free ride," that is, to not contribute or pay. If the community does not tie contributions to swing set use, the Grusaks may be tempted not to contribute at all or to contribute less than what might be requested by the community.

Second, because individual preference for a good is not necessarily related to price, individuals have an incentive to "understate" their true preferences. In market economics, individuals have no incentive to hide their preference since hiding it would only mean they would not acquire the good. For example, if the Grusaks thought the price of the swing set was too high, they might want to bargain until the price was acceptable. When the price is acceptable, their preference has been *revealed*. If the community provides the swing set, however, one does not lose the privilege of using the swing set by understating its value. From the economist's point of view, this understatement of preference leads to problems for optimizing the welfare of the community concerned.

This first issue is ordinarily taken for granted by economists (with the exception of experimental economists, as we shall see), and more attention has been concentrated upon the second issue. But to examine how economists arrive at the two incentive problems and to see how controversy over predictions (and data) occur, we need to consider how expected utility theory is used and what commitments occur because of its use.[2]

EXPECTED UTILITY THEORY (EU)

Perhaps the most fundamental notion underlying the discipline of economics is the *preference relation*. To examine exchange, there must exist some rationale for why people might exchange, and why goods and services acquire value. The concept of preference deals with this crucial issue. Preferences express relations among different goods. These preferences then translate to choices through which preferences are *revealed*. Suppose, for example, that an actor is confronted with a particular choice among three goods: spending x amount to protect the fringe-toed lizard, spending x amount to support desert development and spending x amount to take a vacation. According to the relations of revealed preference, given the same set of circumstances, the same budget constraints, and so forth, the choice made at one choice point will be the same as the choice made at another choice point. Further, the relationships between the three preferences are supposed to remain asymmetric and transitive. In the example above, asymmetric means under conditions c_1, if fringe-toed lizards are chosen first, a vacation second, and land development third, these choices remain constant and in the same order. Under the same conditions, c_1, it is not allowed (and, theoretically, should never be the case) that desert development would be chosen before the fringe-toed lizard. Further, the relations are *transitive*. When the preferences are revealed under conditions c_1, it should be the case that, because fringe-toed lizards were chosen before vacations and vacations before desert development, fringe-toed lizards should be chosen before desert development. In other words, the transitivity relation preserves the ordering between and among the preferences. Utility functions are abstract, formal ways to depict what preferences affect actors' decisions, and the general manner or function in which they do so.

The underlying ideas of preferences and preference bundles refer to certain outcomes. That is, when the choices are presented and when the actor makes those choices, all the properties of the goods are perfectly known. The certainty of saving the fringe-toed lizard or the certainty of the vacation are absolute. Often, however, the environment is not perfectly predictable and the actual quality or value of the good is not really known. In fact, some of the most important decisions we make involve great amounts of uncertainty. For example, when money is donated for the preservation of the fringe-toed lizard, whether or not the money will actually save the habitat, or how much of the habitat will be saved, or how many lizards will be maintained, is all uncertain. When uncertainty is a theoretically important aspect of the environment, then the concepts of preferences and utility can be translated with the use of probability.

How can this be done? One way to represent uncertainty is in terms of the likelihood of an event. Unlikely events would have lower probabilities than more likely events. When events are not certain, their value or worth is a function of their value under certain conditions *and* their probability of occurrence. If the probability of saving the fringe-toed lizard was very low (and thus uncertain), while the probability of a personal vacation or land development was quite high, the value or utility of the lizard would have to be very high to preserve the revealed preference illustrated above (lizards preferred to vacations preferred to land development). Using the probability of an occurrence and its original value of preference ordering is called *expected utility*. Expected utility theory (called EU) is a way to preserve and build on the potent, fundamental concept of preference relations.

Furthermore, these preferences can be interpreted as utilities and the value of the probability distribution as equivalent to the expected utility it will provide to actors. Often the utility representation is referred to as von Neumann-Morgenstern utilities, from their *Theory of Games and Economic Behavior* (1944), but it is generally attributed to Daniel Bernoulli in the eighteenth century. So, the application of probability distributions to preference relations preserves the underlying attributes of preference relations. Among these attributes are asymmetry and transitivity.

In addition, Bernoulli recognized and addressed the issue of risk perceptions. An actor who prefers a sure amount over a risky amount is *risk averse*. As a consequence, this risk averse actor's utility function would be concave, as in Figure 1. This curve indicates that if an actor did not like to take risks, he or she might choose a sure thing of less initial value than an uncertain thing. If an actor were *risk neutral* and risk had no effect, his or her utility functions would be linear. Finally, an actor could be *risk-seeking*, in which case, his or her utility functions would be convex. In this latter case, risk or uncertainty actually increases the value of the uncertain good. Typically, risk aversity is assumed in economics and there is an extensive literature which deals with how it affects differing circumstances.

PROSPECT THEORY

The title "prospect theory" is sometimes given to the collective set of findings suggesting that, under some conditions, expected utility theory does not predict

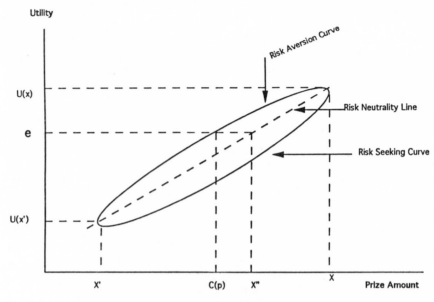

For a lottery p that yields an outcome of
prize x with probability 2/3 and x' with
probability 1/3, the expected value is x'', the
expected utility of the lottery is e, and the
certainty equivalent of the lottery is C(p).

Source: Adapted from Kreps (1990).

Figure 1.

actors' behaviors well. The most discussed disagreements with expected utility
theory center upon reference dependence, loss aversion and diminishing
sensitivity (see Tversky and Kahneman 1991).

Remembering that expected utility theory proposes that decisions can be
characterized as transitive and asymmetric, numerous findings suggest this is
not the case. And deviations from EU are not random; in fact they are clearly
patterned. In examining these deviations, it is clear that they often bear upon
the issue of "giving" versus "taking." In turn, it seems evident that this should
affect comparisons of resource goods versus public goods, since in public goods
the decision involves contributing or paying, while in resource dilemmas the
decision involves refraining from taking what already exists.

The primary principle that seems to counter EU theory is loss aversion. It
is not that EU theory does not address some types of aversion. As discussed
above, it does; and, as a result, utility functions under conditions of uncertainty
or risk are generally conceptualized as concave (as shown in Figure 1).
However, prospect theory claims that the standard treatments of expected

utility and risk aversion are incomplete because losses are psychologically different from gains. Specifically, they are different with respect to loss aversion: *In the loss domain, individuals become risk-seeking.* This is different from the risk-seeking allowance mentioned in discussion of expected utility because the prospect theory claim is not that certain individuals are risk-seeking but, rather, that the same individual who is risk-aversive for gains or acquisitions is risk-seeking for losses. This difference leads to the much used "typical value function" featured in many of the discussions of prospect theory and demonstrated in Figure 2. In comparing Figures 1 and 2, the important difference is in the domains represented. Since the ultimate arbitrator of expected utility function is the preference and the probability associated with that preference, only the outcome value is important. Consequently, only a single graph is necessary. For prospect theory, the claim is that mathematically equivalent outcomes may not yield the same utility. And the reason this can occur is that gains and losses are differentially evaluated. Consequently two graphs are necessary—one representing gains and one representing losses. So, if a particular situation is framed as one in which gains are involved—gains in biodiversity for example—individuals are most often risk-averse. This would mean that under conditions of potential risk (say, for example, if creating a protected area for the fringe-toed lizard were problematic because of the weather conditions), actors are more likely to act conservatively, so that the amount of protection possibilities would have to be quite high to take the

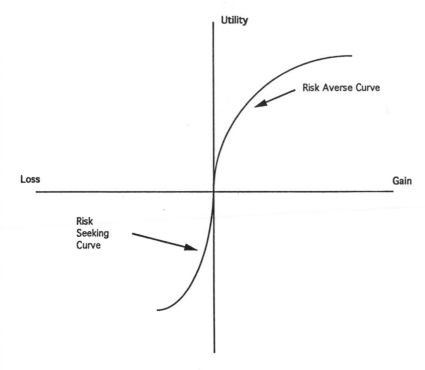

Figure 2.

chance on contributing to such a project. On the other hand, given the same problematic weather conditions, if the problem was the prevention of the loss of an already-created protected area, actors would be more likely to value the project and thereby contribute more money.

Reference dependence and loss aversion are closely related. Reference dependence means one's reaction to a choice is dependent upon one's position or state of acquisition. In particular, if an actor acquires a particular good, it becomes more valuable *because of the acquisition*. So, for example, if we buy an alligator, the moment we acquire the animal, its value increases. Thaler (1980) has labeled this phenomenon the "endowment effect," and there have been numerous tests of the phenomenon reported (Kahneman, Knetsch, and Thaler 1990; Knetsch 1989; Knetsch, Thaler, and Kahneman 1988).

The endowment effect is one way in which the "status quo bias" can evolve. That status quo bias (a concept named and discussed by Samuelson and Zeckhauser 1988) means that, in choice situations, actors seem to prefer (over and above what EU would predict) what they already have versus what they could have. Tversky and Kahneman (1991) note that the status quo bias seems to be a subset of loss aversion, but note that Samuelson and Zeckhauser (1988) mention that, even in the absence of loss aversion, status quo bias could occur.

Indeed, social psychologists find evidence of such a status quo bias in a wide range of phenomena. For example, the "burden of proof process" (Berger, Fisek, Norman, and Zeldith 1979), which underlies stereotyping and labeling, is a type of status quo bias. The development of a stereotype can occur quite easily, for example, from a characteristic's consistent association with resources. However, once formed, it is very difficult to dampen. In fact, unless there is specific information to prohibit stereotyping, stereotyping should occur. The burden of proof rests with disconfirming evidence; the status quo of the stereotype is generally stronger than other types of information.

According to Tversky and Kahneman (1991) *diminishing sensitivity* implies that the marginal value of gains and losses decreases with their amount. This is much like the concept of marginal utility (meaning generally that the value of each additional unit of a good decreases with respect to that good's increase), except that it is reference dependent. This exception is important because standard economic models assume that preferences themselves do not depend on current holdings or reference points.[3] Reference dependence also ties the concept of diminishing sensitivity to endowment effects. If someone has been given a gift of a wild animal (an alligator for example), that acquisition changes the reference point for acquisition of other wild animals. If someone has just kidnapped a most prized alligator, that would also change the reference point. And, consistent with loss aversion, the kidnapping would affect the value of the good more than would the gift. So, the effect of a change in the value of the good or resource is greater the closer to the reference point and is less the more distant the point. In particular, to point out the distinction between this concept and marginal utility, Tversky and Kahneman note that "diminishing sensitivity does not imply that the indifference curves are concave below the reference point" (p. 1049).

It is apparent that, *under some conditions*, prospect theory and expected utility theory suggest different predictions. What is not so apparent is exactly what those conditions are. Part of the difficulty in detecting when these two formulations might give different predictions rests in the specification of the reference point and the values associated with different outcomes. (See Levy [1992] for a discussion of problems in determining conditions under which prospect theory might be used in political science contexts.) However, two related areas in which it seems clear that differing outcomes would be predicted are: (1) willingness to pay versus willingness to accept and (2) public good contribution versus resource use-restraint. While issues related to willingness to pay have been investigated quite a bit, these issues as they relate to different kinds of social dilemmas have been investigated little.

SOCIAL DILEMMA ISSUES RELATED TO PROSPECT THEORY AND EXPECTED UTILITY

Willingness to Pay versus Willingness to Accept

If the endowment effect operates, then resources acquired have disproportional value to the owner. In reported tests of private good exchanges, Knetsch, Thaler, and Kahneman (1988) and Knetsch (1989) find clear evidence that once actors acquire a good, they are less likely to trade it for another, and do not trade it unless the amount offered is considerably higher than its original value. It is important to note that this effect is quite strong, in spite of very little time lapse in acquisition (literally minutes).

The effect this could have on public good or resource dilemmas is clear. One way in which actors' value of a public good is estimated is through willingness-to-pay measures. Willingness to pay implies that one does not already possesses the good or resource in question. To elicit how valuable a particular resource might be, individuals are often asked how much they would be willing to pay to acquire it. For example, individuals might be asked how much they would be *willing to pay* to create a protected amount of acreage of the Coachilla Valley to be maintained for the fringe-toed lizard. On the other hand, once again in pursuit of measuring valuations, individuals might be asked how much they would be *willing to accept* if the acreage was used for desert land development and the existing biodiversity was *reduced*. Remembering that economists need some measure of actors' valuation, various measurement strategies have been developed (see Cumings, Brookshire, and Schulze 1986). However, a fairly consistent anomaly occurs. Often willingness-to-pay measures are quite a bit less than the willingness to accept, for equivalent goods or resources. For example, in *Waterfowl and Wetlands*, Hammack and Brown (1974) report that hunters indicated that they would be willing to pay an average of $247 to implement a program to prevent the wetlands loss, but would demand $1,044 to "accept" or create compensation for the loss. If individuals are experienced at using the two different techniques, the differences lessen, and some specific kinds of measurement techniques seem to be more successful in reducing the differences (see Brookshire and Coursey 1987). However, differences remain, and they are in the same direction: Willingness to pay elicits lower valuations than willingness to accept. This difference leads credence to the prospect theory claim.

Public Goods versus Resource Dilemmas

Public goods are created through contributions. In the language we have been using, actors must take their endowments and contribute them to create the public good. The public good itself will be nonexcludable so that each actor knows that all can consume whether or not they contribute. Resource dilemmas on the other hand involve the existence of a good that is already nonexcludable. In this case, the good can be considered as a portion of the actors' endowment. The social dilemma here is that actors must refrain from taking. Why might the decisions be different?

From the prospect theory perspective, asking individuals to give up goods they already possess activates the endowment effect. Additionally, loss aversion should come into play, since actors are being asked to lose a sure thing (their money or their goods) to gain a less sure good—the public good. Notice that the reverse is true for resource dilemmas. In this case, if there is an endowment effect, it rests with the resource itself, since it already exists. In this case loss aversion also should reside in the resource. In other words, if prospect theory does provide a framework in which to examine social dilemmas, we should expect that, other things equal, sustaining resources will be easier than creating public goods. Is this true? What evidence can we bring to bear on this issue?

Empirical Studies of Social Dilemmas

Very few studies directly compare public goods and resource dilemmas. We first discuss general findings from each of the separate empirical literatures and then discuss the three experimental studies that do directly address differences.

Public Goods.   Both the public goods literature and the resource dilemma literature contain case studies and experimental studies. It is the nature of case studies to consider the complexity of issues, and so public goods cases as well as resource dilemmas cases spend much time sorting through differing incentive structures.

One recent example of public good case studies is Anthony Downs' *New Visions for Metropolitan America* (1994). In this book, Downs presents evidence of public goods problems associated with growth management policies. According to Downs, growth management policies are explicit sets of rules designed to limit or constrain in some ways new housing, businesses, roads, social infrastructures, and increases in population and jobs. Such growth management policies are public goods because lower density development would help limit environmental degradation (which might include reduction of pollution and retention of ground cover and trees to reduce erosion, etc.), help reduce traffic and congestion problems, and potentially provide more adequate city services. If growth management policies provide such obvious benefits, why are successful policies so difficult to implement? According to Downs, such implementation involves giving up much of what Americans value, or "the dominant vision." Components of this dominant vision are: ownership of detached single-family dwellings; ownership of cars; working in low-rise workplaces with their own parking lots; residence in small communities with strong local government; and, an environment free of signs of poverty (Downs mentions that this is the little-talked about or acknowledged component). In other words, Americans highly value individualism. Growth management policies, on the other hand, require that individuals give up some of this individualism for the good of the whole community. Downs argues that this is rarely done.[4]

From the prospect theory perspective, the failures of such policies might be traceable to three problems. First, individuals are asked to give up what they already have (their endowment), and endowments are highly valued in the American culture (notice the first factor combines the endowment effect with loss aversion). Second, related to the endowment effect, the dominant vision creates a reference point, so that those things farther from it (in this case the growth management benefits) seem to have less value. Third, the benefits of the policies themselves are not clear and hence uncertain.

Experimental studies of public goods often are characterized as either one-shot, one-time decisions or decisions over time. Most public goods studies begin with the common economic explanation that invokes the characterization of a dominant strategy. If a public goods setting is characterized by nonexcludability and if, at each point in time, any given actor can gain more by not contributing to the good than by contributing, then not contributing is a dominant strategy. At any given point in time, the decision is clear-cut and, regardless of what others do, it is always the best strategy to not contribute. Economists then would predict that public goods settings would have no contributions if participants had no anticipation of future interaction. This prediction or derivation is sometimes labeled the strong free-riding hypothesis. It should be noticed that this derivation assumes that the utility function has been correctly specified. In this context, correctly specified means that factors other than specific individual gain do not contribute to the utility function.

Empirical (and mostly experimental) studies of one-shot settings can be found in economics, sociology and political science (see Bohm 1972; Dawes, McTavish, and Shaklee 1977; Marwell and Ames 1979, 1980, 1981; Alfano and Marwell 1980; Dawes, Orbell, Simmons, and van de Kragt 1986). The conclusions from these varied settings are similar: Free-riding is not total. These studies examined various payoff characteristics, but most find that without communication, contributions vary between about 30 percent to 60 percent of the possible total. Why might contributions be so high, when the dominant strategy prediction is no contributions at all?

There are several explanations. One, offered by some economists, is that the research is basically a flawed test of the economic prediction (for discussion, see Ledyard forthcoming). Repetition is necessary, some have argued, because repetition allows subjects to learn about the setting (or the "game"). This has been done in two quite different ways. One is to utilize subjects who have been in similar studies (e.g., Isaac, Walker, and Thomas 1984) and the other is to repeat trials over time (e.g., Isaac, Walker, and Thomas 1984; Isaac, Schmidtz, and Walker 1988). A theoretical question which must be addressed here really concerns the theory being tested. If the utility is clearly specified, why should repetition be necessary? If experience is an important component, why is it important? In other words, if repetition is an important factor, then there is an implicit theory about learning invoked. Because the theory is implicit not explicit, different variations are allowed. In fact, these different variations or interpretations of repetition are clear: Bringing in subjects who have been in similar studies emphasizes decreasing the "newness" associated with the setting, but it also creates for subjects a "past history" that is difficult to characterize.

Repetition, with knowledge of outcomes, seems to create a characteristic pattern: Although the pattern fluctuates some, contributions to the public goods fall (Isaac, McCue, and Plott 1985). As pointed out by Sell and Wilson (1991), however, the precise reason for this characteristic pattern is not clear. In their study they find that when subjects have information about each individual member's contributions over time, subjects contribute more than when they have information only at the aggregate group level. This suggests that the repetition many economists had associated with familiarity with the setting represents something more than simple repetition.[5] The conclusion then seems justified that, even in one-time interactions, any characterization of a dominant strategy seems inadequate.

When *theoretical repetition* is a factor, game theory asserts that strategies can change dramatically. These assertions do not change any of the fundamental assumptions about expected utility previously mentioned. Even though the dominant strategy, at each point in time, is noncooperation, it has been theoretically established that cooperation or contribution to the public good can be sustained under certain conditions. Fudenberg and Maskin (1986), Friedman (1986), Raub (1988), and Taylor (1987) all demonstrate that if actors have an infinite time horizon, discount their future gains, and can somehow negatively sanction a defecting actor without sanctioning themselves in exactly the same way, then some level of cooperation can be maintained. While the notion of "an infinite time horizon" sounds particularly daunting, it is equivalent, theoretically, to applications in which actors may know the probability (or range of probabilities) of future interaction. To see why this is equivalent, note that if the probability of an event is truly one-half, it is always one-half and the events preceding have no logical consequence for the subsequent events. So, the fact that the probability is always one-half is logically comparable to infinity: There is no beginning point at which the probability is not one-half, and there is no end point at which the probability is not one-half. The problem with this game-theoretical prediction is that it rules out very little—there are multiple equilibria possible, and without additional theory it is impossible to determine which outcomes might occur under particular circumstances.

Resource Dilemmas.   Most likely because most economists view resource dilemmas and public goods as equivalent, there seem to be few economic explorations of resource dilemmas. The two disciplines that seem more involved in examinations of these settings are psychology and political science.

Lin Ostrom's Book, *Governing the Commons* (1992), examines a series of case studies of commons maintenance. In her discussions she emphasizes the danger of over-generalizing based on models. In particular, she argues that her case studies indicate far more cooperation occurs than would be predicted from Hardin's writings concerning the tragedy of the commons. Her case studies emphasize institutional arrangements that have facilitated the maintenance of such diverse resources as the Sri Lanka fishing village of Mawlle (illustrated by Paul Alexander [1977, 1982]) and the Zanjeras irrigations communities in the Philippines.

In her discussion of the Zanjera irrigation communities, Ostrom details the manner in which the Zanjeras were formed and how they protect the interests of the community and the resources themselves. Zanjeras were first documented in 1630 and are still in place. They were established both by landowners interested in a common irrigation system and by individuals hoping to acquire property rights. A particular type of contract, *biang ti daga* ("sharing of the land"), allows a particular community access to an irrigation system created by the Zanjera, on land that previously had not been irrigated and is privately owned. When Zanjeras are organized through such a contract, land is divided symmetrically, so that all members own some of the more fertile land close to the mouth of the system and some less fertile land near the tail. In times of drought, burdens can be equally shared by deciding not to irrigate the bottom section of the land. In addition, some officials are given extra land for their service to the Zanjeras. The most important job for the members is the maintenance and, in times of emergency, rebuilding of the dams. (In some years the dam will be destroyed three or four times.) In her discussion, Ostrom points out that some of the most important reasons for the Zanjeras success rest with the high control and autonomy of the local participants. Because the decision making is local, solutions can be easily fit to the specific conditions. Such solutions are often complex and, in fact, some are examples of public goods such as cooperative self-enforced agreements.

How might the comparison of prospect theory and expected utility theory be related to the Zanjera example? As just mentioned, the case studies involve complex sets of issues in which public goods and resource goods are entangled. However, there are some aspects to the irrigation case that might be analyzed with prospect theory. First, the river exists, and its value is very clear. The effects of drought and flooding are also clear (either to the individuals themselves or clearly transmitted through family history). So, the endowment effect can operate, and so can loss aversion, *in favor of* resource maintenance.

Psychologists and social psychologists have examined resource dilemmas experimentally as well as through case studies. Sometimes these resource dilemmas have been one-shot or one-time decision contexts (see Allison, McQueen, and Schaerfl 1992; Messick, Allison, and Samuelson 1988; Samuelson and Allison 1994; Suleiman and Rapoport 1988), but most often they have involved a replenishable resource pool (e.g., Brechner 1977; Cass and Edney 1978; Jorgenson and Papciak 1981; Kramer, McClintock, and Messick 1986; Messick, Wilke, Brewer, Kramer, Zemke, and Lui 1983; Samuelson 1991). These studies are characterized by pools that seem to mirror many actual resources, such as water or fish, in that pool size is affected by actors' withdrawals and a pool replenishment or growth rate. In this way, pool size at $t + 1$ depends on actors' withdrawals and the growth rate that affects the pool after all these withdrawals. This creates a *dynamic* setting in which history of interaction is critically important. This is quite different from a *static* situation in which there may be a sequence of decisions, but the decisions themselves are the same at each point in time. While these investigations of dynamic resource pools have examined a number of factors, there seems to be a very common finding or pattern: When the resource is declining, subjects decrease their own withdrawals and thus demonstrate higher levels of cooperation. This decrease appears to be very robust, even occuring when subjects are classified as noncooperative in prior settings (see Roch 1994).

Direct Comparisons of Public Goods and Resource Dilemmas

We find only three published studies to date that compared give-some and take-some games directly. In an experimental study, Brewer and Kramer (1986) examined the effects of both group size and social identity on levels of participation in situations where the public good (or resource) was declining. In this experimental scenario, subjects could give to the resource or take from the resource. The situation was a dynamic one. Subjects cooperated more in replenishable common pool resource situations than in "give some" public goods situations. In addition, group size and social identity had different effects in the two situations. Increased group size was found to have no effect on cooperation for the replenishable common pool resource, but led to decreased levels of giving to the public good. In the commons dilemmas (and in small group public goods games), individuals cooperated more as resource depletion became acute during situations of high group identity. Brewer and Kramer (1986) conclude that these findings are consistent with prospect theory's propositions that the two situations would differ and that cooperation would be higher in resource dilemmas than in public goods dilemmas.

The second study, by Fleishman (1988), examined "give some" versus "take some" resources in a static setting. In this study, no differences in overall cooperation emerged. However, Fleishman concludes that the type of social dilemma did make a difference. Specifically, for resource dilemmas, when other group members took more on the first trial, subjects took more; when others took less, subjects took less. For public goods resources, when other group members took more on the first trial, subjects took less and when others took less, subjects took more.

The third study also considered a static setting, in particular, a one-time decision. Messick, et al. (1988) examined issues related both to communication and to framing. The manipulation that concerned prospect theory involved framing the decision in terms of giving or taking. In terms of giving, subjects were given an endowment ($8) and then had to decide whether to give some or all of this amount to the group. If the four group members returned sixteen dollars or more, group members were entitled to keep whatever money remained. If the group total was less than sixteen dollars, then they could keep what they possessed if a coin flip resulted in their favor. In the "give some" or public goods setting, subjects were told that the money available was either $16 or $32. If the group requested $16 or less they would receive it with certainty. If they requested an amount between $16 and $32, they could keep the requested amount if a coin flip was in their favor. The researchers also varied communication availability. No differences between the "give some" and "take some" settings emerged.

COMPARISONS AND CONCLUSIONS

It is problematic to draw conclusions from the studies that directly compared resource dilemmas because different kinds of resources were considered. In one case a replenishment or growth rate was used, while in the other two it was not. Theoretically, this difference might be important for several reasons. First, the resources themselves are different and so may create different incentives for their maintenance. (See Sell [1988] for discussion of the possible differing types of resources.) Second, the nature of the difference between the resource may give rise to differing levels of uncertainty: If a replenishment function is unknown, group members cannot directly project how their individual withdrawals or investments will affect that resource on the next trial. The element of uncertainty is eliminated if a replenishment function is not involved. However, the Messick et al. (1988) study introduced another source of uncertainty in terms of the probability of outcomes. Finally, dynamic settings are extremely different from static settings—so different that any comparison seems misleading.

Of course, if these comparison problems are present with studies that attempt direct tests, comparisons drawn from studies not designed to address each other seem impossible. However, several general findings or patterns are so clear that they must at least be noticed. First, for one-time decisions about resource dilemmas and public goods, contributions are quite high—too high for any serious support for the dominant strategy. This does not suggest that expected utility theory is wrong necessarily, but it does suggest, at the least, that the utility function is not well specified (for suggestions of possible different specifications, see Ledyard forthcoming). It is important in this context to note that these findings seem to bear little on the prospect theory versus utility theory argument.

Second, a pattern that often obtains for resource dilemmas seems to contradict a pattern that often obtains for public goods. Repetition with information about the aggregate group contributions seems to lead to decreasing cooperation in public good settings, presumably because subjects become familiar with the setting (or perhaps familiar with others' lack of cooperation). However, in replenishable resource dilemmas, even when others are known to be noncooperative, subjects become more cooperative. At first glance it might seem that this would support the prospect theory argument. However, as we discussed, the settings are too different to support automatically such a conclusion. In particular, it seems that the dynamic settings in which each decision potentially carries a different set of decision options are dramatically different from static settings in which each decision has the same set of options.

Based on our discussion of prospect theory and expected utility theory, we would expect that commons dilemmas might be easier to solve than public goods dilemmas. Our reasoning is based on the factors of loss aversion and the endowment effect. The examination of studies, however, does not allow us to conclude support for our expectation. While some of the case studies and empirical evidence seem to suggest support, too many factors vary. In case studies, factors that vary include the value of the resource, the special incentives, and the layered externalities (and public goods). Additionally, it may appear that public goods are more difficult to build because there may be tremendous "start-up" fees. Experimental comparisons should allow more direct, clean comparisons, but as discussed, here too the settings vary.

Finally, while the differences between expected utility theory and prospect theory seem clear-cut, there are definite problems in determining when the differences should appear. The differences between loss aversion and loss seeking seem clear. But it is a nontrivial problem to assess at what point differences should occur. Another examination of Figure 2 shows that under some conditions (and some prizes or lotteries), there is little difference between prospect theory and expected utility theory. So, further studies need to address the points at which the two theories would be most different and then to determine a metric of comparison.

Conclusions about the equivalence of public goods and resource goods are important in two differing but related ways. If the two types of social dilemmas are, indeed, different, theory development must be approached differently. In particular, the economic literature which assumes equivalence would need to be refocused. If theory development is to be changed, the application literature needs to be similarly changed. It may be that some of the "dilemma" components of social dilemmas can be dampened or transformed both by the conditions surrounding the dilemma and the way in which information about those conditions is presented.

ACKNOWLEDGEMENTS

The authors are listed in random order. We thank Ray Battalio, Philip R. Berke, Carrie Frazier, and Rick K. Wilson for their comments on earlier drafts.

NOTES

1. Messick and Brewer (1983) distinguish these two types of social dilemmas as social traps and social fences. This distinction is based on the incentive structure and in most cases corresponds to goods versus resources. Social fences (usually equivalent to public goods) are those situations in which members have an incentive to refrain from doing something which, if done by more people would result in more desirable outcomes. These might include for example, the conflict between the time and emotional energy expended in "getting involved" and the social benefit derived from reporting accidents or other incidents in which you were not directly involved, to the police. Social traps, on the other hand are those situations in which group members have an incentive to do something which, in the long run, has unpleasant consequences if enough group members engage in the behavior. The incentive of keeping more than your limit of muskies in northern Wisconsin benefits you in the short run, but if enough people do this the fish population will be depleted, the ecology of the lakes and future muskie fishing will be affected. While traps and fences almost always coincide with public goods and resource goods, they do not quite fit

in the most-used economic terminology that frames the theoretical distinctions between prospect theory and expected utility theory. That is, they do not deal with the *public* nature of these goods. For this reason our terminology follows economics.

2. Of course, there is much discussion over definition. Many formulations (e.g., Cornes and Sandler 1986) suggest that another defining property of public good and common pool resources is nonrivalness—that is, the consumption of one actor does not detract from the consumption of another actor. Of course, most actual public goods or resources possess some variation of both nonrivalness and nonexludability. For our purposes, however, we follow the logic of Sell (1988). She notes that some form of nonexcludability is necessary for distinction from private goods. She then considers issues of nonrivalness in terms of degrees of congestion and resource stratification.

3. Tversky and Kahneman (1991) assert that reference dependence is quite different from transaction cost matters and income effects.

4. For examples of cases that are generally viewed as a growth management success, see Brower, Godschalk, and Porter (1989).

5. Sell, Griffith, and Wilson (1993) ran some experiments in which decisions were repeated over time but with no information supplied regarding how others in the group contributed. They argued that this creates an overtime baseline with which to assess the impact of other factors.

REFERENCES

Alexander, P. 1977. "South Sri Lanka Sea Tenure." *Ethnology* 16: 231-255.
_____ . 1982. *Sri Lankan Fishermen: Rural Capitalism and Peasant Society*. Australian National University Monograph on South Asia 7 Canberra: Australian National University.
Alfano, G. and G. Marwell. 1980. "Experiments on the Provision of Public Goods III: Nondivisibility and Free-riding in 'Real' Groups." *Social Psychology Quarterly* 43: 300-309.
Allison, S.T., L.R. McQueen, and L.M. Schaerfl. 1992. "Social Decision Making Processes and the Equal Partitionment of Shared Resources." *Journal of Experimental Social Psychology* 28: 23-42.
Berger, J., H. Fisek, R. Norman, and M. Zelditch, Jr. 1979. *Status Characteristics and Social Interaction: An Expectation States Approach*. New York: Elsevier.
Brechner, K.C. 1977. "An Experimental Analysis of Social Traps." *Journal of Experimental Social Psychology* 28: 23-42.
Brewer, M. and R.M. Kramer. 1986. "Choice Behavior in Social Dilemmas: Effects of Social identity, Group size and Decision framing." *Journal of Personality and Social Psychology* 50: 543-549.
Bohm, P. 1972. "Estimating Demand for Public Goods: An Experiment." *European Economic Review* 3: 111-130.
Brookshire, D. and D. Coursey. 1987. "Measuring the Value of a Public Good: An Empirical Comparison of Elicitation Procedures." *American Economic Review* 77: 554-566.
Brower, D.J., D.R. Godschalk, and D.R. Porter. 1989. *Understanding Growth Management: Critical Issues and a Research Agenda*. Washington, DC: Urban Land Institute.
Cass, R.C. and J.J. Edney. 1978. "The Commons Dilemma: A Simulation Testing the Effects of Resource Visibility and Territorial Division." *Human Ecology* 6: 371-386.
Cornes, R. and T. Sandler. 1986. *The Theory of Externalities, Public Goods, and Club Goods*. Cambridge: Cambridge University Press.
Cummings, R.G., D.S. Brookshire, and W.D. Schulze. 1986. *Valuing Environmental Goods: An Assessment of the Contingent Valuation Method*. Totowa, NJ: Towman & Allanheld.
Dawes, R.M. 1980. "Social Dilemmas." *Annual Review of Psychology* 31: 169-193.

Dawes, R.M., J. McTavish, and H. Shaklee. 1977. "Behavior, Communication and Assumptions About Other People's Behavior in a Common Dilemma Situation." *Journal of Personality and Social Psychology* 35: 1-11.

Dawes, R.M., J. Orbell, R. Simmons, and A. van de Kragt. 1986. "Organizing Groups for Collective Action." *American Political Science Review* 8: 1171-1185.

Downs, A. 1994. *New Visions for Metropolitan America.* Washington, DC: The Brookings Institute.

Fleishman, J.A. 1988. "The Effects of Decision Framing and Others' Behavior on Cooperation in a Social Dilemma." *Journal of Conflict Resolution* 20: 162-180.

Friedman, J. 1986. *Game Theory with Applications to Economics.* Oxford: Oxford University Press.

Fudenberg, D. and E. Maskin. 1986. "The Folk Theorem in Repeated Games with Discounting or with Incomplete Information." *Econometrica* 54: 533-544.

Hammock, J. and G.M. Brown. 1974. *Waterfowl and Wetlands.* Baltimore, MD: The Johns Hopkins University Press.

Hardin, G. 1968. "The Tragedy of the Commons." *Science* 162: 1243-1248.

Isaac, R.M., K. McCue, and C. Plott. 1985. "Public Goods Provision in an Experimental Environment." *Journal of Public Economics* 26: 51-74.

Issac, R.M., D. Schmidtz, and J.M. Walker. 1989. "The Assurance Problem in a Laboratory Market." *Public Choice* 62: 217-236.

Isaac, R.M., J. Walker, and S. Thomas. 1984. "Divergent Evidence on Free-Riding: An Experimental Examination of Possible Explanations." *Public Choice* 43: 113-149.

Jorgenson, D.G. and A.S. Papciak. 1981. "The Effects of Communication, Resource Feedback and Identifiability on Behavior in a Simulated Commons." *Journal of Experimental Social Psychology* 17: 373-385.

Kahneman, D., J.L. Knetsch, and R.H. Thaler. 1990 "Experimental Tests of the Endowment Effect and the Coase Theorem." *Journal of Political Economy* 98: 325-1347.

Knetsch, J.L. 1989. "The Endowment Effect and Evidence of Nonreversible Indifference Curves." *American Economic Review* 79: 1277-1284.

Knetsch, J.L., R. Thaler, and D. Kahneman. 1988. "Experimental Tests of the Endowment Effect and the Coase Theorem." Simon Fraser University Working Paper.

Kramer, R.M. and M.B. Brewer. 1986. "Choice Behavior in Social Dilemmas: Effects of Social Identity, Group Size and Decision Framing." *Journal of Personality and Social Psychology* 50: 543-549.

Kramer, R.M., C.G. McClintock, and D.M. Messick. 1986. "Social Values and Cooperative Response to a Simulated Resource Conservation Crisis." *Journal of Personality* 54: 576-592.

Kreps, D.M. 1990. *A Course in Microeconomic Theory.* Princeton, NJ: Princeton University Press.

Ledyard. J. Forthcoming. "Public Goods: A Survey of Experimental Research." In *Handbook of Experimental Economics*, edited by J. Kagel and A.E. Roth. Princeton, NJ: Princeton University Press.

Levy, J.S. 1992. "Prospect Theory and International Relations: Theoretical Applications and Analytical Problems." *Political Psychology* 13: 283-310.

Marwell, G. and R.E. Ames. 1979. "Experiments on the Provision of Public Goods, I: Resources, Interest, Group Size and the Free-Rider Problem." *American Journal of Sociology* 84: 1335-1360.

—————— . 1980. "Experiments of the Provision of Public Goods, II: Provision Points, Stakes and Experience and the Free Rider Problem." *American Journal of Sociology* 85: 926-937.

—————— . 1981. "Economists Free Fide, Does Anyone Else? Experiments on the Provision of Public Goods IV." *Journal of Public Economics* 15: 295-310.

Messick, D.M., S.T. Allison, and C.D. Samuelson. 1988. "Framing and Communication Effects on Group Members' Responses to Environmental and Social Uncertainty." Pp. 677-700 in *Applied Behavioural Economics*, Vol 2, edited by S. Maital. New York: New York University Press.

Messick, D.M. and M.B. Brewer. 1983. "Solving Social Dilemmas: A Review." *Review of Personality and Social Psychology* 4: 11-44.

Messick, D.M., H. Wilke, M.B. Brewer, R.M. Kramer, P.I. Zemke, and L. Lui. 1983. "Individual Adaptations and Structural Change as Solutions to Social Dilemmas." *Journal of Personality and Social Psychology* 44: 294-309.

Olson, M. 1965. *The Logic of Collective Action: Public Goods and the Theory of Groups.* Cambridge, MA: Harvard University Press.

Ostom, E. 1992. *Governing the Commons: The Evolution of Institutions for Collective Action.* New York: Cambridge University Press.

Raub, W. 1988. "Problematic Social Situations and the 'Large Number Dilemma': A Game-Theoretical Analysis." *Journal of Mathematical Sociology* 13: 311-357.

Roch, S.G. 1994. "Environmental Uncertainty and Social Value Orientation in Resource Dilemmas." Masters Thesis, Texas A&M University.

Samuelson, C.D. 1991. "Perceived Task Difficulty, Causal Attributions, and Preferences for Structural Change in Resource Dilemmas." *Personality and Social Psychology* Bulletin 17: 181-187.

Samuelson, C.D. and S.T. Allison. 1994. "Cognitive Factors Affecting the Use of Social Decision Heuristics in Resource Sharing Tasks." *Organizational Behavior and Human Decision Processes* 58: 1-27.

Samuelson, W. and R. Zeckhauser. 1988. "Status Quo Bias in Decision Making." *Journal of Risk and Uncertainty* 1: 7-59.

Sell, J. 1988. "Types of Public Goods and Free-Riding." Pp. 119-140 in *Advances in Group Process*, Vol. 5, edited by E.J. Lawler and B. Markovsky. Greenwich, CT: JAI Press.

Sell, J., W.I. Griffith, and R.K. Wilson. 1993. "Are Women More Cooperative Than Men in Social Dilemmas?" *Social Psychology Quarterly* 56: 211-222.

Sell, J. and R.K. Wilson. 1991. "Levels of Information and Public Goods." *Social Forces* 70: 107-124.

Suleiman, R. and A. Rapoport. 1988. "Environmental and Social Uncertainty in Single-Trial Resource Dilemmas." *Acta Psychologica* 68: 99-112.

Taylor, M. 1987. *The Possibility of Cooperation.* Cambridge: Cambridge University Press.

Thaler, R. 1980. "Toward a Positive Theory of Consumer Choice." *Journal of Economic Behavior and Organization* 1: 39-60.

Tversky, A. and D. Kahneman. 1991. "Loss Aversion in Riskless Choice: A Reference-Dependent Model." *Quarterly Journal of Economics* 106: 1039-1061.

von Neumann, J. and O. Morgenstern. 1944. *Theory of Games and Economic Behavior.* Princeton, NJ: Princeton University Press.

COMMON AND PRIVATE CONCERNS

Bonnie J. McCay

ABSTRACT

"Tragic" and "comic" views about human relations with nature appear in the science and practice of natural resource management. In recent years a critique of the dominant "tragedy of the commons" perspective has appeared, a critique here labelled "comedy." After a discussion of the fundamental arguments in that critique, I offer suggestions about ways to conceptualize regimes and forms of user-participation. The goal is to clarify concepts and raise issues that may contribute to the further development of theory concerning property rights and the performance of natural resource systems. In closing, I offer some "private" concerns, the alternative metaphor of "romance," and a challenge to focus on culture and the commons.

THE TRAGEDY OF THE COMMONS:
INACCURATE HISTORY AND HARMFUL POLICY

A popular and powerful way of understanding environmental problems is to blame them on either freedom or open access or both. This argument was cast as the metaphor "the tragedy of the commons" by Garrett Hardin (1968), who called for strong government intervention or privatization to avert such tragedies. To make his point about the workings of the tragedy of the commons,

Advances in Human Ecology, Volume 4, pages 89-116.
Copyright © 1995 by JAI Press Inc.
All rights of reproduction in any form reserved.
ISBN: 1-55938-874-9

Hardin offered the image of the old English village common pasture. The animal owners in the village have to decide how many animals to put on the pasture, and, Hardin argues—following the early nineteenth-century essayist William Forster Lloyd ([1837] 1968)—that each will be inclined to put more animals on the pasture than the pasture can sustain because the immediate benefit of doing so for each animal owner is higher than the immediate costs, which are spread among all pasture users (and, we might add, into the next year). The costs are "social costs," or "externalities." Forster Lloyd offered this image in 1832 as an analogy to the overbreeding of the poor, and Hardin offered it in 1968 in the same vein, but both were also thinking of the actual situation as the rationale for enclosure—the abandonment of the commons in favor of private land tenure in the British Isles.

Neither was a very good historian. The traditional English commons was very different: It was "community property subject to community control" (Hanna 1990, p. 159), and matters such as the number of animals one could put on the common grazing land, or on the fields after harvest, were often strictly controlled by community regulations known as "stinting" rules. The Faroese grazing commons in the "outfield" and on the in-field after harvest were and are governed this way (Torben Vestergaard, personal communication, October 27, 1993). It was a prime example of exactly what Hardin said is needed to better manage both population and natural resources: "mutual coercion, mutually agreed upon" (see also Cox 1985). Moreover, the demise of the commons took place through internal agreements within communities and also with the help of Parliament, over many centuries; the evidence suggests that, despite the rhetoric of landlords, the reasons had nothing to do with the inability of the community to control individual use (Hanna 1990, p. 163).

The view of the commons as a situation of free and open access is not only historically inaccurate. It is also profoundly misleading to attempts to understand environmental problems and propose solutions. Reinterpreting the rich experience of common property management as little more than open access, even to make an analytic point, has the effect of narrowing possible solutions.

Hardin and others usually talk of only two possible solutions to the problems of open access: strong, centralized governmental imposition and enforcement of rules; or, where possible, changing the system to one of exclusive property rights. In practice, this has meant, for example, nationalization of forest lands in Nepal, Thailand and elsewhere (Thomson, Feeny, and Oakerson 1986; Arnold and Campbell 1986), and attempts to create individual ranches where pastoralists had wandered in southern Africa (Peters 1987). Such events have often undermined or destroyed the option of communal management of common property and generated tragedies of both the commons and the commoners.

A seventeenth-century English couplet suggests an alternative point of view, about the "tragedy of the commoners" (see McCay 1987, 1989):

The law locks up the man or woman Who steals the goose from off the commons But the greater villain the law lets loose Who steals the commons from the goose.[1]

Models and Morals

More formal thinking about the dilemma of the commons is derived from studies of fisheries. Indeed, the problem of common property resources is also known as "the fisherman's problem" (McEvoy 1986). For fishes and other renewable living resources there are relationships between mortality and production, or effort and yield, that look like a logistic Lotka-Volterra curve. In theory there is a level of mortality that results in maximum sustained yield (MSY). Those using this model assumed that management involved government rules that kept fishing mortality at the MSY level, more or less, and important fisheries today are managed roughly in this way.

H. Scott Gordon (1954) and Anthony Scott (1955) added to the biologists' concern with maximum sustained yield the economists' concern with maximum economic yield, or profitability, and showed how open access affects both. The point of marginal returns to capital, where money made from fishing is no greater than the cost of fishing, is the point at which people will stop, but that is far beyond both MSY and the point of maximum sustained profitability. This is the basis for a long-standing argument for limiting access to fisheries that, in the past decade, has become an enthusiastic chorus for creating exclusive rights to fish or rights to fish, that is, the "private concern" of this paper.

Almost always, the models used to understand the interactive dynamics of fisheries stop at this point, wedded as most of us in America are to two paradigms: conservation and rationalization (Charles 1992, pp. 384-385). The first is concerned with taking care of the fish (or birds or forests); the second with the pursuit of economic returns. Conservation in America has long been marked by tension between the two. But there is a third paradigm, "the social/community paradigm," involving questions about distributional equity, community welfare, and other social and cultural benefits. For some reason we do not publicly talk about this one as much in America, even though it too underlies much of the politics of conservation and environmentalism.

The "social/community" paradigm is absent in most discussions of tragedies of the commons and natural resource management. It is, however, expressed in the metaphor "comedies of the commons"—people, as social beings, trying to come to some collective agreement about common problems. In the bioeconomic model, people are asocial beings, responding as individuals to incentives from the natural environment and the market; the limits, if any, on their behavior (such as TACs or limited licenses) implicitly come from the outside, from a wiser government. But we know that even fishers care and try to do something about the resources on which they depend, and they may play important roles in the creation and enforcement of rules and regulations.

This alternative perspective is reflected in research that attempts to bring human values into the bioeconomic values, such as job satisfaction research (Gatewood and McCay 1990; Smith 1981). It is important in recognizing disproportionality and inequality in both the causes and consequences of environmental problems. And it points to a focus on collective action and other social responses to environmental problems.

BAD HABITS AND A NEW TAXONOMY

Scholarly writing, thinking, and practice concerning problems of the commons have been in a tangle. One reason is the practice of using the phrase "common property" to refer to resources that share certain features—for example, fluidity, mobility, and extensiveness. The error is the failure to recognize that property derives not from nature but from culture. It does not refer to things but to social agreements about how humans relate to things (Furobotn and Pejovich 1972; Bohannan 1962). A key argument of the revisionist perspective on "commons" issues is, therefore, that one should distinguish between the features of the resource and those of the ways people choose to relate to the resource and each other (Ciriacy-Wantrup and Bishop 1975; Feeny, Berkes, McCay, and Acheson 1990; Berkes et al. 1989; Ostrom 1990). Vincent Ostrom and Elinor Ostrom (1977) long ago argued for the use of the term *common pool*, rather than *common property*, for that class of resources that are particularly problematic to human institutions because of the difficulties of bounding or dividing them, the likelihood that one person's actions may affect another's enjoyment of the resource, and so forth.[2] Examples of common *pool* resources would then include large bodies of water, rivers, fishes and other wildlife, air and the airwaves, even information and genetic material, all of which have certain natural features in common.[3] Simpler and other definitional schemes abound. The point here is that common pool is not the same as common *property*; there might be cases of common property for noncommon pool resources (e.g., condominium housing), and of private property for common pool resources (e.g., buying tickets for access to camping in public wilderness areas).

The Fisherman's Problem: Interdependence and Open Access

The two horns of the commons dilemma—damned if you do, by yourself, and you're all damned in the long run if you don't, collectively—can be seen in the following scenario.

A large number of East Coast commercial and recreational fishermen try to catch summer flounder or fluke, a valuable fish. When I interviewed commercial fishermen in New Jersey in the mid-1980s, the fish were getting scarcer and it was harder to find the larger, more valuable ones. So each of the fishing crews put more effort into fishing (more time, more tows of the net) and most had started using nets with a smaller mesh size to catch the smaller fish. It became even harder to find the "jumbo" and large sizes of fluke. Most of the people involved knew what was happening, and some were heard to say: "This is crazy, we should be using large-mesh nets."

There are three reasons they did not use large mesh nets, one that reflects the unpredictable variability of wild fisheries, and two which bear directly on the "commons" problem. First, they could not be certain that switching to larger mesh nets would actually work because they did not know for sure that the reason for the decline was an increased take of smaller fish. They would have to accept declining catches in the short run in exchange for a very risky bet that changing mesh size would result in increased catches in the long run. In other words, it was a situation of high risk and uncertainty, which in and of itself promotes a take-it-while-you-can strategy, or what economists describe as a high rate of discounting the future.

Added to the troubling challenge of coping wisely with risk and uncertainty, as well as ignorance (see Ludwig, Hilborn, and Walters 1993) are the two "commons" problems. The second disincentive for switching to larger-mesh sizes derives from the *open access* feature of many fisheries. If everyone agrees to fish with larger mesh nets now, there is little to prevent a lot of other people from coming into the fluke fishery and competing for the fish in the near future. This problem and the expensive competition that follows are among the reasons more and more fisheries are being managed with some form of *limited entry*, ranging from local residency requirements or territoriality to limited licenses or even creating private property out of the right to fish.

The third disincentive is that any who switch to large mesh nets also risk losing money and being seen as foolish. Smaller flounders that wriggle through the meshes of their nets are probably going to be caught in the nets of those who use small mesh. This is because of the *interdependence* of those using a common pool resource. The interdependence leads to a challenge for truly collective action, else private gain leading to collective disaster, Hardin's (1968) "tragedy of the commons." As the summer flounder fishermen of New Jersey say, "We can't do it unless the others do." In Hardin's terms, what is needed is mutual coercion, mutually agreed on.

At the risk of cutting the argument short, I must note that in the 1990s the summer flounder fishing industry—recreational and commercial— cooperated with government agencies to develop a set of regulations that include larger mesh sizes. This was mutual coercion, mutually agreed on. However, the analytic frameworks used in theoretical resource management models are more closely based on Hardin's more pessimistic conclusion that when dealing with common pool resources, people will not be able to come up with collective solutions unless forced by an outside government. And in those frameworks it is often assumed that common pool or common property resources are also open access resources.

Common Property, Open Access

A second reason for an intellectual muddle consists in treating "common property" as synonymous with "open access" (e.g., Christy and Scott 1965), or the same as "no property rights" (e.g., Demsetz 1967). Although *open access* is a distinctive commons problem, it is not definitive of common property. The "comedy" perspective insists that there is an important difference (Ciriacy-Wantrup and Bishop 1975). Common property is about property rights. In common property systems there can be restrictions on who is a proper commoner and what people do, or even a social agreement that there will be no restrictions and open access.

To reiterate, *common property* is a cultural artifact, socially constructed and contested, not a natural or necessary condition. In this way it is distinct from the condition of *open access* as this appears in economic models, even though some common property regimes may have been specified, or socially constructed, as open access. In the "thin" (cf. Little 1991) version of this perspective, neo-institutional economists emphasize the contingency of economic behavior on legal-social contexts (Schmid 1987; Bromley 1989). Property is not created because one or two individuals behave certain ways. Rather, property arises from public choice, requiring some degree of community consideration and agreement. Anthropologists are likely to "thicken" the analysis with more detailed specification of content, context, and culture.

Property Rights and Management Regimes

The "thin" way of looking at these issues has been very important to comparative and interdisciplinary work. The revisionist view recognizes that the natural environment may be dealt with in many different ways, with many different consequences. *Common pool* resources may be under a variety of management regimes, not adequately indicated by the term *common property*. In a recent set of articles, we used regimes loosely identified as *open access* (or no governance), *communal property, state property*, and *private property* (Berkes et al. 1989; Feeny et al. 1990, p. 4 [listing many other references to similar distinctions]). In traditional analyses, the first three types of management regime are more often lumped as common property. Splitting the category and examining case studies shows that there is no simple one-to-one relationship between regime and outcome and whether the outcome is sustainable exploitation. This revisionist perspective leads one to doubt that environmental problems are due to the common property attribute of some resources plain and simple (Feeny et al. 1990, p. 13).

Table 1.   A Typology of Resources, Property, and Management Regimes

Types of Resources
Common Pool
Non common Pool

Types of Property
Private Property
Common Property
Open Access

Types of Management Regimes
Laissez-faire
Market Regulation
Communal Governance
State Governance
International Governance

I propose a somewhat more complex way of ordering the study of "the commons," distinguishing between property claims (one class of institutions) and management regimes (another institutional class). To keep the analysis simple, in Table 1 only three general types of property are listed: open access, private property, and common property. The management regimes are laissez-faire, market, communal, state, and international.

Open access is the null condition of no property claims. For some purposes it may be appropriate to distinguish this case from a socially-constructed agreement that all citizens, inhabitants, or members of the public have rights of use.

Private property is usually defined in terms of exclusivity and transferability (e.g., Regier and Grima 1985). Private property rights are more exclusive and generally (but not universally) more transferable than are common property rights. It is essential to recognize the potential variability of the "bundles of rights," as the lawyers say, for private as well as common property (see Dowling [1975] for an African case study of limits to transferability of private property).

Common property refers to a large class of property rights that can incorporate much of what is otherwise thought of in these schemes as "state property" (as in Feeny et al. 1990). One of the anthropological points to be made is that it is dangerous to generalize given the specificity of particular property systems and their embeddedness in other dimensions of social, economic, and political life. However, we can draw some general outlines of what is often meant. Among the features typically found in that class are a right to use something in common with others; or, a right not to be excluded from the use of something (Macpherson 1978); and some expression of equality or equitability in the allocation of rights (Ciriacy-Wantrup and Bishop 1975). It is often defined as a situation in which people have use rights but not exchange rights (Schmid 1987, p. 55).

Much more variable are the boundaries of common property. They may be virtually nonexistent, as for example in the Swedish custom of *allmennsretten* allowing anyone to harvest wild mushrooms or berries on private lands. They may be very tightly circumscribed, as in some village communal systems, where common rights may be contingent on citizenship or land ownership. The boundaries of "the commons" and "the commoners" vary in their permeability (Pollnac 1984). They may be very permeable in terms of access, that is, where a local community takes care of a resource but allows others to come in to harvest it by community rules—a system fairly typical of aboriginal American Indian management of wildlife (Berkes 1987; Feit 1973), wild rice (Cizek 1993), and salmon netting at Celilo Falls, on the Columbia River; but also found more widely, as in the case of municipal care of a coastal beach to which the larger public has access, on paying a beach fee or parking fee, as is the New Jersey system. But common property boundaries can be very tightly circumscribed, so that only legitimate members of certain communities have any rights at all, such as the high alp grazing lands and forests of Switzerland (Netting 1976), some coral reef and lagoon fisheries in the Pacific (Johannes 1981; Carrier 1987), or the Coast Salish reef net fisheries for salmon in the Straits of Juan de Fuca (Suttles 1987). These common property systems are not restricted to native Americans. On the Columbia River, for example, the Scandinavian and Mediterranean immigrants formed "drift net associations" to clear snags and provide exclusive drift net access to cleared areas (Martin 1971). Again, to broaden the example, devices such as land trusts or conservation foundations (Hilts and Mitchell 1993) are also common property systems.

Property Rights, Management Regimes

For purposes of comparative analysis, property rights should be separated from management regimes (Table 2). Property rights are among the institutional conditions that influence management regimes but are not the same as management regimes. Following is an initial sketch of a typology that might emerge from making a distinction betwen property rights and management regimes.

Laissez-faire, or the condition of no management regime, replaces open access in the original scheme. The management significance of open access for common pool resources is that there is virtually no governance nor is there effective market-based regulation. This combination of property rights and management regime is particularly prone to tragedies of the commons if pressure on resources is high enough. Fishermen sometimes argue for laissez-faire approaches to natural resource problems, saying that the system is self-regulating because when the resource becomes scarce, the fishers will switch to something else. However, the commons problem is that, where access is open, that point of switching may be too late to avoid biological or economic losses and even irreversible disaster.

Table 2. Property Rights and Governance Systems

	Laissez-faire	Market	Communal	State	International
"Open Access"	XX	?	X	X	X
Private Property	X	XX	X	X	?
Common Property	X	?	XX	XX	XX

Notes: X = Possible.
XX = Most Obvious.
? = Problematic or Unlikely.

Market regulation replaces private property in the original scheme. Private property is relevant to management insofar as it allows market mechanisms to work more effectively. On the other hand, governance is required to uphold private property claims and other conditions of the market. This combination may be a source of tragedies of the commoners as well as tragedies of misplaced faith in market remedies, particularly where externalities and long-term and indirect ecological effects are involved. In a very general sense, the market is also at work in tragedies of the commons. Markets can have perverse effects: When market demand is high the price of a natural product, for example, salmon or flounders, will likely increase as the resource gets scarcer, stimulating more effort rather than less.

Communal governance replaces common or communal property in the revisionist scheme. It highlights the existence and potential of user-governance and local-level systems of common pool resource management, irrespective of whether rights are common or private or a mixture. Collective action challenges may or may not be met in a wide variety of ways. Communal governance is of special interest where the interests of people and the sustainability of their resource use are not well served by governments and where privatization is not feasible or politically acceptable.

State governance replaces state property in the original scheme, recognizing the central role of the state or central government to most common pool systems whether state-owned or not. State property can be the property owned outright and used exclusively by agents of the state, on the one hand, and property deemed public over which the state exercises governance. The latter is most important (see Marchak 1988-89), and the concept of state governance reflects that fact.

A very important addition to the scheme is *international governance* (Young 1989). It has features and challenges to common pool management that differ from state governance, if not communal governance, such as the absolute lack of centralized enforcement. The free-rider problem is a very sore point for international institutions as is their reliance on suasion and indirect penalties for breaking the rules.

In sum, property rights are not the same as management systems, although they are logically connected. Open access is not the same as laissez-faire. Although most laissez-faire systems are open-access, there are many open-access systems in the fisheries, particularly, where rules and regulations abound. Private property is not the same as market regulation, even though the "tragedy of the commons" theory is that market regulation does not work. Market forces certainly apply across the board, wherever the activity is linked to markets, but the regulatory incentives of markets do work best where there is something like private property. On the other hand, private property rights are no guarantee that their owners will care about resource conservation. Moreover, a tragedy of the *noncommons* (May 1990) can occur when privatization benefits the few but further marginalizes the many, who are forced to increase their uses and weaken their management of common pool resources.

Common property is not the same as communal regulation, either. It is possible for communal regulation to exist while access is open. It is also very possible that a community can regulate how private property owners use their properties (e.g., zoning), because of concern about externalities and shared community values. But communal regulation probably works best where members of a community have special rights, property rights. For example, after independence from colonial domination, many new nations did away with communal or common property rights because these were linked with clans and other groups that were seen as problematic to the emerging nation-state, and this weakened and destroyed customary systems of resource management (for a Somalia example, see Shepherd 1990).

State and international management regimes—which is what is usually meant by "governance"—cross-cut all forms of property. The state—meaning the centralized government that holds a virtual monopoly on the use of force and is the final arbiter of law—is critical to the existence of both private and common property. It legitimizes and protects (or can be used to challenge) such property claims. The international level of governance (cf. Young 1989) is particularly challenging for the solution of regional and global environmental problems, because the so-called "free-rider" problem inherent to all commons dilemmas is writ large, and there is no real centralized system of enforcement.

Problems With The Typology

The virtue of this typology, like the simpler one that preceded it (Berkes et al. 1989; Feeny et al. 1990), is that it underscores the tremendous diversity of management regimes that can and do exist beyond the laissez-faire commons, and that can be used to ask questions about the ecology, economics, and sustainability of natural resource systems. However, both are misleading in suggesting that there is something universal about each of its categories, that there is something homogenously known as private property and common property (versus recognition of complex, varying "bundles of rights" as the lawyers say), and that the market and the state are homogeneous and virtually the same in form and effect everywhere.

Moreover, they virtually beg for additions and subtypes, and one is quickly led to the point that they are all potentially interrelated. For example, there can be no market regulation without private property, and no private property without some level of governance. Communal regulation is often dependent on authority granted from central government powers. Examining relationships between communal and state governance leads to further questions. For example, what is "the community?" Some communities may be defined in terms of the geography of people's residences and working places; others in terms of occupations or occupational specialization (such as tuna fishermen versus clam fishermen); others in terms of interest groups (harvesters, processors, environmentalists, tour operators, consumers). Some common property governing communities may in fact be comprised of members of a local elite rather than the larger populace (Rodman 1989; Vondal 1987), raising questions about how social, economic, and political hierarchy and heterogeneity affect the nature and success of common property governance (McKean 1992; Hackett 1992).

How do we conceptualize and understand overlapping, changing, and contentious property and governance claims? There are also trickier questions about what "community" means in experiential, moral, and social-organizational terms and how it affects various forms of common property governance (Taylor 1987; Singleton and Taylor 1992; Ostrom 1992). On a more theoretical level, questions about how to specify the nature of communities and to understand relationships between different and changing communities and how people behave vis-à-vis common pool resources are extremely important to the development of an understanding of what economists call nonprice signals to the change of behavior.

COMEDIES OF THE COMMONS

The tragedy of the commons view leads to arguments for strong, centralized governance or for privatization, that is, letting the market do the job. From the revisionist point of view, a broader and more complex range of alternatives comes into view. Alternatives include a stronger emphasis on the potentials of people as social actors to manage their affairs and on more decentralized and cooperative management—what is here meant by "comedy of the commons" (cf. Smith 1984; Rose 1986). Tragedy in the classic Greek sense is the drama of an individual, with a tragic flaw or relationship with the gods, who is inevitably propelled to some tragic destiny. In a comedy, people recognize that something is wrong and try, for better or worse (often comically), to do something about it. The funny part of comedy may be that we recognize ourselves in these situations only too well, and that we see their irony given the very real difficulties of knowing what we are doing and getting people to go along.

Range of Comedies of the Commons

Anthropologists are among those who advocate self-governance and local-level autonomy in resource management. In fact, few local communities are fully autonomous, particularly with respect to the management of valuable natural resources such as fish stocks and forests. The "comedy" perspective does not preclude government management. In nation-states the right to make and enforce decisions about the commons is often centralized, often taken by government leaders, legislatures and their agencies. This can be seen as a kind of common property, a system of public trust whereby the interests of the true owners of common rights—rights not to be excluded and/or rights to share in the benefits—are taken care of by political representatives.

The comedy of the commons thus would include the political process of determining how these public stewards should manage the common resources, with varying degrees and forms of participation by resource users and other interested groups. At the other end, this comedy would be about how a local community of resource users decides to allocate and manage rights to common resources.

Communal Management

Much of the promise of the "comedy" perspective derives from case studies of communal regulation of the commons. Chiefs, elders, town councils, shamans and other ritual specialists, irrigation committees, boards of directors of cooperatives, "cofradias," unions, others have in fact been involved in the management of common property resources. It is clearly not the exclusive provenance of centralized government.

Very important research is leading to an appreciation of the characteristics of communal management systems, past and present, that may be applicable to the design of new common property management regimes. For example, Margaret McKean recently compared what she has learned about common property land management on the north slope of Mount Fuji, Japan, over two centuries, with what others have learned from studying landed commons in medieval England, Nepal, Switzerland, Morocco, Nepal, India, and the Andean highlands, as well as some irrigation and fisheries management cases, to find out what makes for successful communal management (McKean 1992, pp. 258-261; see also Ostrom 1987, 1990):

1. a clear understanding of who is and is not eligible to use the commons;
2. some way that the eligible users or their representatives regularly meet to air grievances, adjudicate problems, and make decisions and rules;
3. jurisdiction mostly independent of larger government powers;
4. limited transferability of common property;

5. ability of the system to handle social and economic differences; and
6. close attention to monitoring and enforcement.

A good example can be found in New Jersey in the late 1970s and early 1980s (McCay 1980). The Fishermen's Dock Cooperative of Point Pleasant had developed a complex system of catch limits for two species that were critical to the fishery during the winter months and were subject to sharp price declines when the market was glutted. The system met all of the criteria emphasized by McKean (1992): Only members of the cooperative were eligible; they met regularly to make decisions and air grievances; rights to sell through the cooperative were not transferable; complex ways of administering the catch rules were created to handle differences in capital and skill, while rewarding both and yet maintaining a sense of fairness; and both monitoring and enforcement were relatively easy. The boats had to land their catches and follow the rules to stay in the coop. In addition—speaking to a question not handled very well by most scholars of common property management—the Point Pleasant fishermen were capable of expanding the boundaries of their self-regulation to others within the larger region when it seemed important and necessary.

Some might say the system was too specific and limited to be applicable elsewhere and, therefore, to be of interest to fisheries managers in government agencies. However, this very same factor may also be used to suggest that a reasonable alternative or adjunct to centralized, large-scale systems of fisheries management does exist. Some management systems may persist and work best where they remain on a scale small and flexible enough to be adjusted to the particular problems and circumstances of the people inherent in them, and yet capable at times of being extended to a regional level [as I had shown in the description] (McCay 1980, p. 36).

There are many other systems of communal management, including some that are relatively new. A general notion arising from the case studies is that if a group of people has some sort of territorial or jurisdictional claim to a valuable resource, they will be motivated and empowered to manage it better. This is critical where government resources and the political will required for enforcement of regulations are scarce. Some systems are experiments introduced by outsiders. Experiments have begun in some areas of the Philippines to create or restore self-governance of coral reefs in admittedly desperate attempts to find ways to motivate people to stop, or dare to make others stop, destructive practices that include dynamiting of the reefs (Christie, White, and Buhat 1990). Others have developed locally. In the wake of "fish wars" between commercial fishers and local subsistence users of the great floodplain lakes of the Amazon, communities there have developed local management programs (Castro, personal communication, 1993). Research in Nepal on systems of managing irrigation suggests that locally-generated systems are more likely to be effective and equitable than even well-meaning systems planned by government agencies and World Bank-type outsiders (Ostrom 1992).

Major obstacles exist to the self-governance way of managing the commons. It may be impractical where resources are migratory or overlap jurisdictions, as in the Newfoundland fisheries and most of the other temperate and northern fisheries of the world. For example, in the midst of the ecological tragedy of the near demise of northern cod in the mid-1990s, it was very difficult for even the province of Newfoundland, much less local communities, to claim and exercise management jurisdiction because of the broader claims of the nation of Canada and of foreign countries with "historic" and other rights.

In addition, self-governance may be unacceptable where it excludes people with claims to common use-rights based on historical use or other notions of right. For example, it is possible to interpret New Jersey's system of giving municipalities the power to regulate access to coastal beaches as a good example of self-governance: People who go to the beach must pay for beach badges and/or parking, and that money is used by the towns to maintain the beaches. Very little of the coast is a state or federal park. However, courts have accepted that the intent and consequence are often exclusionary, favoring local residents, and courts have delimited the power of the towns because under public trust law all citizens have common rights of access to the tidewaters and oceans. Similarly, but back at the smaller scale that we normally think of as self-governance, the Amazonian *varzea* or floodplain communities that exhibit self-governance are doing so illicitly because of national laws that protect the rights of citizens to fishery resources (Stocks 1987).

Nonetheless, much of what is being learned about the workings of the smaller-scale systems is also applicable to the design of improved systems at the national and international levels. Susan Hanna (1990) presented information about the eighteenth-century English commons as an example of a successful resource management institution, and then posed challenges to the design of ocean management institutions that could, like many of the eighteenth-century English village or manorial commons, coordinate multiple resource uses, be flexible to changing environmental conditions, and embody community control.

Co-Management and User Participation

The revisionist perspective emphasizes communal management and self-governance, but clearly there are limits and drawbacks to self-governance, including the migratory or fugitive nature of some resources, overlapping jurisdiction, and competing claims (such as the special rights of local people who depend on a particular resource, versus the rights of citizens or the public to the use of the resources). Put another way, the question is about the autonomy of the state, and the ways that common pool resource users (and members of other interest groups) interact with the state in developing and changing systems of governance. Like it or not, the fact remains that central governments are major actors with respect to common pool resource use and management.

The term *co-management* has come to be used to introduce the topic, but it can be seen that co-management is but one of a variety of forms of interaction between a government and its public (Table 3). This discussion will focus on fisheries. As noted earlier, the problem of the commons has been called "the fisherman's problem" (McEvoy 1986) because open-access fisheries provided important early illustrations of the commons dilemma (Scott 1955; Gordon 1954).

The wider domain of citizen involvement in environmental and social issues (Hance, Chess, and Sandman 1988; Arnstein 1969) provides a useful schema. In a happy case of independent discovery and adoption, Berkes et al. (1991) have also used the model developed by Arnstein (1969), in the context of community empowerment in the War on Poverty. As I have adapted it (see Table 3), the extremes of fisher/user/public participation in public policy would be, at one end, *Government Power*, and at the other end, *Fisher Power*. Either the government acts unilaterally, as it seems to do from time to time, for example, in the State Department's relations with foreign countries that affect fish markets or in closures of fisheries due to public health concerns; or the fishers completely ignore government, creating their own systems of resource allocation and management, or subverting government programs.

More common in democratic polities is the vast "in between" arena, whereby the fishers (or other users) and the government (or whatever agencies are involved) are interacting. An imaginary "ladder of fisher participation" as shown in Table 3 would have a number of rungs, according to the level and degree of fisher (or fishery community) power in the interaction process. Following Hance et al. (1988), I have simplified the model first proposed by Sherry Arnstein (1969), based on observations of community action politics in poor urban areas, to six rungs—the two extremes already mentioned and then the "in between" steps: Inform, Consult 1, Consult 2, and Co-Management. Elsewhere (McCay, in press), I have analyzed in some detail the differences among these stages, with illustrations from observations of the fishery management process in the United States. A brief commentary on this focus on microsociological relationships between "fishers" and "governments" is provided below.

The three rungs of the ladder following Government Power represent situations where members of the community are allowed to listen to what is happening and perhaps to have a voice, but their power is weak. At the *Inform* level of fisher participation, the government agency talks, the fishers listen. This is what many officials believe to be the most appropriate way of involving

Table 3. Ladder of Participation in Fisheries Management

Fisher Power:
Fishers Act Independently

Co-Management
Fishers and Government Work Together

Consult 2
Government Asks for Input and Intends to
Listen

Consult 1
Government Asks for Input, Prefers Not to
Listen

Inform
Government Talks, Fishers Listen

Government Power
Government Acts Without Communicating
with Fishers

---

citizens because they view the problem as one of education and the means to education as one-way communication. Press releases and newsletters are vehicles, as are many public hearings and other meetings held by fishery management agencies, councils and committees. This style of interaction is promoted by bringing people in at a late stage in planning, so that people have little opportunity to influence the plans. One-way communication is also promoted at meetings by "the simple device of providing superficial information, discouraging questions, or giving irrelevant answers" (Arnstein 1969, p. 219; see Smith [1982] for a fisheries case study).

People quickly become frustrated and angry when restricted to the *Inform* level of citizen-government interaction over a matter that concerns them, such as developing new mesh sizes and closed seasons for a fishery. They demand at least the right to be heard, and they often are accorded that right. In *Consult 1*, the government agency asks for limited input but seems to prefer not to listen. Public hearings are required for fishery management plans in the U.S. regional management system; often they are run in a pro forma way, for example, industry members rising to speak or read prepared statements, members of the council committee sitting with little sign of active involvement in listening.

In *Consult 2*, members of the fishery community are asked for meaningful input and the agency indicates that it intends to listen and take what it hears into account in developing policy. Many advisory committees are run this way: The government agency or management council with the mandate to manage fisheries is genuinely concerned to get advice from the industry. This kind of consultation is usually best nurtured at more informal meetings, where people feel freer to express themselves and there can be ongoing dialogues. However, people are rightly suspicious even when the meeting becomes open and communication appears to be two-way (or more). They may be confused about whether they are in a *Consult, 1* or *Consult 2* situation, depending on their expectations about whether the government officials really will listen. Those expectations are affected by a longer history of interactions that affect credibility and trust.

Another rung in the ladder, not shown in the table, represents the situation in which citizens are brought into the decision-making process as members of advisory and planning committees. It can be a style of nonparticipation (Arnstein 1969), used to legitimize programs that are required to have public participation but without actually granting any power or authority to members of the public. Consequently, it can be a very empty gesture, a fact that can embitter participants, who leave the system (see Hanna's [1992] portrayal of the risks of "exit" from the system including noncompliance, and hence the importance of ensuring loyalty to the system by giving fishers "voice"). If, on the other hand, participation is structured so that the advice and expertise of fishers is used and actually influences the decision-making process, this can be a step toward full participation, even co-management.

Co-Management entails a power-sharing partnership between government agencies and citizens with a stake in the common pool resource. Examples of co-management would be situations in which meetings are called jointly by fisher organizations and government officials; where fishers have oversight and monitoring powers in relation to a specific fishery management system; and where fishers are funded to hire technical consultants (see Hance et al. [1988] for parallels in environmental protection matters). American Indian tribes in the West have formal co-management powers in fisheries that often include those features (see Pinkerton 1989 for specific cases and a thorough introduction to co-management). Successfully co-managed fisheries that are now well documented include some with historical depth, like the inshore fisheries of Japan, managed by cooperatives (Ruddle 1989) and the Lofoten winter cod fisheries of Norway, managed and enforced by groups of fishers (Jentoft and Kristoffersen 1989). Newer examples include the user of European Community producer organizations as vehicles for allocating individual quotas among fishers in the UK (Jentoft and Kristoffersen 1989; see also Meltzoff and Broad 1992), as well as a variety of arrangements between state agencies and tribal groups in North America, where courts have upheld the sovereignty of the tribes (Cohen 1986). Even more recent is the co-management system used for an individual transferable quota (ITQ) for fisheries in Nova Scotia, Canada. The decision to use ITQs was made unilaterally by the Minister of Fisheries in 1989, but the details of the system and many of the details of its implementation and change are done by a committee intended to represent both industry and government (Apostle, McCay, and Mikalsen 1993).

Co-management promises an institutional response to the commons problem, which is essentially the question of how private interests can better intermesh with collective interests. In theory (Jentoft 1989; Pinkerton 1989), co-management will improve both the effectiveness and the equitability of fisheries management. Co-management may also improve compliance with agreed-upon rules. If decisions are made by fishers themselves, that is, by majority rule, then there is internal coercion to follow the rules, versus top-down rule-making that often results in rampant and gleeful violation. Once rules become the government's, even the fishers who asked for them or agreed to them may be compelled to find ways to break them (for a telling case in Iceland, see Durrenberger and Pálsson 1987). However, if fishers have a clear and important role in making and implementing the rules, and if a majority agree to them, they are more likely to follow them and to coerce others to do the same.

Effectiveness is partly a question of accurate appraisal of the situation and the effects of changing the rules. Resource assessment is critical. It seems logical that under a co-management system, resource users would be more likely to share accurate information than they are under other systems. This would reflect more fundamental changes in behavior and attitudes as fishers become and are treated as responsible co-managers. The recent disaster in Newfoundland, where one of the major cod stocks has come close to extinction, is traceable in part to faulty science, and that in part to the failure to take into account the knowledge, experience, and catches of inshore fishers (Steele, Andersen, and Green 1992). Co-management is one of the ways that "indigenous" and nonexpert knowledge and interests can be meaningfully brought into management.

There are other arguments for co-management systems, such as the likelihood that they will be more equitable, based on the premise that resource users are more familiar with the intricacies of local social and economic situations and, therefore, are more able to respond to the special needs and interests of different groups or individuals than are governments, which usually try to treat everyone alike (but see McCay [1988] where an experiment in co-managed resource enhancement failed to meet local criteria of equity). In addition, a co-managed regulatory process may be more responsive to changing conditions. The organizations of resource users involved may be able to change rules more quickly, and are in general more flexible and responsive than government (Jentoft 1989; see McCay [1980] for the flexibility of a New Jersey fisheries cooperative).

PRIVATE CONCERNS

Few would disagree with the proposition that open access can generate resource abuse and economic losses. This is really what Garrett Hardin (1968) was modelling in his sketch of the tragedy of the commons and what H. Scott Gordon (1954) meant by common property fishing in his seminal article on the dynamics of overfishing. Nor is there much to argue about concerning the value of delineating and enforcing property rights when conservation is a problem. *Some* specification of property rights is a necessary foundation to the development of regulation. What is of concern is the rapid jump over Gordon's prescription of limiting access (which is often done in true common property systems, particularly the English village commons that remains the archetype [Cox 1985; Hanna 1990]), to the prescription of creating private property in rights to resources.

The term *privatization* is usually avoided in the fisheries economics and policy literature, as it is in environmental literature. In fisheries it is replaced by euphemisms such as "rights-based fishing" (Neher, Arnason, and Mollett 1989), but what is advocated clearly has the earmarks of private property: the creation of exclusive use-rights in fish stocks (typically as percentages of a quota), with more or less freedom to transfer these rights—the hallmarks of a marketable commodity. The idea rests on work by economists on problems of environmental pollution, including the idea of tradeable emissions permits, then extended by Christy (1973) and Moloney and Pearse (1979) to fisheries (Lanfersieck and Squires 1992). These individual transferable quotas are widely praised as solving the problems of the commons, combining a quota for conservation purposes with a way of restoring the ability of the market to generate efficiencies in the use of a resource.

There is nothing inherently right or wrong, bad or good, about market-based solutions to environmental and resource management problems. They enable the use of market regulation for common property, but they change the property rights in the direction of exclusion. Whether right or wrong, good or bad, depends on the specifics of a particular situation, including the goals of management, framed within the goals and expectations of a society. Studies are now underway in a variety of regions to look at the implications of ITQs and related measures in fisheries. We are doing this for the sea clam fisheries of the East Coast of the United States, the first fishery in federal waters to be managed with ITQs (McCay and Creed 1994). Preliminary analysis shows that, since 1990, the number of vessels has declined by more than 50 percent and the number of firms by 20 percent; that ownership of vessels and of rights to fish is being concentrated in fewer larger firms, including banks and other "outsiders"; and that large numbers of people have lost their jobs, some of whom are still wondering what hit them. The big are getting bigger and the small smaller. Parallels with the social consequences of agrarian enclosure in rural Europe cannot help but spring to mind.

In fisheries, as in other domains, agents and agencies of the central government appear eager to try out various market-based solutions to environmental problems, in part because of the high costs and demonstrably poor effectiveness and well as inefficiencies of strictly regulatory solutions. Another motivating force is the desire of some government workers, trained in the sciences, to get out of the messy business of resource allocation; with privatization, after the initial cut, the market takes the responsibility for allocation. The Clean Air Act of 1990 and the system it enables, just underway, of tradeable pollution emissions, is another instance (Feder 1993). In addition, some of the national and international conservation groups, such as the World Wildlife Fund and the Center for Marine Conservation, are investigating ITQs for fisheries conservation. It is difficult to discern the mechanisms by which privatized fishing rights translate into conservation. ITQ systems are still dependent on government-imposed or co-managed regulations on catches and technology (Mace 1993).

One argument is that those who hold exclusive rights are more likely to engage in conservation-oriented behavior: Landless, tenant farmers with uncertain futures are not very likely to plant or care for trees on their tenant farms. But private property owners are quite willing and able to over-exploit and push to extinction "their" resources, if the price is right and the future holds other options, as Colin Clark (1973) long ago demonstrated for whaling. Moreover, privatization can create new pressures on the remaining commons, as shown throughout the world, where the privatizing accumulation of property by the few pushes the majority to more marginal lands or to overexploit their customary, communal lands. This has been called the tragedy of the noncommons (May 1990). Will there be fisheries parallels in the wake of ITQs? Can this method of resource allocation narrow the gap between individual and collective interests that is at the core of the commons dilemma, or might it, in some circumstances, widen the gap or keep it open?

CULTURE AND THE COMMONS

The culture of the commons is a strong and unifying perspective from which one can approach the problem of property rights and natural resources. It concludes both the "high" culture of academics, politics, and law, and the "low" culture of people who claim, contest, and exercise property rights in the course of their lives. A number of research questions and topics follow. For example, how do these two cultures interact? What about the contested terrain of privatizing common property rights? What about the nature of community?

Culture includes the realm of people's expectations about nature, themselves, and each other, for example, whether people are seen as far too greedy and selfish to ever get together on anything common, whether they see themselves as significantly affecting the natural world and its resources, and how these things affect how people behave, including their ability to come to terms with the management of common property. We could and should also include expectations about the relationships between citizens and their governments, with respect to the management of natural resources—expectations which, when not met, may lead to unexpected responses (cf. Krauss [1983] on citizen activism in the wake of discovery of poisonous chemicals at Love Canal, New York). Culture also includes the values and beliefs people hold about social and ecological relationships, how they are prioritized and linked to each other, and how these affect how people behave. Can we even imagine a world in which people actually cooperated with each other and sacrificed their immediate self-interests to achieve a better balance with the rest of the natural world? These and other dimensions of culture are both various and changing, and should be incorporated into any theory about human ecology and the commons.

A DIFFERENT METAPHOR

The metaphors we use not only reflect but also help mold the ways we explain and respond to environmental problems. The tragedy of the commons discourse is profoundly modernist, based on the asocial individual who is naturalized and individualized in the model. The self-seeking behavior of the herdsman is only "natural," given his identity as both Economic man and Everyman, and there is, in the model, only one possible alternative to atomistic, mutually destructive social relations: government intervention. A particular view of the nature of human nature leads to a view of the process of environmental abuse as inevitable and inexorable. And natural greed must be harnessed if natural greed is the cause.

One alternative, suggested above, is comedy. In literature, as Donald Donham has pointed out, comedy is a common plot or persistent theme of neoclassical economic analyses, "so-called Pareto optimality typically providing the healthy resolution to apparent contradiction" (Donham 1990, p. 192).[4] It may be appropriate to use the concept of comedy for the focus and narrative style of the revisionist approach to the question of the commons, where game theory, public choice approaches, and other economistic approaches are used to show conditions under which cooperation to prevent or resolve problems of the commons, occurs Elinor Ostrom's *Governing the Commons* (1990) is an instructive example (see also Berkes 1989; Bromley 1989; Schmid 1987).

However, that set of approaches has the risk of being interpreted as being prescriptive (thou shalt be small-scale and self-governed) and overly optimistic (when left to their own devices people will reach viable solutions to their collective dilemmas). In addition, it is still squarely modernist, with but a shift in assumption about human nature and the degree of social interaction. A more satisfying approach would add concerns about the interplays of conflicting interests, contested and agreed-upon meanings and definitions. It would look at the "thick" specification of property rights and other "institutional arrangements"—in particular intersections of history, politics, culture, time and space (McCay and Acheson 1987).

For an example of the cultural and historical specifity and embeddedness of the commons, note that misuse of the term common property as equivalent to no property rights at all is, arguably, a distinctive part of the American experience.[5] In language and culture Americans have generally lost a sense of common property as property. With the rise of radical individualism, capitalist practice, and liberal economic theory, property came to be seen *only* as an individual right to exclude others from the use or benefit of something—that is, private property—when logically and historically it pertains to a broader class of individual rights, including the individual right not to be excluded from something (Macpherson 1978, p. 202). Telling is the fact that the Library of Congress cataloging system does not have a subject heading for common property excepting the very recent use of "commons" and "natural resources, communal," for the "revisionist" literature I have cited. This is at the core of one of the major political problems affecting environmentalist goals in the United States today: The rise of a private property rights movement in reaction to attempts to use the common property dimensions of the legal doctrine of public trust for environmentalist objectives. Common property has lost its status as anything other than the general power of the state, under the rubric of legal doctrines and the general sentiment of "public trust," reducing the issue to one of compensable "taking" versus private property rights.[6]

When I first ventured using the metaphor of comedy what I had in mind was what M. Estellie Smith (1984) had defined as comedy in an encyclopedia's version of classic Greek comedy: the drama of humans "as social rather than private beings, a drama of social actions having a frankly corrective purpose." It might be better to try the metaphor of the romance of the commons. In romance, conflict drives the narrative and is not overcome in the manner of neoclassical analyses. Thus, Marxist narratives include a "romance of oppositional consciousness and of future hope" (Donham 1990, p. 193) as well as ironic unmasking of the present condition. Romance implies a far more complex development of character, situation, and plot and hinges upon the tension of not knowing what the outcome will be, but hoping for the best. As a literary metaphor, it comes closer to the anthropological endeavor.

WHICH TRAGEDY?

A shift in metaphor, to either comedy or romance rather than tragedy, underscores the importance of thinking about fishers and other people not just as competitive, greedy individuals—which they are and can be in many contexts—but also as social beings, capable of and interested in collective action on behalf of the resources and habitats upon which they depend—which also they are and can be in many contexts. If the property rights they hold are common property, they are not necessarily, inextricably, destined to create "tragedies of the commons." Self-governance, co-management, and a variety of other systems of collective action are and can be used. They—and our ethnographic narratives about them—may provide comic relief and, potentially, happy outcomes. Or they may be romances structured around conflict and opposition—between the individual and the collective, among interest groups, communities, classes; or within the individual struggling to do what seems right. If we are yet unwilling to switch metaphors, consider the possibility that there are many potential sources of tragedy affecting people in relation to their environments. We should at least try to be more specific when talking about environmental problems. Are they tragedies of the commons, or of ineffective or incomplete communal management? Or tragedies of open-access and laissez-faire management? Are they tragedies of government mismanagement (Marchak 1988-89) and inadequate science (Steele et al. 1992)? Or tragedies of the noncommons—of privatization? Are they tragedies of the loss of communal institutions? Or are the tragedies really beyond the scope of human cause and response, tragedies caused by the vengeance of fate and the gods, or by uncaring and chaotic natural systems?

ACKNOWLEDGMENTS

This paper was developed out of several talks. Parts of this paper were part of a talk given at the Plenary Session, 123rd Annual Meeting, American Fisheries Society, Portland, Oregon, August 30, 1993. Other parts are from a document called "Management Regimes," prepared for the Meeting on Property Rights and the Performance of Natural Resource Systems, September 2-4, 1993, The Beijer Institute, Royal Academy of Sciences, Stockholm, Sweden; from a paper prepared for a Seminar in the Program in Agrarian Studies, Yale University, October 8; 1993, and from a paper given at a symposium "Antropologien og naturen" at Tórshavn, Faroe Islands, Denmark. I am indebted to those who listened and criticized, in particular David Nugent, James Scott, Carol Rose, and Angelique Haugerud at the Yale Seminar and to Gísli Pálsson, Torben Vestergaard, and Poul Pedersen at the Faroe Islands symposium. Research for the paper was supported in part by the National Sea Grant College Program and the New Jersey Agricultural Experiment Station. It was also sponsored by the Beijer International Institute of Ecological Economics, the Royal Swedish Academy of Sciences, Stockholm, Sweden, with support from the World Environment and Resources Program of the John D. and Catherine T. MacArthur Foundation and the World Bank. The research was conducted as part of the research program Property Rights and the Performance of Natural Resource Systems.

NOTES

1. Courtesy of P. Fricke (personal communication, April 15, 1993).

2. As Schmid (1987) has argued, a focus on the characteristics of the resources is essential to an understanding of how different institutions (or property rights) affect behavior, and thus we might further elaborate a typology of resources, or goods. Schmid emphasizes a number of features that are critical to theory, chosen it would seem because of their implications for exclusion costs, interdependence, or the extent to which one person's choice affects another's, and the limitations of solely competitive market solutions: incompatibility of use; different economies of scale; degrees of jointness of impact (also known as rivalry, where "public goods" become "nonrival" goods [Dixon and Sherman 1990, p. 27]); features that affect transaction costs—contractual, information, and enforcing; and the existence of surpluses as well as fluctuations in supply.

3. This discussion is awkward because of the essentially reflexive nature of our ways of depicting and interpreting natural phenomena. For instance, the reason that common pool resources are defined as such is that they share properties that make it difficult to bound them and to keep one person's actions from affecting another person's opportunities—that is, the "natural" properties of interest are defined and salient because of cultural and social issues. However, for the purposes of the argument I use a distinction between natural and cultural.

4. I am indebted to Angelique Haugerud, Yale University, for directing me to Donham's discussion of the dramatic forms in relation to social theory.

5. For example, Demsetz (1967) and other economic historians depict the historical development of what they call property rights, but what is more accurately rendered as *exclusive* property rights ranging from territoriality to private property.

6. Attempts to account for this phenomenon in both England and the United States can be found in the works of the historian E.P. Thompson (1975, 1991) and the legal scholar Carol Rose (1986). Rose makes the particularly intriguing observation that the legal status of communal "custom" did not travel very well across the Atlantic, from English common law to American law, in part because Americans seemed determined to have nothing between the individual and his or her political representatives. Thompson's work cannot be easily summarized. One point he made is worth recounting here, though: The rise of capitalism meant the objectification of property rights that had often before been parts of communal understanding—moral sentiment in his terms; nonmonetary use rights, converted into objective property rights, seemed to have fared poorly in courts of law.

REFERENCES

Apostle, R., B. McCay, and K.H. Mikalsen. 1993. "Overcapacity and Privatization: The Case of ITQs in the Scotia-Fundy Groundfish Fisheries." Paper presented to the 12th Anniversary Conference of the International Society for the Study of Marginal Regions, Swansea and Gregynog, Powys, July 17-24.

Arnold, J.E.M. and J. G. Campbell. 1986. "Collective Management of Hill Forests in Nepal: The Community Forestry Development Project." Pp. 425-454 in *Proceedings of the Conference on Common Property Resource Management, April 21-26, 1985*. Washington, DC: National Academy Press.

Arnstein, S. 1969. "A Ladder of Citizen Participation." *Journal of American Institute of Planners* 4: 216-224.

Berkes, F. 1987. "Common-Property Resource Management and Cree Indian Fisheries in Canada." Pp. 66-91 in *The Question of the Commons: The Culture and Ecology of Communal Resources*, edited by B.J. McCay and J.M. Acheson. Tucson: University of Arizona Press.

_____ . ed. 1989. *Common Property Resources; Ecology and Community-Based Sustainable Development*. London: Belhaven Press.

Berkes, F.D. Feeny, B.J. McCay, and J.M. Acheson. 1989. "The Benefit of the Commons." *Nature* 340: 91-93.

Berkes, F., P. George, and R. Preston. 1991. "Co-Management: The Evolution of the Theory and Practice of Joint Administration of Living Resources." TASO Research Report, 2nd Series, No. 1, Research Program for Technology Assessment in Subarctic Ontario, McMaster University.

Bohannan, P. 1963. "Land Tenure." Pp. 110-115 in *African Agrarian Systems*, edited by D. Biebuyk. Oxford: Oxford University Press For IAI.

Bromley, D.W. 1989. *Economic Interests and Institutions: The Conceptual Foundations of Public Policy*. New York: Basil Blackwell Inc.

Carrier, J.G. 1987. "Marine Tenure and Conservation in Papua New Guinea: Problems in Interpretation." Pp. 142-167 in *The Question of the Commons: The Culture and Ecology of Communal Resources*, edited by B. McCay and J. Acheson. Tucson: University of Arizona Press.

Charles, A.T. 1992. "Fishery Conflicts; A Unified Framework." *Marine Policy* (September): 379-393.

Christie, P., A.T. White, and D. Buhat. 1990. "San Salvador Island Marine Conservation Project: Some Lessons for Community-Based Resource Management." *Tropical Coastal Area Management* (ICLARM Newsletter) 5(1/2): 7-11.

Christy, F.T., Jr. 1973. "Fishermen's Quotas: A Tentative Suggestion for Domestic Management." Occasional Papers 19, Law of The Sea Institute, University of Rhode Island.

Christy, F.T., Jr. and A. Scott. 1965. *The Common Wealth in Ocean Fisheries: Some Problems of Growth and Economic Allocation*. Baltimore, MD: The Johns Hopkins University Press.

Ciriacy-Wantrup, S. and R. Bishop. 1975. "'Common Property' as a Concept in Natural Resources Policy." *Natural Resources Journal* 15: 713-727.

Cizek, P. 1993. "Guardians of Manomin: Aboriginal Self-Management of Wild Rice Harvesting." *Alternatives* 19(3): 29-32.

Clark, C.W. 1973. "The Economics of Overexploitation." *Science* 181: 630-634.

Cohen, F.G. 1986. *Treaties on Trial; The Continuing Controversy Over Northwest Indian Fishing Rights*. Seattle: University of Washington Press.

Cox, S.J.B. 1985. "No Tragedy on the Common." *Environmental Ethics* 7: 49-61.

Demsetz, H. 1967. "Toward a Theory of Property Rights." *American Economic Review* 62(2): 347-359.

Dixon, J.A. and P.B. Sherman. 1990. *Economics of Protected Areas: A New Look at Benefits and Costs*. Washington, DC: Island Press.

Donham, D. 1990. *History, Power, Ideology*. Cambridge: Cambridge University Press.

Dowling, J.H. 1975. "Property Relations and Productive Strategies in Pastoral Societies." *American Ethnologist* 2(3): 419-426.

Durrenberger, E.P. and G. Pálsson. 1987. "The Grass Roots and the State: Resource Management in Icelandic Fishing." Pp. 370-392 in *The Question of the Commons: The Culture and Ecology of Communal Resources*, edited by B.J. McCay and J. Acheson. Tucson: University of Arizona Press.

Feeny, D., F. Berkes, B.J. McCay, and J.M. Acheson. 1990. "The Tragedy of the Commons: Twenty-Two Years Later." *Human Ecology* 18(1): 1-19.

Feder, B.J. 1993. "Sold: $21 Million of Air Pollution." *New York Times* (March 3): D1, D22.

Feit, H.A. 1973. "The Ethno-ecology of the Waswanipi Cree; Or How Hunters Can Manage Their Resources." Pp. 115-125 in *Cultural Ecology*, edited by B. Cox. Toronto: McClelland and Stewart.

Furubotn, E.G. and S. Pejovich. 1972. "Property Rights and Economic Theory: A Survey of Recent Literature." *Journal of Economic Literature* 10: 1137-1162.

Gatewood, J. and B.J. McCay. 1990. "Comparison of Job Satisfaction in Six New Jersey Fisheries; Implications for Management." *Human Organization* 49(1): 14-25.

Gordon, H.S. 1954. "The Economic Theory of a Common Property Resource: The Fishery." *Journal of Political Economy* 62: 124-142.

Hackett, S.C. 1992. "Heterogeneity and the Provision of Governance for Common-Property Resources." *Journal of Theoretical Politics* 4(3): 325-342.

Hance, B.J., C. Chess, and P.M. Sandman. 1988. *Improving Dialogue with Communities: A Risk Communication Manual for Government*. New Brunswick, NJ: Environmental Communication Research Program, New Jersey Agricultural Experiment Station, Rutgers University.

Hanna, S. 1990. "The Eighteenth Century English Commons: A Model for Ocean Management." *Ocean and Shoreline Management* 14: 155-172.

————. 1992. "Creating User Group Vested Interest in Fishery Management Outcomes: A Case Study." Paper presented to World Fisheries Congress, Athens, Greece, May.

Hardin, G. 1968. "The Tragedy of the Commons." *Science* 162: 1243-1248.

Hilts, S. and P. Mitchell. 1993. "Bucking the Free Market Economy: Using Land Trusts for Conservation and Community-Building." *Alternatives* 19(3): 16-23.

Jentoft, S. 1989. "Fisheries Co-management: Delegating Government Responsibility to Fishermen's Organizations." *Marine Policy* (April): 137-154.

Jentoft, S. and T. Kristoffersen. 1989. "Fishermen's Co-management: The Case of the Lofoten Fishery." *Human Organization* 48(4): 355-365.

Johannes, R.E. 1981. *Words of the Lagoon: Fishing and Marine Lore in the Palau District of Micronesia*. Berkeley: University of California Press.

Krauss, C. 1983. "The Elusive Process of Citizen Activism." *Social Policy* 14(Fall): 50-55

Lanfersieck, J. and D. Squires. 1991. "Planning Models for Individual Transferable Quota Programs." *Canadian Journal of Fisheries and Aquatic Sciences* 49(1): 2313-2321.

Little, D. 1991. *Varieties of Social Explanation: An Introduction to the Philosophy of Social Science*. Boulder, CO: Westview Press.

Lloyd, W.F. (1837) 1968. *Lectures On Population, Value, Poor-laws, and Rent, Delivered in the University of Oxford During the Years, 1832, 1833, 1834, 1835, & 1836*. Reprints of Economic Classics. New York: Augustus M. Kelley.

Ludwig, D., R. Hilborn, and C. Walters. 1993. "Uncertainty, Resource Exploitation, and Conservation: Lessons from History." *Science* 260(April 2): 17,36.

Mace, P.M. 1993. "Will Private Owners Practice Resource Management?" *Fisheries* 18(9): 29-31.

Macpherson, C.B. 1978. "The Meaning of Property." Pp. 1-13 in *Property: Mainstream and Critical Positions*, edited by C.B. Macpherson. Toronto: University of Toronto Press.

Marchak, M.P. 1988-89. "What Happens When Common Property Becomes Uncommon?" *BC Studies* 80(Winter): 3-23.

Martin, I. 1994. *Legacy and Testament: The Story of Columbia River Gillnetters*. Pullman: Washington State University Press.

May, P.H. 1990. "A Tragedy of the Non-Commons: Recent Developments in the Babaçu Palm Based Industries in Maranhao, Brazil." *Forests, Trees and People Newsletter* 11: 23-27.

McCay, B.J. 1980. "A Fishermen's Cooperative, Limited: Indigenous Resource Management in a Complex Society." *Anthropological Quarterly* 53: 29-38.

————. 1987. "The Culture of the Commoners: Historical Observations on Old and New World Fisheries." Pp. 195-216 in *The Question of the Commons: The Culture and Ecology of Communal Resources*, edited by B.J. McCay and J.M. Acheson. Tucson: University of Arizona Press.

_____. 1988. "Muddling through the Clam Beds: Cooperative Management of New Jersey's Hard Clam Spawner Sanctuaries." *Journal of Shellfish Research* 7(2): 327-340.

_____. 1989. "Sea Tenure and the Culture of the Commoners." Pp. 203-226 in *A Sea of Small Boats*, edited by J. Cordell. Cambridge, MA: Cultural Survival, Inc.

_____. 1994. *Social Impacts of ITQs in the Sea Clam Fishery*. Final Report to the New Jersey Sea Grant College Program, New Jersey Marine Sciences Consortium, Fort Hancock, NJ.

_____. In press. "Participation of Fishers in Fisheries Management." In *Fisheries Utilization and Policy; Proceedings of the World Fisheries Congress, May 1992; Theme 2 Volume*, edited by R.M. Meyer, C. Zhang, M.L. Windsor, B. McCay, L. Hushak, and R. Muth. New Delhi: Oxford & IBH Publishing Co. Pvt. Inc.

McCay, B.J. and J.M. Acheson. 1987. *The Question of the Commons: The Culture and Ecology of Communal Resources*. Tucson: University of Arizona Press.

McEvoy, A.F. 1986. *The Fisherman's Problem: Ecology and Law in the California Fisheries, 1850-1980*. Cambridge: Cambridge University Press.

McKean, M.A. 1992. "Success on the Commons: A Comparative Examination of Institutions for Common Property Resource Management." *Journal of Theoretical Politics* 4(3): 247-281.

Meltzoff, S.K. and K. Broad. 1992. "The Rise of Women in Fisheries Management: The Marisquadoras of Illa de Arousa, Galicia." Paper presented to World Fisheries Congress, Athens, Greece, May.

Moloney, D.G. and P.H. Pearse. 1979. "Quantitative Rights as an Instrument for Regulating Commercial Fisheries." *Journal of the Fisheries Research Board of Canada* 36: 859-866.

Neher, P.A., R. Arnason, and N. Mollett, eds. 1989. *Rights Based Fishing*. Proceedings of the NATA Advanced Research Workshop on Scientific Foundations for Rights Based Fishing, Reykjavik, Iceland, June 27-July 1, 1988. Dordrecht: Kluwer Academic Publishing.

Netting, R. McC. 1976. "What Alpine Peasants Have in Common: Observations on Communal Tenure in a Swiss Village." *Human Ecology* 4: 135-146.

Ostrom, E. 1987. "Institutional Arrangements For Resolving The Commons Dilemma: Some Contending Approaches." Pp. 250-265 in *Capturing The Commons: The Culture and Ecology of Communal Resources*, edited by B.J. McCay and J.M. Acheson. Tucson: University of Arizona Press.

_____. 1990. *Governing the Commons: The Evolution of Institutions for Collective Action*. New York: Cambridge University Press.

_____. 1992. *Crafting Institutions for Self-Governing Irrigation Systems*. San Francisco: ICS Press.

_____. 1994. "Neither Market Nor State: Govenrance of Common-Pool Resources in the Twenty-First Century." International Food Policy Research Institute (IFPRI) Lecture Series No. 2, presented June 2, 1994, Washington, D.C.

Ostrom, V. and E. Ostrom. 1977. "A Theory for Institutional Analysis of Common Pool Problems." Pp. 157-172 in *Managing the Commons*, edited by G. Hardin and J. Baden. San Francisco: W.H. Freeman.

Peters, P.E. 1987. "Embedded Systems and Rooted Models: The Grazing Lands of Botswana and the Commons Debate." Pp. 171-194 in *The Question of the Commons: The Culture and Ecology of Communal Resources*, edited by B.J. McCay and J. Acheson. Tucson: University of Arizona Press.

Pinkerton, E., ed. 1989. *Cooperative Management of Local Fisheries; New Directions for Improved Management and Community Development*. Vancouver, BC: University of British Columbia Press.

Pollnac, R.B. 1984. "Investigating Territorial Use Rights Among Fishermen." Pp. 285-300 in *Maritime Institutions in the Western Pacific*, Senri Ethnological Studies, 17, edited by K. Ruddle and T. Akimichi. Osaka: National Museum of Ethnology.

Regier, H.A. and A.P. Grima. 1985. "Fishery Reserve Allocation: An Explanatory Essay." *Canadian Journal of Fisheries and Aquatic Sciences* 42: 845-859.

Rodman, M.C. 1989. *Deep Water; Development and Change in Pacific Village Fisheries.* Boulder, CO: Westview Press.

Rose, C. 1986. "The Comedy of the Commons: Custom, Commerce, and Inherently Public Property." *The University of Chicago Law Review* 53(3): 711-781.

Ruddle, K. 1989. "Solving The Common-Property Dilemma: Village Fisheries Rights in Japanese Coastal Waters." Pp. 168-198 in *Common Property Resources*, edited by F. Berkes. London: Belhaven Press.

Schmid, A.A. 1987. *Property, Power, and Public Choice.* New York: Praeger.

Scott, A. 1955. "The Fishery: The Objectives of Sole Ownership." *Journal of Political Economy* 63: 116-124.

Shepherd, G. 1990. "The People Have Something to Say." *Forests, Trees and People Newsletter* 11.

Singleton, S. and M. Taylor. 1992. "Common Property, Collective Action and Community." *Journal of Theoretical Politics* 4(3): 309-324.

Smith, C.L. 1981. "Satisfaction Bonus from Salmon Fishing: Implications for Economic Evaluation." *Land Economics* 57(2): 181-194.

Smith, M.E., 1982. "Fisheries Management: Intended Results and Unintended Consequences." Pp. 57-93 in *Modernization and Marine Fisheries Policy*, edited by J.R. Maiolo and M.K. Orbach. Ann Arbor, MI: Ann Arbor Science Publishers.

————. 1984. "The Triage of The Commons." Paper presented to annual meeting of The Society for Applied Anthropology, March 14-18, Toronto, Canada.

Steele, D.H., R. Andersen, and J.M. Green. 1992. "The Managed Commercial Annihilation of Northern Cod." *Newfoundland Studies* 8(1): 34-68.

Stocks, A. 1987. "Resource Management in an Amazon Varzea Lake Ecosystem: The Cocamilla case." Pp. 108-120 in *The Question of the Commons: The Culture and Ecology of Communal Resources*, edited by B. McCay and J. Acheson. Tucson: University of Arizona Press.

Suttles, W. 1987. *Coast Salish Essays.* Seattle: University of Washington Press.

Taylor, L. 1987. "The River Would Run Red With Blood: Community and Common Property in an Irish Fishing Settlement." Pp. 290-307 in *The Question of the Commons: The Culture and Ecology of Communal Resources*, edited by B.J. McCay and J. Acheson. Tucson: University of Arizona Press.

Thomson, J.T., D.H. Feeny, and R.J. Oakerson. 1986. "Institutional Dynamics: The Evolution and Dissolution of Common Property Resource Management." Pp. 391-424 in *Proceedings of the Conference on Common Property Resource Management, April 21-26, 1985.* Washington, DC: National Academy Press.

Thompson, E.P. 1975. *Whigs and Hunters: The Origins of the Black Act.* London: Allen Lane.

————. 1991. *Customs In Common.* New York: The New Press.

Vondal, P.J. 1987. "The Common Swamplands of Southeastern Borneo: Multiple Use, Management, and Conflict." Pp. 231-249 in *The Question of the Commons: The Culture and Ecology of Communal Resources*, edited by B.J. McCay and J. Acheson. Tucson: University of Arizona Press.

Young, O.R. 1989. "The Politics of International Regime Formation: Managing Natural Resources and the Environment." *International Organization* 43(3): 349-375.

FROM COMMONS TO TRAPS:

NATURAL BALANCE AND HUMAN ECOLOGICAL SERIES

Lee Freese

ABSTRACT

For the purpose of developing human ecological theory, the dilemma of the commons as conceived to date is too simple a problem to bear the weight that has come to be expected of it. The problem is not unique to humans. It is not a problem of decision making, or of rationality. It is not really a dilemma. It is not even a single problem. The commons metaphor is an incomplete formulation of what here is characterized as an ecological trap condition, in which increasingly irreversible ecological changes for biosociocultural regimes cascade out of serial progressions. Formulated so, *Garrett Hardin's problem*—namely, the overshooting of human ecological carrying capacities due to population growth and the unsustainable exploitation of biophysical resources—can maintain its empirical status as a presumed tragedy in the making. However, its logical status in the theory of human ecology is suspect: Hardin's problem presumes a human imbalance with nature and presumes a balance can be restored, but the implicit concept of balance is anthropocentric and therefore untenable.

Advances in Human Ecology, Volume 4, pages 117-140.

INTRODUCTION

Modern environmentalists show great concern for the shifting balance of nature caused by human activities. The concern may be more accentuated now, because the effects are more transparent and serious now, but the concern is not new and the process itself most certainly is not. Marston Bates observed, in 1960, that "the whole course of man's [sic] cultural development turns on shifting the balance of nature" (p. 162). Bates might have gone further to say that shifting the balance of nature provides the principal story line of human sociocultural development, has been its whole purpose actually, insofar as it may be said to have had a purpose, and is the whole idea behind humans forming what they call communities. Human communities are extensions of nature inasmuch as they take root in the need for a material subsistence that must be drawn from natural communities that take no pity on humans without communities of their own. The existence of human communities in itself implies no human-natural imbalance. But in the present, it seems, *Homo sapiens* has become what W.R. Catton, Jr. (1986) so aptly named *Homo colossus*, for its colossal appetites and unconstrained penetration and dominance of natural biota. Put otherwise, the balance qua dominance has shifted against nature even more than what Bates had in mind, when he had it in mind.

But, we should consider whether to conceive this concept of balance of nature otherwise, and consider whether to employ it at all. The concept of natural balance and imbalance, as a point-counterpoint of opposing ecological forces, in which humans are the principal forcers, derives from the ecologists and environmentalists of Bates' generation and earlier. Today it informs or undergirds virtually every discourse on environmental affairs, practically every discourse on the ecological sustainability of human sociocultural systems, and is a root for interminable arguments about limits to economic growth and to population growth that can not be settled in the terms of the arguments themselves. Meanwhile, although they have not abandoned the concept of a balance to nature, bioecologists are now casting serious aspersions on it and are striving to employ more dynamic and sophisticated concepts to describe the interaction of ecological phenomena (Wiens 1984; Botkin 1990; Pimm 1991; Allen and Hoekstra 1991, 1992).

In this paper I suggest that human ecologists should do likewise. To persuade, I examine the concept of ecological commons, which is sometimes held up as a paradigm for human ecological analysis. The world view that underwrites the concept of a commons implicitly contains a concept of human-natural balance. I undertake to show how the commons idea, though a very good first approximation for human ecological analysis, is much too simple and incomplete to accomplish what its principal exponent himself wished for, namely, an effective grounding for the analysis of human ecological predicaments. The grounding is not effective, I argue, just because it is constrained in its world view by the concept of a balance to nature in which humans are supposed as the centerpieces. Without this constraint a fuller explication in ecological terms of the intent of the commons model can be found in the concept of an ecological trap. With this concept there is no tragedy of the commons, but humans have so trapped themselves now, indeed, there may be a tragedy in the making.

THE PROBLEMS OF THE PROBLEM OF THE COMMONS

We may consider just the theoretical highlights of the commons problem as posed by Garrett Hardin (1968). All modern treatments flow from this seminal piece,[1] which seemed to pose an inherent dilemma for the interaction of human ecological and economic forces.

In general theoretical terms, assume a set of resources that are not individually owned but, rather, are common property. Let there be incremental increases in the numbers of persons who are permitted to withdraw the common resources at a constant rate or, should the number of users remain constant, incremental increases in the rate of withdrawal. Either way, how shall we construe the benefits and costs that accrue with each incremental increase in the use of the commons? The benefit obtained from each additional withdrawal for each person is near unity: There is a direct gain per unit of increased consumption, but the costs are fractional for any individual because the costs—eventual depletion of the common resources—are borne by all its users and, thus, are divided among them. It therefore is in the self-interest of persons to consume but not conserve. Should this be done without limit for common resources that themselves are not without limit, eventually of course the commons and its communities will be destroyed by overuse. On this analysis, the unrestrained freedom of individuals to use common property resources brings ruination to all, in Hardin's phrase, which is why he called it the tragedy of the commons. It is a tragedy noticed long ago in the annals of human thought. Aristotle had said that "what is common to the greatest number gets the least amount of care" (Barker 1962, p. 44).

The tragedy of the commons has often been interpreted as a beacon for the overshooting of ecological carrying capacities due to human population and economic growth. Ecological processes provide resources for humans, and they are "common to the greatest number." But the very existence of these resources is thought to encourage their unfettered consumption as commons are converted into, or utilized in connection with, the economic production of material wealth. The commons model implies there is an incentive to use common property resources for economic purposes without regard for whether that use is sustainable.

Depending on where one finds oneself in the process, the destruction of the commons may actually be economically profitable, as Fife (1971) pointed out. Just as those who enter a pyramid scheme to scam money from the unsuspecting stand to profit should they enter at the base of the pyramid and get out early, so it is with ecological commons. For instance, it benefits corporate executives of the timber industry to cut old growth forests as quickly as they can, presuming there is a market for the product (which there is); such a practice will produce quick and handsome corporate profits, a portion of which is then siphoned into bloated executive compensation. This does not benefit the next generation of timber workers who stand to be unemployed very shortly because of overharvesting, nor the next generation of the general public that might have some diffuse interest in sustaining old growth forests, but these executives do not belong to the next generation. The costs, remember, are spread about. It is through comparisons such as these that the metaphor of the commons model is both enticing and depressing.

But before we seek therapy we might first seek clarification. First, what is to count as a common property resource? Whatever some legally constituted sociopolitical entity is inspired to define as such—a national park, for instance—counts. But the problem of the commons would not be interesting if that were its only intended interpretation, and it is not. Also counted are fisheries, forests, groundwater, wildlife, and the like. Note that all these resources are the products of evolutionary and ecological processes, to which the concept of commons also extends. The ecological processes include virtually all of the human life support systems that ecological dynamics create—for instance, the atmosphere and all that goes into the making of it. Note now that the processes that generate the common property resources, like the resources themselves, are also degradable and vulnerable to a commons tragedy.

So commons come in at least two kinds: The first is the sociopolitical kind, wherein some natural habitat is defined by the human imposition of boundaries defined intentionally to serve social, political, or cultural purposes. The second is the purely ecological kind of which there are also two: (a) processes that respect no human social, political, or cultural boundary, intentions, or purpose whatever, which I take to be the heart of the commons question; and (b) products of the processes, from which derive the problem of common property resources, since the products may be deemed worthy of management or exploitation by humans. The intended application both to sociopolitical and ecological commons makes the problems of the commons and of common property resources appear to be distinct, significant, and intractable.

Clearly, if we distinguish matters so, it is rather odd to think of ecological commons as property, since the constituents of ecological commons are not, in general, capable of being owned. Governments can own national parks, so to speak, just by claiming to, and they can claim fishes and the grounds that spawn them. Nobody—no individual, no sociopolitical entity—owns the nitrogen-fixing bacteria or the stratospheric ozone, nor could they. Nevertheless, the thought that ecological commons provide common *property* resources persists. The thought has taken root in the confusing of ecological processes with ecological *products*, which are economically coveted; and, in the recognition that the products need to be sustainably managed and regulated so that human activity does not degrade their economic utility or esthetic value.

The use of sociopolitical commons may be amenable to regulation by whatever sociopolitical entity "owns" it, and regulation is the buzzword for protecting this kind of commons. Plainly, however, regulating the use of ecological commons is orders of magnitude more difficult. This is not just because this would require the cooperation of distinct sociopolitical entities that may have competing interests in governing processes that do not respect national boundaries. It is also because it is much easier to regulate a fixed habitat than it is to "regulate" a set of interacting biogeochemical processes. At best sociopolitical entities can try to regulate behavior that affects the processes, and then only within the purview of their political authority, moral community, and economic leverage.

There is no significant problem of ecological commons apart from the economics of subsistence. Ecological dynamics provide resources for human life-support that economic activity presumes when economic markets organize and function to provide goods and services that human societies demand. The dependence of economic organization on ecological organization has, unfortunately, been known to perturb ecological organization by generating so called externalities—costs external to an economic transaction and borne externally to it. Thus ecological commons can be imperiled by economic activity even when the resources obtained from the commons are not directly consumed in economic production or consumption. The nub is that economic price may not reflect true ecological cost. It is sufficient that the resources of ecological commons are implicated in economic production and consumption either before or after the fact—for example, nitrogen-fixing bacteria in agricultural production or the stratospheric ozone in industrial consumption. The resources of an ecological commons need not enter at all into a given economic transaction, and the processes typically do not, and their role as external parameters may be obscured or unrecognized even though they might provide vital boundary conditions. A possible solution? Factor in to the economic price the assessible ecological costs or, in the jargon of the day, internalize the externalities. Whatever the case-by-case merits of that, the standard analysis of the commons tells us that there *shall* come a time when external ecological parameters are affected for the worse because it will be in no economic agent's self-interest to protect them.

The ecological-economic dilemma now begins to take shape: Every economic transaction occurs within some ecological system within which economies are organized and upon which they depend. But there is a mismatch. Economic markets, which set prices for goods and services, use the processes and resources of ecological commons without pricing *them*. These are free goods in the sense that the costs are borne by ecological systems, in the form of degradation, but are not reckoned in to the prices paid for the goods and services obtained from the systems. Thus, life sustaining ecological processes, which are shared human resources and can be thought of as common property only in a loose sense, can not be thought of as *economic* property in any sense. They cannot be commoditized or divided. Being economically unpriced, thus it seemingly is rational for individuals to convert the ecological commons to their own economic uses; but, as they continue to do so without limit, that becomes seemingly irrational as the commons eventually are degraded. Ecological commons do, after all, have finite carrying capacities—or so it is assumed.

The commons dilemma as originally construed was thought early to have no technical solution (Stillman 1975), although various ethical, political, and policy solutions have periodically been proposed. The solutions have ranged from radical centralization (Ophuls 1977) to radical decentralization (Fox 1985) to the opinion that there are no political solutions (Crowe 1969). Hardin himself considered various solutions and eventually settled on a disguised Social Darwinism (Hardin 1993). Ostrom's (1990) examination of numerous case studies indicates a far wider range of practical solutions may be effective than privatization or central regulation, which are the major themes that undergird most theoretical proposals set forth to date. Edney (1980, 1981) assessed the range of alternatives, and some indication of current thinking about the problem can be had from McCay and Acheson (1987) and Feeny, Berkes, McCay, and Acheson (1990).

The problem of the commons is a metaphor to describe a biospheric condition that some believe poses this irreconcilable dilemma: The pursuit of individual economic self-interest in the short term, other things equal, is inimical to the collective ecological interest in the long-term. And on the face of it this would, indeed, appear to be ultimately irrational: The defeat of any long term collective interest eventuates in the defeat of individual self-interest at some point which, for the individuals affected at that point, then is the short term.

Short-term and long-term time frames and segments of them are crucial to interpreting the dilemma of the commons. Here, however, is where the metaphor disappoints. The commons metaphor as originally formulated is altogether too vague on this matter of time frames. It just states a condition of conflict between individual and collective interest that is supposed to eventuate in harm to the collectivity. It arrives at this conclusion based on its assignment of utilities to individuals and its assumptions about those utilities. But there is more than this to take into account in analyzing what, if any, dilemma the metaphor poses.

There are numerous reasons not to fix on the commons dilemma as a problem in its own right. As McCay (1995) showed, this is far too indiscriminate a model to generate any serious proposals that might be useful to deal with the very complex problem of managing common-pool resources, and far too simple a model to enable us to tell when and how ecological conditions may come into conflict with economic conditions. When explicated and analyzed as follows, we shall see that the original problem of the commons can be set aside. However, when its true ecological import for humans is appreciated in evolutionary context, the problem can be developed to maximum effect. Let us begin by analyzing the supposed dilemma the problem is believed to represent.

SOCIAL DILEMMAS

The commons dilemma is one member of a larger class of problems that social psychologists call social dilemmas. In an early review Robyn M. Dawes (1980) defined social dilemmas by the presence of two properties that may be temporarily present in human social orders whether or not ecological matters are at issue. One property is that persons taken as an aggregate are better off if they cooperate with each other than if they do not. The other is that *each* person is better off for not cooperating regardless of what the other implicated persons do. These are the properties of the classic prisoners' dilemma, long a favorite tea party distraction of social psychologists and game theorists; and they are the properties of the commons dilemma as we just saw. The difference is that in the prisoners' dilemma information is usually lacking as to how another person will act to affect the collective welfare, whereas the commons dilemma results from the negligible impact that individual choices have on the collective welfare.

The trail of the social dilemmas is long and wide.[2] Some investigators have sought to incorporate explicit ecological properties into social dilemmas. Edney and Harper (1978b), for instance, permitted experimental resource pools to be replaced at a constant rate known to experimental subjects (and found that subjects depleted the resource pools anyway). However, the social dilemmas are a sidebar. It suffices here to show that by following the social dilemmas, whether or not they have ecological parameters, we can expect no serendipitous result useful for solving the commons dilemma. To the contrary, a problem *with* the commons dilemma, as distinct from the problem of it, should be easier now to highlight if we consider just a few noteworthy properties pertaining to all the social dilemmas, the commons included.

The social dilemmas are not true dilemmas in the classic philosophical sense. The classic sense is a dilemma of logic—an implication with a double bind obtained from an argument constructed usually with enthymematic premises whose solution requires changing or enriching the premises. A classic philosophical dilemma is a classic philosopher's trick. It poses a problem that can not be solved in the form posed. When philosophers cast these baited hooks, they usually react by cutting each others' lines. There are two ways to do that. One is to analyze the language in which the dilemma is posed and recast it. The other is to change the logic of the dilemma by supplying the missing premisses. Either way, the dilemmas are not usually solved. They are dissolved. But the social dilemmas are not like that at all.

The social dilemmas relate the psychological decision making of individual agents to undesirable social outcomes, but the dilemmas are apparent not real. Besides no dilemma of logic, there is no dilemma of social psychology either. An illusion of dilemma appears from missing social prerequisites. As a matter of sociology, for any social structure to function it requires some predictable patterns to the behavior of individuals if the interdependencies the structure has evolved to organize are to be managed and the functions executed. A social structure is defective without social norms to serve as parameters for human conduct, on pain of suffering the arbitrariness, unpredictableness, and chaos of social disorder. In the absence of social norms, human beings undertake to contrive some always.

Why bring up these tidbits of introductory sociology? Because the so called social dilemmas are defective social structures. The prisoners' dilemma is defective because it lacks a norm for cooperation; the prisoners are permitted none. That structural flaw virtually guarantees that individual benefit will take precedence over collective benefit when the prisoners are forced to choose. They have been tricked into a condition of interdependence with no social relations to define and manage it, and so they have to "defect." Iterated plays of the game, as Amnon Rapaport (1967) early showed, remove the so called dilemma by supplying the missing condition: the development and functioning of social norms with their patterns of reciprocal exchange. Likewise, iterated conditions of interaction for other kinds of social dilemmas tend to induce cooperation not defection depending upon the time frame, group size, and cost-benefit conditions that are provided to decision making agents (Glance and Huberman 1994).

Without iterative trials, the commons dilemma, when interpreted as a variant of the prisoners' dilemma, is defective in a homologous way. In the case of the commons at issue are free, public goods and how to manage them. The point had already been made that common ownership is the same as no ownership at all (Olsen 1965; Gordon 1954). Then Buchanan (1971) persuasively argued that the existence of public goods is equivalent to the absence of law (statutory social norms). With statutory regulation of common property, he thought, individuals would have an incentive to act in terms of the collective welfare. Without statutory regulation, the incentive wasn't there. The core of the matter was thought to be this: With any common property there is built in to the circumstance a psychological incentive that promotes free riding[3]—an intellectually polite term for freeloading at the expense of others. There being no apparent cost to an individual to consume free or public goods, in the absence of law there is therefore no social constraint on those who would derive benefits from common property without contributing to its preservation. Clearly, statutory regulation in principle can provide social constraints on free riders of sociopolitical commons. Ecological commons are not so amenable to statutory fixes. But let us note the intent: to buttress a defective social structure with just what it lacks, a kind of (enforceable) social norm, for the purpose of providing incentives (and disincentives) for persons to make altruistic choices.

An alternative means to buttress a defective social structure where wants enter in is to locate the desiderata in economic markets. For the case at hand, this could in principle be done by removing some kinds of common property from the public realm and placing it in private ownership. Should common property be privatized, then markets could price it presuming there were markets for it. Disregarding the very serious problem of monopoly formation that would be certain to arise with the privatization of certain kinds of common property, it is necessary to observe again that not all common property has common properties: Ecological commons—all the fundamental biogeochemical processes and interactions—cannot be privatized. With ecological commons there arises the intractable problem of measuring and assigning economic values. It is one thing (and by no means easy) to assign economic values to a national park. That is an ecological system, but a sociopolitical commons. How does one assign economic values to human life supporting *processes*, such as autotrophic production or the hydrologic cycle? Can we put a price on the sun and the rain?

COMMONS DILEMMAS DIVERSIONS

Those are just some reasons why the commons problem has no political, technical, or logical solution in theory. There are additional reasons, and they get more to the heart of why there can be no theoretical solution in the terms in which the problem has been posed. The development of the problem of ecological commons has been writ anthropocentric, posing a conflict of individual versus collective benefit and short-term versus long-term rationality. This tacitly conceives an inherently ecological problem as a problem of human social psychology and economics. Why should we expect this can be coherent?

The problem of ecological commons, as construed above, is not one of individual versus collective benefit. The problem has application to nonhuman systems in which that thought could not be reasonably entertained. The conditions defined for the commons problem apply to other species in habitats not dominated by humans. Should a biologist such as Hardin observe a decline in the numbers or well-being of a population of a nonhuman social species in its natural habitat, the declines would not be attributed to the failure of the members of the population to act in concert for the collective welfare!

Instead, the declines would be attributed to some combination of circumstances concerning selection pressures operating on the population or its competitors, the reproductive and adaptive strategies the species had evolved, the energy flows and food chains of the ecosystem on which the population depended, whether species population growth was self-limited, predator-limited, or resource-limited, the local and bioregional capacities—all this and more. Now, in the case of human dominated ecosystems it could be observed that human population growth and economic consumption tend to be resource-limited and can, indeed, be controlled by human decision making. While it is *true* that *Homo sapiens* can control its ecosystemic behavior, it is ecologically diversionary to conceive this as a dilemma of decision making that leads to irrational consequences. Numerous organic species have a tendency to eat themselves out of house and home. It is not selfish, antisocial, or unecological for some rodents sometimes to reproduce beyond the means able to sustain them. Why, then, should it be so regarded for humans? Because humans "know" the consequences and rodents do not?

The commons problem has application to species wherein "rationality," whatever that is, cannot possibly apply to long-term consequences, for some implicated species have no concept of such. It is not irrational, it is routine, that algae bloom and crash. Is it irrational when humans do this? In applying the question to humans we should note there is a risk of contradiction in talking about short-term rationality and long-term irrationality. If behavioral choices are irrational in the long run, then they must have been irrational in the short run whether humans *know* it or not, perceive it or not, or model it or not, because the long run is made up of a series of just so many short runs (or of disjointed and not necessarily linear segments of them). Discussions of rationality in the context of commons often leave the time parameter unspecified, and they fail to note that some short-term rewards, supposedly rational, have long-term hidden costs (Lepper and Greene 1978). It is not necessarily in the rational self-interest of humans to be rewarded when that reward is to be followed by a series. It depends on the nature of the series. It therefore confuses, and may sometimes mistake, issues to interpret human behavioral choices that have immediately reinforcing qualities as indicators of rational choice.

It diverts the development of human ecological theory to interpret ecological commons when applied to humans as problems of utilitarian decision making—in effect, as problems of social psychology and economics. That tacitly equates a problem of human ecology with the environmental survival implications for humans. But—that was the point all along. My point is that the problem of ecological commons is a problem of human *ecology*, not one of human social psychology and economics. That the social psychological dynamics and the economic relations of humans may *cause* environmental problems does not imply that the corresponding problem of human ecology can be solved by conceiving it in the terms of the respective social sciences.

However, since human ecology has to include humans somewhere and the commons analysis does this, it deserves to be developed to its fullest. For, the significance of Hardin's parable has not been the least bit disturbed. The significance is that ecological commons incorporate the biosphere from which all humans draw resources for subsistence, and from which humans are supposed now to be drawing at unsustainable rates. So, to keep in the spirit of things, let us temporarily retain the method of thinking about ecological commons as a matter of human decision making just long enough to consider iterated decision making—the condition in which the outcome at trial n depends on the outcome at $n-1$, and so on, consecutively. It happens there is a useful idea to cover this circumstance, and it enhances the quality and sophistication of the commons model.

TRAPS

With the idea of a trap comes social psychology's most serious and useful contribution to human ecology. John Platt (1973), a psychologist thinking to keep with the theory of his discipline, defined a trap as a sequence of repeated behaviors that have rewarding consequences in the short term and so get reinforced, but that have punishing consequences in the long term. One-person traps, exemplified by the behavior of alcoholics and chain smokers, are ecologically irrelevant. But *social* traps, in which collective action that is reinforced in the short term but punished in the long term, have numerous interpretations to ecological concerns. Population growth rates that exceed environmental levels of subsistence create a social trap condition, for eventually people shall go hungry. An economy whose growth depends on nonrenewable energy supplies is clearly a social trap, too. It commits the economy to dependence on something that eventually cannot be depended on. Overgrazing, monocropping, and the overplowing of arable land, though economically profitable in the short term, create a social trap in the long term because such practices eventually undermine the very function they are intended to promote. Economic dependence on any kind of overharvesting is a trap because eventually there is little or nothing to harvest.

Unlike the social dilemmas the social traps have the idea of iteration built in. Time is incorporated as a variable so that radical changes can be described over the course of a repeated sequence as a function of the sequence itself. That makes the concept useful for ecological applications, especially for drawing out the logic of the commons problem. Following its logic, an ecological commons becomes a social trap whenever human adaptive strategies for obtaining subsistence transform a habitat until the strategies become maladaptive. But this logic has not been entirely drawn out.

Social psychologists following Platt continued to anchor the idea of a social trap in the theory and problematics of psychology (Cross and Guyer 1980), and focussed on reinforcement schedules (Brechner 1977), information contingencies (Edney and Harper 1978b), and traps of different kinds (Messick and McClelland 1983). For the purpose of finding useful ecological applications of the idea, these too are diversions.

So, what shall we do? Let us take some initiative and define the idea of an *ecological trap*. A trap may be said to be ecological if, and only if, the following conditions apply to some system with respect to some dominant species and one or more biophysical resources critical for its functioning: (1) the resources are replaced over a series at a constant rate; (2) the exploitation of the resources exceeds their rate of replacement; (3) the depletion of the resources has a cumulative effect leading to an exponential increase in their relative scarcity; and (4) as the series proceeds, the probability that the system can return to its original state declines or, put another way, the degradation of the system becomes increasingly irreversible.

This, it seems to me, is the set of conditions that Hardin intended (and still intends) to address. An ecological trap is an evolving condition that results from an iterated series in which dependent events produce a cascade in which the distribution of biophysical resources is irreversibly changed. The condition of irreversibility does not have to apply for all time—just for enough time as measured by the species' organic bounds. The same caveat applies to the condition of relative scarcity: It is sufficient if some critical resource is unavailable for some critical time frame. One or more of the following effects may be expected to result from an ecological trap, depending on how long the series has proceeded and the magnitude and extent of its connections with other ecological networks: diminished species interactions, diminished population sizes and altered distributions, degraded biogeochemical interactions, and the simplification of social organization, if any. Conceived as a serial progression of iterated episodes building to a cascade, an ecological trap need not be terminal. It depends on where one's observations are located in the series. Assuming some arbitrarily chosen starting point as an original system state, early in the series perhaps many steps can be retraced and the system nearly restored; later in the series, fewer and to a lesser degree; at the end of the series, none and not at all. If, as time proceeds, the degradation effects within the system become more cumulative, exponential, and irreversible, the probabilities decline that the affected species can escape the trap.

The original problem of the commons is a vague, imprecise, and incomplete formulation of an ecological trap. If the cover of the dilemma is removed by supplying a remedy for the social structural defect, the genuine problem concealed by the apparent dilemma remains in full form though it remains unsolved. Attempts to deal with it *as a dilemma* leave untouched the serial trap its ecological properties implicitly define. Theoretical solutions to the commons dilemma have focussed on conditions to promote social cooperation, and the management of public goods and free riders. But an ecological trap can materialize under conditions of total cooperation, no free riders, and any system or no system for managing public goods: Every organic species is subject to getting caught in ecological traps that may be evolutionarily inevitable. Ecological traps may develop their own momentum from natural selection or ecosystemic succession. These effects are not normally predictable or controllable. They most certainly need not arise from defective social structures, nor need they present any inherent "dilemmas." Dilemmas arise just when humans have to make decisions and behavioral choices that affect the stability of their habitats. Mostly, however, this is done without humans making any real choices at all, insofar as cognition is a factor in choice. Mostly, it seems, humans act without forethought for ecological consequences. Only afterthoughts give us pause, and not always then.

We may reasonably wonder afterwards whether *Homo sapiens* did not enter an ecological trap 10 thousand years ago with the beginning of agriculture. This, after all, represented an enormous increase in energy capture, which was correlated with increased environmental impacts—a human ecological threshold of monumental consequences. With agriculture, more people could be fed, and more were. We may further wonder whether a more encompassing trap did not ensnare us as we crossed the threshold of industrialization. Now even more energy could be captured, and it was, with proportional environmental impacts and hyperbolic population growth that is now leveling off to *merely* exponential levels[4] (and will not top off until at least one more doubling). With the twentieth century we got even more of the same effects, combined now, through the "wonders" of industrialized agriculture. The increased environmental impacts now have to be measured in extraordinary terms: Recently *Homo sapiens*, in virtue of their sociocultural, economic, and demographic tendencies, have caused and are continuing to cause the extirpation of other species the magnitude and rate of which the planet has not seen in 65 million years (Wilson 1988). All this gives stark merit to Hardin's original and continuing concern.

Assuming, with Hardin, that the human species evolved as resource-limited, sociocultural evolution and development may be expected to result in ecological traps of greater or lesser severity as a matter of course. The typical local pattern of adaptation to resource depletion, when it succeeded, appears often to have been intensified extraction (Harris 1977). Such a pattern is a temporary fix, at best, for it puts days of reckoning into the future while commiting future generations to repeating the pattern. The pessimistic slant on human history, on a short view, as one emergency following on another may be valid if, on a long view, humans move from one ecological trap to another along a cumulative series. Without stretching matters too much, one could interpret global patterns of human socioecological adaptation as processions down an avenue of no return—into ecological traps something like a box canyon. Unlike in the cinema serials of yesteryear, there is no escape from these.[5]

If we think of commons problems as cumulative series of ecological traps, then some properties attributed to the original model are no longer useful. What does it profit us to think of the development and spread of agriculture as the sum total effect of so many individual choices? Or the origin and spread of industrialization as rational then but irrational now? If agricultural and industrial modes of human subsistence together with the sociocultural traditions and institutions that support them represent a long-unfolding ecological trap in which humans have become progressively ensnared, with less and less chance of reversing the course, what is the dilemma to be resolved here? If humans have now trapped themselves by their means of subsistence, we must consider that thresholds were crossed and changes at the thresholds were anything but linear; that sociocultural evolution has its own momentum and trajectories in which individual decision makers are channeled by their cultures; and that the connections between individual decision making and nonlinear sociocultural evolutionary trajectories are largely unknown.

NATURAL BALANCES AND ANTHROPOCENTRISM

The tendency to view problems of ecological commons as problems of social psychology and economics resides in the tacit placing of *Homo sapiens* at the center of the ecological universe, then proceeding to analyze current human environmental predicaments in terms that suggest an imbalance between humans and the rest of nature—an imbalance that will supposedly reverberate to the ill effect of humans. But I think an impartial judge must rule that the marriage of an ecological balance to nature with anthropocentrism is irreconcilable.

Hardin and most who followed him conceived anthropogenic ecological degradation as a matter of the aggregated effects of countless individual human decisions the incentive for which issued from, we have seen, defective social structures that permit the consequences of individual decision making to aggregate without cost to individuals until harmful collective results come due. The worrisome problem is the supposed tendency, which can certainly be documented at times and places, of humans to overshoot their carrying capacities. If the concept of natural imbalance applies at all to this, it applies to some possibly maladaptive tendency of our species to evolve sociocultural systems that are out of whack with the conditions of human organic evolution (Rappaport 1990). If there is such a tendency and it is irreversible, then the human species is something of an evolutionary shooting star or, as some biologists have put it, one very lethal mutation. But if that is true, no human-natural balance can be restored.

At times a concept of natural balance using certain special closure conditions, especially concerning time frame, scale, and nature of ecological interaction, can be interpreted to the well-known population equilibria observed in various biota. Population equilibria, when observed, represent stabilities for a time, but just for a time. They do not imply any restoration of species demographics to some "original state" when perturbed, for the choice of any original system state is arbitrary (see Botkin 1990). It is always uncertain just how long any temporary population equilibrium will hold. For some species, observed equilibria fail and instabilities appear with monotonous regularity. Shall we say the commons in which population dynamics with instabilities appear are unbalanced, or just that they are dynamic? If just dynamic, what shall we say when humans are brought in?

The problem of ecological commons as applied to humans explicitly presumes an inherent population instability or disequilibrium. The instability presumed is that humans reproduce according to the logistic growth curve that describes monocultures.[6] From this is derived the Malthusian expectation that humans will tend to reproduce beyond the means available to sustain them (indeed, that we have already done this). The standard explanation is that the economics of population growth create this imbalance of human systems with natural systems that cannot be indefinitely sustained. With this follows an injunction that properly informed human agency, collectively organized, can and should resist the tendency—should resist logistic population growth and its consequent economic exploitation of biophysical resources—that puts humans "out of balance" with nature. Thus we have an explicit presumption that humans can act to overcome a presumed *inherent* tendency toward ecological overshoot. Also presumed implicitly is the Western worldview that humans are technically and morally empowered to rearrange nature, including their lawful relationships to it, to suit their interests—including the interest of avoiding the Malthusian outcomes associated with a condition of overshoot.

The entire line of thought originates in a motive to preserve and enhance human material standards of living. But there comes a hidden agenda that serves the motive of material well-being and enhancement: to maintain the ecological position of the human species relative to other species. Given the current and anticipated size of the total human population, the maintenance of human ecological dominance is the only way to serve the motive of preserving and enhancing material standards of living. If the overshooting of carrying capacities is an inherent human ecological tendency, the wish to avoid that fate is a hidden wish to maintain an unbalanced human biotic dominance. The dominance serves subsistence needs for large populations and the economic interests of well-capitalized corporations, since so much of the production of economic systems depends on direct or indirect biotic consumption. Why propose solutions to commons problems that call on persons' volition or governments' force, if needed, to act rationally for the collective human welfare? The motive is not just to provide for what humans need but also to protect what we have. We already have 40 percent of the net primary production of terrestrial ecosystems (Vitousek, Ehrlich, Ehrlich, and Matson 1986.) The wish to extend the advantages of industrial development to undeveloped nations in the South is the wish to have more—for humans to capture even more energy in the form of biomass. More energy can be converted into more wealth.

Is the concept of human balance and imbalance with nature beginning now to unravel? If so, it is because these lines of thinking and wishing about current human environmental predicaments do not connect well to human evolutionary and ecological origins. Let us suppose the Malthusian expectation to be valid. If it is, then it is so in virtue of the ecological relationships out of which the human species and its cultures have been evolutionarily defined. Those relationships considered in their entirety cannot permit us to place human interests front and center; to do so would be contrary to the nature of ecological organization and therefore inimical to human ecological interests. The design of natural selection does not have humans at the front or the center or the top of anything. (It has them last, or most recent.) For the time being humans are ecologically at the top of the *food chain only*, an inherently unstable condition for such a gross population of large fierce animals. Yet, if the ecological positioning is only temporary and the anthropocentric positioning is not valid, then the problem of ecological commons is not even a current environmental dilemma. Now *Homo sapiens* becomes just one more species acting out its evolutionary fate—a shooting star or lethal mutation that evolutionary design cannot long accomodate. On that attitude the "rational" conclusion is to accept without complaint the consequences of an inherent imbalance between human sociocultural development and the well-being of ecological commons. Humans cannot, logically or empirically, be placed to the front, center, and top of ecological systems that are presumed to do a balancing act, with the expectation that humans' priveleged position can be maintained. The problem of the commons asks an anthropocentric question and seeks a self-serving answer it therefore cannot find.

IMBALANCES IN HUMAN ECOLOGICAL SERIES

If the problem of human ecological commons is interpreted in evolutionary terms there has to be defined a different set of problems pertaining not to the summed interactions of individuals but to the synergistic interactions of coevolving biophysical and sociocultural systems. These may be considered to be unitary systems in their own right. Call them *biosociocultural systems*. Now, talk about humans being "out of balance" with nature has to be circumscribed, for here the idea of some "original" system condition of balance has no empirical interpretation. However, we may compare alternative biosociocultural systems, or the same system over time, for changes in critical parameters. Then some coherent, if limited, meaning may be found for the idea of imbalance to human ecological series.

One major human ecological series in particular, mentioned earlier, may be used to illustrate the uses and limitations of a concept of human-natural imbalance: the sporadic but relentless replacement of traditional agroecosystems with agro-industrial ecosystems. The imbalance is reflected in increased magnitudes of energy capture by humans, which came to pass because a mode of adaptation *to* nature eventually became a mode of adaptation *of* nature.

Consider a traditional agroecosystem. Remember it is solar powered. Because it renders less stable the natural ecosystem in which it is designed and is more vulnerable to disturbances whose effects may be immediate, humans have to be more attuned to its interactions. Normally exploited by draft animals and assorted gear to harness muscle power for sowing, plowing, harvesting, and terracing, and to engineer irrigation or other forms of water management, within an economy whose prime energy base is wood, as was the case for so long, a traditional agroecosystem itself and the relations humans have to it must be respected. Built-in biogeochemical controls ensure that human interference, though far from trivial, is nevertheless checked. Apart from the controls afforded by the seasons and the weather, biotic interactions exert their own. Crops must be rotated with respect for their differential capacity to host nitrogen fixing bacteria. Nutrient cycles must be respected by setting aside some land as fallow. Natural competitors may command just a grudging respect, but they have their ecological functions. Animal dung may be accorded serious respect for its fertilizing properties. Most of all, the ratio of energy input to energy output must be respected: With only so much net food energy to be gotten, given the energy invested, traditional agroecosystems have to be managed in terms of biogeochemical interactions and processes whose natural cycles lend the systems a certain stability and predictability only just within the human reach to manipulate. Natural biogeochemical cycles are manipulated in traditional agroecosystems, and therefore constitute socially organized disturbances of natural ecosystems, but they are controlled more by those natural systems than by social organization. The relative power of an environmentally-based economy itself, therefore, has to be respected. If it is not, then traditional agrarian ways of life, already adapted to the cycles of agroecosystems, are threatened when the systems fail—a fact immediately impressed upon those who work the land. It talks back to them.

Now add the products of fossil hydrocarbon technology and derivative or correlated technologies, in order to release and amplify the potential energy stored in fossil fuels. Add complex organic compounds unknown in nature. Eliminate natural competitors with insecticides and herbicides, finesse nutrient cycles with nitrogen fertilizers, and introduce new genetic strains. Extend planting into otherwise inhospitable temperate grasslands or scrublands, tapping their underground aquifers or damming their regional rivers to irrigate. Replace animals with tractors, substituting mechanical power for muscle power and, most important of all, utilize the internal combustion engine. In other words, to a solar powered agricultural system from which you intend to derive energy in the form of food, *add* a technologically derived energy subsidy.

Then none of the above has to be respected in the short or intermediate term because the weight of control in human ecological interactions has shifted. Now when the land begins to "talk back" its message can be ignored because more energy can be pumped in to maintain or increase its yields. Now, instead of adapting a sociocultural system to a natural system, a natural system can be adapted to a sociocultural system: The cycles that manifest themselves in traditional agroecosystems, whose governors are the cycles of the larger natural ecosystems in which they are situated, can now be finessed with the proper energy-intensive technologies *for a longer time than the natural systems would ordinarily permit.* With fossil hydrocarbon technologies the ratio of energy input to output is so substantially altered that the balance of control now passes to humans, who can extend the period of exploitation for the purpose of increasing the output. The differences will be exploited to the hilt because of purely economic motives that surface in virtue of the physical properties of the fossil fuels themselves: They are so concentrated in their energy content that their exploitation affords a substantial economic return, given their abundance, relative to the investment of initial energy inputs. That generalization holds not just for agroecosystems, but for just about any system to which fossil hydrocarbon technology can be applied, which is why it was applied so much and why the transition from agroecosystems to agro-industrial ecosystems continues still. The transition has been, more or less, a "natural" trajectory, unless one wishes to argue that something about human culture is "unnatural."

Looking at this major human ecological series from the angle of sociocultural sciences we have the discontinuous but persistent appropriation of rural production activities with the eventual substitution of a food industry, as described by Goodman, Sorj, and Wilkenson (1987); and from the angle of ecological sciences, the transformation of food chains, the appropriation of biomass by humans, and the alteration of natural systems by the introduction of energy subsidies. Now, combining them into a biosociocultural angle, into what does the concept of human-natural imbalance resolve in this instance? Not much, for no nonarbitrary, natural equilibrium point can be defined and no scale of balance constructed for evolving systems of this kind, in which energy is increasingly (and nonlinearly) appropriated for the system's sociocultural subassembly.

With the replacement of traditional agroecosystems by agro-industrial ecosystems we have serial alteration of biosociocultural regimes, in which sociocultural practices systematically have sought to preempt biophysical processes in such a way that the processes are not completed. Generally, the plan and the practice have been to alter biophysical regimes so that they become adapted to the needs of sociocultural regimes, rather than the other way round. We could call that changing the balance of nature, which in the present instance can mean that humans have become so empowered with respect to biophysical systems that we now have more control over them than the systems have over us. However true, that thought should not be expected to bear much weight. In the long run there is no doubt where "control" lies: It lies with natural selection and whatever is made available for selection by ecological regimes and biogeochemical conditions. Now, it is clear that sociocultural regimes are modifying all that, and the effects have begun to boomerang. Is this because there are too many people and not enough to go around—too many people in the lifeboat, as Hardin was fond of saying?

Sociocultural regimes that are no longer inclined to adapt to natural systems but are intent on adapting natural systems to their own proceed as if human technological, social, cultural, and organizational design can finesse the design of organic evolution and physical thermodynamics. On a long-term systemic view, a major *purpose* of industrialization and technological development has been to transcend human evolutionary and ecological relationships—to learn how to do what nature does not otherwise permit us to do. The assiduous pursuit of this goal, a realization of the Biblical command to exercise dominion in the sense of power and control, has long and often been hailed as virtuous. In technocratic industrial societies this injunction has turned into an overweening self-confidence, an attitude of ecohubris at the root of technocratic cultures' world views, in which natural laws are regarded as inconvenient and temporary obstacles to be overcome. Encouraged by the mystique of science and the domination of human subsistence activities by interlocking political economies, there is little thought now that natural laws might afford unseen protections from tendencies to excess. Ecohubris is a symbolic value that supports multiple, interwoven series of political-economic and technocratic-sociocultural evolutionary developments that seem to have set the species on an irreversible trajectory. If there is some human-natural imbalance, how much of it issues from the disrespect that tehcnologically-empowered cultures have shown for the operation of natural laws? If we really believe the laws of biology and physics, which are the same laws we employ to hubristically rearrange the world around us so as to continue the modern trajectory ever deeper into ecological traps, eventually a natural price should be exacted. It may be the price that Hardin feared, but not for the reason he feared it. Catton's (1995) reason is more logical: "by fulfilling the potential inherent in ... a culture-bearing species" (p. 24). Humans, who might have gotten away with farming the land, almost certainly will not escape the trap of industrialization. But if there is a tragedy in the making (and if there is, it is not just for humans), this is not because there are too many of us in the lifeboat and now it is listing out of balance. It is because we are never content with the uses of lifeboats. The lifeboat perhaps could hold over five and one-half billion *poor* horticulturalists. It cannot possibly hold that many well-to-do industrialists.

Hardin objects. While hesitating to affirm a notion of ecological balance, he recently wrote:

> Any theory that deals with any one of the millions (ten million?) of species *cannot escape presuming* an inherent drive toward positive exponential multiplication of every species (with varying exponents)....I challenge you to imagine a species that does not have the potential of exponential growth. Any exception would soon become extinct. It is on this basis that the theory of the commons—and all other theories of animal behavior—are based (1994, personal communication, emphasis in original).

Setting aside the question of what all theories of animal behavior are based on, we can certainly agree that the theory of the commons is so based. And that is why it seems to contain an implication—issuing, perhaps, more from the rhetoric of the discourse than from the logic of the theory—that an ecologically balanced human imbalance is possible and desirable. If ecological commons are analyzed into ecological traps, the implication is otherwise: The human species will assume whatever ecological niches and functions that currently constituted evolutionary regimes (organic and sociocultural) permit, as a perfectly natural development in the trajectory of evolutionary series— even if the trajectory leads to irreversible ecological traps so that the species becomes evolutionarily cornered. If we really believe in evolution and evolutionary series, we would not, could not, and should not try to stay the process.[7] Evolution does not do a balancing act.

Insofar as human ecological processes behave in evolutionary series and especially insofar as cumulative serial traps can be characterized, concepts such as balance, imbalance, homeostasis, and the like do not help very much. They cannot be used much to describe serial progressions, especially of a nonlinear variety, that lead to ecological traps. Presuming the mathematical modeling of steady states, such concepts may serve as idealized reference points for the calibration of linear change within tight ranges of closure. But nonlinear, dynamic, macroscopic human ecological series materialize as biosociocultural regimes that change as a function of their own accumulated interaction histories. Such series can hardly be expected to do a balancing act, for there is no standard for them to balance in terms of.

ACKNOWLEDGMENTS

For suggestions and advice on the exposition of the ideas contained herein, I am indebted to William R. Catton, Jr., C. Dyke, and Garrett Hardin.

NOTES

1. Hardin's paper, originally a presidential address delivered to a regional society of the American Association for the Advancement of Science, is believed to be the most cited paper in the 100-plus year history of the publication of *Science*, the official journal of the AAAS. Hardin was not the first to conceive the problem of the commons, as he acknowledged at the time. H. Scott Gordon (1954) anticipated Hardin by arguing that everybody's property is nobody's property, and so there is no incentive for self-interested persons to act in the common interest; for, should they do so, the common resources would be expropriated and depleted by other self-interested individuals who are not so altruistic. Hardin's formulation was more general and more timely, and it generated an intellectual growth industry all its own, and eventually even a professional association, the Association for the Study of Common Property, devoted exclusively to addressing commons questions.

2. Some points of observation can be found in Kelley and Grzelak (1972), Meux (1973), Kahan (1974), Foddy (1974), Rubenstein, Watzke, Doktor, and Dana (1975), Stern (1976), Dawes, McTavish, and Shaklee (1977), Edney and Harper (1978a), Cass and Edney (1978), Edney (1979), Baird (1982), Gifford (1982), Powers and Boyle (1983), Edney and Bell (1984), Samuelson, Messick, Rutte, and Wilke (1984), Yamagishi (1986), and Glance and Huberman (1994).

3. The literature on free riders, public goods, and common resource management extends from economics to political science and social psychology. Often, but not always, these matters are discussed in the context of social dilemmas. These lines of thought owe much to the work of Mancur Olson (1965), and a sorting of the various lines that attempts to formally synthesize some basic ideas can be found in Sell (1988).

4. For a hyperbolic growth curve doubling times are halved with each doubling, while with an "ordinary" exponential curve the doubling times are constant. A hyperbolic function is a special case of an exponential function.

5. Numerous grade-B serials were produced in Hollywood in the 1930s in which something like this could be seen: The heroes, often cowboys wearing white hats, chased by villans wearing black, would ride through a canyon entrance and dynamite the entrance closed—only to discover they had entered a box canyon, in which there was progressively less room to manuever and no way out. There an episode would end. But script writers and cinema editors always found a way out for the heroes, usually by changing the conditions from the end of one episode to the start of the next—in effect, by cheating. With standard editing techniques different footage would be substituted so that what had seemed to be inevitable doom for the heroes was turned to their advantage. In real traps, it should be obvious, there is no way to cheat by rewriting the script. Real human ecological traps, if undetected and extensive in their effects, materialize from conditions that can not be rescripted or reversed much within the time frame of human societies. The cinema industry's creative artists never did find an honest solution to a real trap.

6. The empirical adequacy of the logistic growth curve, along with the adequacy of predator-prey and competition models, has been seriously challenged of late. See Hall (1988).

7. It should go without saying—but I am afraid it may not, in view of the emotional heat that this topic can generate—that my purpose here is to draw out the theoretical logic of alternative arguments. The purpose is not to propound some special ecological principle from which immediate moral or policy implications can be inferred, except to exhibit contrasts to the implications that have been preferred using standard commons logic. The argument developed here applies to time frames that go beyond the immediacies of the moment, and no ideological position applicable to short-term local conditions, especially no "laissez-faire" position, is intended or should be inferred.

That disclaimer may be ineffectual if C. Dyke (personal communication, 1994) is correct in his assessment of the logic implicit in the position I am taking. In the position I express in the text Dyke finds the implication of a false asymmetry between doing something and doing nothing—

false because, at least as regards living things, Dyke observes it is possible only to do something or do something else. In other words, there is no choice for humans *but* to interfere in, or at least to affect, evolutionary processes.

Dyke's assessment reached me only as this manuscript went to press, and it included the following views on the role of humans in evolution, which I quote: "We are part of the process and can't power our way out of it. It doesn't follow that we ought to let ourselves get numerous without limit, or wait for some Malthusian limit to be reached.... Humility doesn't imply resignation, and knowledge doesn't imply manipulation and control." If these views, which I share, are at odds with the argument in the text, then I did not express the argument with sufficient clarity aforethought.

REFERENCES

Allen, T.F.H. and T.W. Hoekstra. 1991. "Role of Heterogeneity in Scaling of Ecological Systems Under Analysis." Pp. 47-68 in *Ecological Heterogeneity*, edited by J. Kolasa and S.T.A. Pickett. New York: Springer-Verlag.

—————. 1992. *Toward a Unified Ecology*. New York: Columbia University Press.

Baird, J.S., Jr. 1982. "Conservation of the Commons: Effects of Group Cohesiveness and Prior Sharing." *Journal of Community Psychology* 10(July): 210-215.

Barker, E., Trans. 1962. *The Politics of Aristotle*. New York: Oxford University Press.

Bates, M. 1960. *The Forest and The Sea*. New York: Random House.

Botkin, D.B. 1990. *Discordant Harmonies: A New Ecology for the Twenty-first Century*. New York: Oxford.

Brechner, K.C. 1977. "An Experimental Analysis of Social Traps." *Journal of Experimental Social Psychology* 13: 552-564.

Buchanan, J.M. 1971. *The Bases for Collective Action*. New York: General Learning Press.

Cass, R.C. and J.J. Edney. 1978. "The Commons Dilemma: A Simulation Testing the Effects of Resource Visibility and Territorial Division." *Human Ecology* 6: 371-386.

Catton, W.R., Jr. 1986. "Homo Colossus and the Technological Turn-Around." *Sociological Spectrum* 6: 121-147.

—————. 1995. "From Eukaryotic Cells to Gaia: The Range of Symbiosis and Its Relevance to Human Ecology." In *Advances in Human Ecology*, Vol. 4, edited by L. Freese. Greenwich, CT: JAI Press.

Cross, J.G. and M.J. Guyer. 1980. *Social Traps*. Ann Arbor: University of Michigan Press.

Crowe, B.L. 1969. "The Tragedy of the Commons Revisited." *Science* 166(November): 1103-1107.

Dawes, R.M. 1980. "Social Dilemmas." *Annual Review of Psychology* 31: 169-193.

Dawes, R.M., J. McTavish, and H. Shaklee. 1977. "Behavior, Communication, and Assumptions about Other People's Behavior in a Commons Dilemma Situation." *Journal of Personality and Social Psychology* 35: 1-11.

Edney, J.J. 1979. "Free Riders En Route to Disaster." *Psychology Today* 13(August): 80-87. 102.

—————. 1980. "The Commons Problem: Alternative Perspectives." *American Psychologist* 35(February): 131-150.

—————. 1981. "Paradoxes on the Commons: Scarcity and the Problem of Equality." *Journal of Community Psychology* 9: 3-34.

Edney, J.J. and P.A. Bell. 1984. "Sharing Scarce Resources: Group-Outcome Orientation, External Diaster [sic], and Stealing in a Simulated Commons." *Small Group Behavior* 15(February): 87-108.

Edney, J.J. and C.S. Harper. 1978a. "The Commons Dilemma: A Review." *Environmental Management* 2: 491-507.

_____ . 1978b. "The Effects of Information in a Resource Management Problem: A Social Trap Analog." *Human Ecology* 6: 387-395.

Feeny, D., F. Berkes, B.J. McCay, and J.M. Acheson. 1990. "The Tragedy of the Commons: Twenty-Two Years Later." *Human Ecology* 18(March): 1-19.

Fife, D. 1971. "Killing the Goose." *Environment* 13(April): 20-22, 27.

Foddy, W.H. 1974. "Shared Resources and Ecological Catastrophes." *The Australian and New Zealand Journal of Sociology* 10(October): 154-163.

Fox, D.R. 1985. "Psychology, Ideology, Utopia, and the Commons." *American Psychologist* 40(January): 48-58.

Gifford, R. 1982. "Children and the Commons Dilemma." *Journal of Applied Social Psychology* 12: 269-280.

Glance, N.S. and B.A. Huberman. 1994. "The Dynamics of Social Dilemmas." *Scientific American* (March): 76-81.

Goodman, D., B. Sorj, and J. Wilkinson. 1987. *From Farming to Biotechnology: A Theory of Agro-Industrial Development.* Oxford: Basil Blackwell.

Gordon, H.S. 1954. "The Economic Theory of a Common-Property Resource: The Fishery." *Journal of Political Economy* 62: 124-142.

Hall, C.A.S. 1988. "An Assessment of Several of the Historically Most Influential Theoretical Models Used in Ecology and of the Data Provided in Their Support." *Ecological Modelling* 43: 5-31.

Hardin, G. 1968. "The Tragedy of the Commons." *Science* 162: 1243-1248.

_____ . 1993. *Living Within Limits: Ecology, Economics, and Population Taboos.* Oxford: Oxford University Press.

Harris, M. 1977. *Cannibals and Kings: The Origins of Cultures.* New York: Random House.

Kahan, J.P. 1974. "Rationality, The Prisoner's Dilemma, and Population." *Journal of Social Issues* 30: 189-210.

Kelley, H.H. and J. Grzelak. 1972. "Conflict Between Individual and Common Interest in an N-Person Relationship." *Journal of Personality and Social Psychology* 21: 190-197.

Lepper, M.R. and D. Greene, eds. 1978. *The Hidden Cost of Reward.* New York: Wiley.

McCay, B.J. 1995. "Common and Private Concerns." In *Advances in Human Ecology*, Vol. 4, edited by L. Freese. Greenwich, CT: JAI Press.

McCay, B.J. and J.M. Acheson, eds. 1987. *The Question of the Commons: The Culture and Ecology of Communal Resources.* Tucson: University of Arizona Press.

Messick, D.M. and C.L. McClelland. 1983. "Social Traps and Temporal Traps." *Personality and Social Psychology Bulletin* 9(March): 105-110.

Meux, E.P. 1973. "Concern for the Common Good in an N-Person Game." *Journal of Personality and Social Psychology* 28: 414-418.

Olsen, M. 1965. *The Logic of Collective Action: Public Goods and The Theory of Groups.* Cambridge, MA: Harvard University Press.

Ophuls, W. 1977. *Ecology and The Politics of Scarcity.* San Francisco: W. H. Freeman.

Ostrom, E. 1990. *Governing the Commons: The Evolution of Institutions for Collective Action.* Cambridge: Cambridge University Press.

Pimm, S.L. 1991. *The Balance of Nature? Ecological Issues in the Conservation of Species and Communities.* Chicago: University of Chicago Press.

Platt, J. 1973. "Social Traps." *American Psychologist* 28(August): 641-651.

Powers, R.B. and W. Boyle. 1983. "Generalization From a Commons-Dilemma Game: The Effects of a Fine Option, Information, and Communication on Cooperation and Defection." *Simulation & Games* 14(September): 253-274.

Rapaport, A. 1967. "Optimal Policies for the Prisoner's Dilemma." *Psychological Review* 74: 136-148.

Rappaport, R.A. 1990. "Ecosystems, Populations, and People." Pp. 41-72 in *The Ecosystem Approach in Anthropology*, edited by E.F. Moran. Ann Arbor: University of Michigan Press.

Rubenstein, F.D., G. Watzke, R.H. Doktor, and J. Dana. 1975. "The Effect of Two Incentive Schemes upon the Conservation of Shared Resource by Five-Person Groups." *Organizational Behavior and Human Performance* 13: 330-338.

Samuelson, C.D., D.M. Messick, C.G. Rutte, and H. Wilke. 1984. "Individual and Structural Solutions to Resource Dilemmas in Two Cultures." *Journal of Personality and Social Psychology* 47: 94-104.

Sell, J. 1988. "Types of Public Goods and Free Riding." Pp. 119-140 in *Advances In Group Processes: Theory and Research*, Vol. 5, edited by E. Lawler and B. Markovsky. Greenwich, CT: JAI Press.

Stern, P.C. 1976. "Effects of Incentives and Education on Resource Conservation Decisions in a Simulated Commons Dilemma." *Journal of Personality and Social Psychology* 34: 1285-1292.

Stillman, P.G. 1975. "The Tragedy of the Commons: A Re-analysis." *Alternatives* 4(Winter): 12-15.

Vitousek, P.M., P.R. Ehrlich, A.H. Erhlich, and P.A. Matson. 1986. "Human Appropriation of the Products of Photosynthesis." *Bioscience* 36(June): 368-380.

Wiens, J.A. 1984. "On Understanding a Non-Equilibrium World: Myth and Reality in Community Patterns and Processes." Pp. 439-457 in *Ecological Communities: Conceptual Issues and the Evidence*, edited by D.R. Strong, Jr., D. Simberloff, L.G. Abele, and A.B. Thistle. Princeton, NJ: Princeton University Press.

Wilson, E.O., ed. 1988. *Biodiversity*. Washington, DC: National Academy Press.

Yamagashi, T. 1986. "The Structural Goal Expectation Theory of Cooperation in Social Dilemmas." In *Advances in Group Processes*, Vol. 3, edited by E. Lawler. Greenwich, CT: JAI Press.

INTERGENERATIONAL COMMONS, GLOBALIZATION, ECONOMISM, AND UNSUSTAINABLE DEVELOPMENT

Richard B. Norgaard

ABSTRACT

As little as two 200 years ago, the world could be thought of as a patchwork quilt of relatively independent coevolving cultures and ecosystems in which sustainability was facilitated through intergenerational commons that protected environmental resources and encouraged their collective transfer to the next generation. Four shortcomings in market reasoning have facilitated the transformation of the world into an increasingly global economy with global environmental dynamics. These incorrect or incomplete arguments implicitly deny the need for commons institutions in general and intergenerational commons institutions in particular. The global economy requires global intergenerational commons institutions for sustainability, but the difficulties of adequate institutions developing and operating at this scale are immense. Economic logic, properly followed, indicates that communities, which necessarily must have some autonomy to be communities, are essential to sustainability.

Advances in Human Ecology, Volume 4, pages 141-171.
Copyright © 1995 by JAI Press Inc.
All rights of reproduction in any form reserved.
ISBN: 1-55938-874-9

INTRODUCTION

Human ecology frequently describes and interprets commons institutions for the management of environmental resources. Neoclassical economic theory is central to this description and interpretation. This fruitful interdependence between the two fields occurs in spite of the clash between the systems perspective of human ecology and the reductionist approach of neoclassical economics. Economic models readily show how, in the absence of common property institutions, the individualist behavior associated with private property and markets leads to the degradation of resources that are available for use by all. Garrett Hardin's (1968) "tragedy of the commons" is now understood to be a misnomer. His argument is correct for open-access resources but, historically, typically incorrect, since commons institutions have long provided social norms specifying the nature of access (Feeny, Berkes, McCay, and Acheson 1990; Ostrom 1990). Economic reasoning also readily explains the very existence of commons institutions for managing resource systems for which access cannot be administered effectively through the creation and distribution of private property. If such environmental resources are being used inefficiently, all might be made better-off by adopting commons institutions. In short, where the atomistic-individualistic requirements of private property and assumptions of market reasoning do not fit the systemic nature of environmental resources and social needs, commons institutions can lead to different outcomes which may be preferred. Knowing that social and environmental systems do not always sufficiently fit the reductionist assumptions behind the logic of private property and markets helps us understand and explain commons institutions by converse reasoning.

Our interpretation of commons institutions can be further enriched through converse reasoning by exploring the nature of economic reasoning in greater depth. This enrichment, however, comes through a complex synthesis of arguments that first must be explicated in their own right. The paper begins by showing how history can be understood as a process of coevolution between social and ecological systems. Furthermore, I give this historical process a spatial dimension, arguing that as little as two hundred years ago, the world could be envisioned as a coevolutionary patchwork quilt of diverse cultures and ecosystems. Through a parable elaborated in the following section, I then argue that commons institutions are needed to assure the transfer of assets from one generation to the next, the essence of sustainability. Commons institutions do not evolve simply to effectively manage resources, but also to assure the transfer of sufficient resources to subsequent generations. The parable continues, indicating how the spatial expansion of markets over the past several centuries broke down local commons institutions without adequate replacement on a broader scale. In the following sections I then systematically expose four logical shortcomings of economics. These shortcomings support globalization, the breakdown of community, and hence the decline of intergenerational commons that facilitate the transfer of assets to future generations. Since these logical shortcomings are phenomena which pervade economic thinking, from academic theorizing to bureaucratic decision making and throughout political discourse, some explanation seemed in order. I label the phenomena of these shortcomings "economism" and, in the following section, return to a coevolutionary framework to explain how incomplete and erroneous thinking are allowed to exist in the most logically well-developed and most thoroughly explored discipline of the social sciences. This coevolution, furthermore, has resulted in both incomplete and incorrect economic arguments which affect our understanding of the commons. In the final section, I summarize the significance of these arguments to our understanding of commons institutions.

COEVOLUTIONARY SOCIAL AND ENVIRONMENTAL HISTORIES AND A PATCHWORK QUILT OF CULTURES

Our understanding of development has drawn on diverse metaphors of change. Economies have been portrayed to develop like embryos grow, to go through stages of growth like the morphogenesis of caterpillars into butterflies, and to progressively improve through increases in the accumulation of physical capital and human knowledge. In earlier works (Norgaard 1981, 1988, 1994), I portrayed development as a process of coevolution between knowledge, values, organizational, technological, and environmental systems (see Figure 1). In this portrayal, each of these systems is related to each of the others, yet each is also changing and affecting change in the others. Deliberate innovations, chance discoveries, random changes, and chance introductions occur in each system that affect the fitness and hence the distribution and qualities of components in each of the other systems. Whether new components prove to be fit depends on the characteristics of each of the systems at the time. With each system putting selective pressure on each of the others, they coevolve in a manner whereby each reflects the other. Coevolution explains how everything appears to be tightly locked together, yet everything also appears to be changing.

To further elaborate the process, imagine that the systems of Figure 1—values, knowledge, social organization, and technology—are made up of different types of ways of valuing, knowing, organizing, and doing things. Similarly, the environmental system consists of numerous different types of species, environmental factors, and relationships between them. The survival and relative dominance, or frequency, of each particular type in each subsystem is "explained" by its historical fitness with respect to the relative dominance of types of things in the other systems. The relative importance, or frequency distribution, of types results from selection processes. Now, imagine that a new

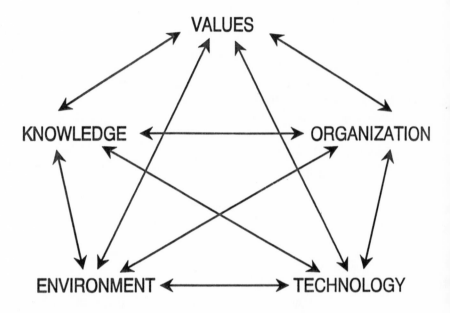

Figure 1.

type is introduced into one of the systems. For example, imagine that a new way of understanding the world, let us call it N for Newtonian, is introduced into the knowledge system of Western culture. The survival and relative importance of N will depend on the selection pressures from the components in the other systems. If N fits by complementing in some way sufficient other components, it survives, and vice versa. If N fits significantly better than other ways of knowing, it will outcompete and replace them, or at least reduce their relative importance. And if N survives, it will begin to put selective pressure on the components of other systems and affect their relative dominance. This process of experiments, discoveries, chance mutations, and introductions within each of the systems drives coevolution across all of the subsystems simultaneously. With each of the systems applying selective pressure on each of the others, they all reflect each other.

The coevolutionary explanation of change acknowledges that people design new elements and introduce them into their cultures, but its emphasis on ongoing change driven by the random nature of mutations and introductions throughout the system helps explain why designs often fail and at other times succeed by evolving into something quite unexpected. From within the coevolutionary perspective, designs are better thought of as deliberate experiments, for the outcomes of experiments are uncertain by definition. New elements which prove fit are successful because they interrelate with other elements in some functional way. While the experiments may be random or designed, those that succeed are not elements in a system of random elements. Quite the contrary, we marvel at how everything interrelates so intricately and proclaim that only a Grand Designer could have accomplished the task.

Coevolutionary processes are occurring at multiple spatial scales all of the time. Some processes are very local, taking place between specific plants and soil bacteria under special mineralogical conditions; other coevolutionary processes are instigated by animal species that migrate over great distances carrying traits which coevolved with relatively sedentary species at one location to affect the coevolution of relatively sedentary species at another location. People, of course, have long been among the most mobile of species and, furthermore, they can carry knowledge, values, technologies, and social organization, as well as other species, with them. Many histories have focused on the transfer of characteristics from one culture to another and the ways in which these characteristics proved fit or not. More recently, environmental histories have emphasized how people have redistributed plant and animal species from one continent to another and thereby affected the subsequent coevolution of ecosystems (Crosby 1972, 1986; Cronon 1983).

Yet, in spite of the ability of people to move and move things with them, until merely a few centuries ago, the world could be thought of as a patchwork quilt of coevolving cultures and ecosystems. The dominant coevolutionary processes occurred within patches associated with distinct human cultures. Boundaries, however, were neither distinct nor fixed within this coevolving mosaic. Knowledge, values, aspects of social organization, technologies, and species spilled from the patches within which they initially coevolved to become exotics in other areas. Some of these exotics proved fit as they arrived and thrived in their new areas, some adapted, and some died out. But to some extent, they all influenced the subsequent coevolution of patch characteristics in their new areas, resetting the dynamics of the change in the composition of characteristics, their structural relations, and spatial area. The possible combinations of spillovers and rooting of exotics into different areas were effectively infinite. The plethora of combinations within each patch kept the global pattern—of coevolving species, myths, organization, and technology—itself patchy, albeit a constantly changing, fuzzy, patchiness.

In each of the patches numerous types of commons institutions seem to have coevolved with people. Diverse experiments with social organization led diverse peoples to similar social forms much the same way as fish and some aquatic mammals both have fin-like structures. Form followed function. Yet, the variation in commons institutions is astounding across cultures as well because the coevolutionary histories in each patch were different. The differences in coevolutionary social and environmental histories make the study of commons institutions across cultures especially rich.

TREES, SAWS, SEVEN GENERATIONS, AND SUSTAINABILITY

In the best tradition of economics (McCloskey 1985)—and in keeping with the perspective of economics as a secular religion (Nelson 1991)—let me develop several further critical arguments through a parable with a few interpretive interruptions.

Imagine a society of near-subsistence farmers with rights to land. Parents can improve the quality of the land by planting trees, which provide other goods and services at various stages of their lives. The parents might choose to reduce their consumption in their youth to invest in trees in order to have more consumption in their older age. When one's objective is to redistribute rewards over time for oneself, such as here, we think of the activity as an investment. One could invest in trees both for oneself and accumulate them for transfer to one's children. Some of the returns from planting trees are enjoyed by the parents, while others go to their children. The extent to which current consumption is foregone, and trees are planted to increase the parents' welfare or to meet the parents' responsibility to transfer assets to their children, would be difficult to determine. Wealth, of course, does not simply accumulate linearly. Some parents choose to cut more wood for timber or firewood than grew during the period they enjoyed the land, transferring less to their children than they had themselves received from their own parents. Natural disasters and war set the process back periodically just as a string of good years might make greedy parents look like misers. And the total amount that can be accumulated at any given time is limited by the cultural knowledge, technologies, and nature of cooperation in the society.

The Iroquois of what is now the northeastern United States are said to have been conscious of seven generations when they made decisions affecting their future. Such a consciousness and whatever institutions maintained and implemented it are so different from modern consciousness and institutions that the very term *seven generations* symbolizes the unsustainability, both environmentally and culturally, of modern life. A central argument of this paper is that over centuries of believing that progress will take care of our progeny, modern peoples lost their sense of responsibility for their offspring and the institutions needed to assure appropriate transfers of assets. Let us consider the institutional aspects that complemented and maintained responsibility.

Protecting the well-being of future generations cannot be accomplished by individuals acting out of self-interest alone. It must be a common responsibility because one's great-great-grandchildren have seven sets of other great-great-grandparents in approximately one's own generation besides oneself and one's spouse. One never knows, however, who these other fourteen people are likely to be (Marglin 1963; Daly and Cobb 1989; Weiss 1989). Furthermore, even if one could enter into an agreement with the other great-great-grandparents, there are numerous relatives in between who must carry out the agreement over time. Thus it is very difficult to assure the well-being of one's offspring beyond one's own immediate children unless the entire community throughout time is playing by a set of rules to achieve the desired outcome (Howarth 1992). Patrilineal, matrilineal, and other rules of inheritance, the awarding of dowries, responsibilities to train youth, and diverse other practices and obligations can be interpreted as intergenerational commons institutions that have facilitated the transfer of assets to the next generation. The social concerns, consciousness, and institutions that promote individual responsibility are coevolved elements that are critical to the conservation of resources and their transfer to the next generation.

An additional element needs to be introduced into the parable. Indeed, economists would be very concerned if human-produced capital were not integrated into the story. Parents might save in order to acquire human-produced capital, for example, more saws, or perhaps a bigger or better type of saw with which they could more easily harvest their trees. The role of saws as capital is different from trees. Our stylized parents know that saws provide a return by reducing natural tree capital but not *conversely*. Note that the existence of two types of assets, trees and saws, considerably complicates the problem of collecting and processing information. It is the mix of trees and saws that is important. The next generation would not be very well-off if it received all trees and no saws and would be in dire straights indeed if it received all saws and no trees. Assets need to be transferred from one generation to the next in the right proportions. Fortunately, in a small, relatively self-sufficient community, the proportion of trees and saws can be readily observed. Furthermore, members of the community can readily monitor the effects of their choices on their cumulative assets and adjust the mix accordingly.

To extend the parable, imagine that our once nearly isolated and relatively self-sufficient community becomes connected to a larger community by the clearing of trails and expansion of markets. While nothing else changes directly, the improvement in travel and introduction of markets open up new opportunities which, by exercising them, affect the community in a myriad of indirect ways. Some people, for example, might specialize by selling their trees and investing in the production of saws while others might invest more heavily in trees. As the community increasingly connects to markets, such decisions would be made in response to price signals from factor, commodity, and financial markets. The community institutions which had maintained a balance between trees and saws and heretofore sustained the community over time would fall into disuse and no longer be maintained.

The dynamics from here could be perverse. There may be an expanding market for saws precisely because, as communities were drawn into the market economy, people were choosing to cut trees, driving tree prices down, while the increased demand for saws would drive saw prices up, justifying greater investment in saws. If the market economy our community has joined has a way of assessing the overall mix of trees and saws within its area, informing everyone, and perhaps enforcing a proper mix, then disaster could be averted. Given the expanded area over which decisions are now interlinked, ultimately new intergenerational commons institutions will be needed to facilitate the appropriate transfer of assets over time. And yet the formation of commons institutions becomes more difficult the larger the community, as now multiple smaller communities are combined into a larger community. One can imagine some efforts initially being made to establish commons institutions on a larger scale, but with the process of market expansion ongoing, such efforts are partially successful at best.

Eventually our community finds itself fully a part of modern society and a still-globalizing economy. Though transfers of real assets in terms of land, housing, and factories from one generation to the next still constitute a significant portion of total transfers, parents are increasingly trying to meet their investment and intergenerational transfer objectives through financial claims to assets, through the education of their offspring and the cohorts they might marry, or through legislation at the state and national, and now even global, levels. In a complexly interconnected, globalizing economy with many types of interrelated assets, such as we have today, comparable information on the mix of assets, let alone the complementarity of the mix, is much harder to assess.

Let us consider markets. Individual investors in financial markets only see interest rates, not the stocks of trees and saws, let alone the stocks of the myriad of natural and human-produced capital supporting modern economies. But let us address the global issue first, the complexity issue second. Economists will argue that the value of a corporation's assets would decline if it cut all of its trees, but corporations can and do move on to other forests. Economic models assume good information. Who is keeping track of the whole picture? While most developed countries have fairly sophisticated monitoring institutions, even many of those nations do not make their data available to the public. Environmental monitoring in less developed countries is improving rapidly at the end of the twentieth century, but history cannot be corrected and our increasing awareness of the importance of biodiversity, among other things, has increased the demand for monitoring far faster than the supply. But even if all investors individually realize they are investing in saws, the net effect of which is deforestation, they may continue to do so if there is not an enforcement institution. They have no alternative but to hope that the returns from an investment that depend on a rapidly depleting resource can be reinvested again in some other sector to the benefit of their children, even if they can see that all in the further future are losing on net. This is the nature of a common pool problem unmatched by commons institutions.

The problem, however, is not simply one of monitoring and enforcement, but one of interpreting as well. With but trees and saws, contemplating the appropriate mix and deciding when there are too few of one or the other is relatively difficult. One must consider the age distribution of the trees as well as of the saws, the multiple uses of the trees, the likely future needs for tree services, and how these factors interact. Real economies, especially modern economies, depend on many more environmental resources and their services, and the interactions greatly compound the difficulties of interpretation. Note that economic theory requires that decision makers be informed, not simply that they have access to great mounds of raw data. This means that global models of the physical interdependencies of the economy are necessary to produce the information required by economically rational investors as we go from relatively self-sufficient communities, where resource monitoring and assessment can be done informally, to global economies.

With respect to trying to achieve our asset transfer objectives through education or the state, the situation is equally bleak. We have given little thought to which types of education complement trees or saws, or which substitute for them, let alone tried to affect the mix of education with the objective of sustainability in mind. Nor have we begun to analyze how modern institutions such as "pay-as-you-go" social security affect asset accumulation and transfers, let alone design new intergenerational commons institutions to facilitate appropriate individual behavior in a global economy.

The parable, of course, is highly stylized and too simple, but the point remains that people historically were closer to the resources they used and in a better position to monitor the overall set of assets on which they depended. Global agencies currently trying to oversee the whole picture with respect to resources and economic processes are very weak, short on conceptual justification, and an anathema to current market ideology. Ironically, the logic of markets in fact justifies information institutions at a minimum. The parable is about the interplay between community, environmental management, asset transfers, sustainability, and how they have been lost in the process of globalization.

Many scholars have begun to address the issues identified by the parable during the last decade. Shiva (1988), Worster (1988), and Guha (1990), among others, are rewriting environmental history, expanding the commons arguments and historical perspective of Karl Polanyi's *The Great*

Transformation (1944) to issues of environmental management as well. While the bequest motives of individuals have been considered by economists for some time (Dasgupta and Heal 1979, chap. 9), more serious arguments (Bromley 1989) and formal economic models that incorporate bequest motives are only now beginning to appear in the environmental economics literature. On the other hand, while there is now considerable interest in the relationships between trade and the environment, economists are still using models of resource use over time that assume each actor is fully aware of the global stock of resources (Dasgupta and Heal 1979) without addressing the implications of this assumption.

The following four sections show how fallacious economic reasoning has distorted our interpretation of the interplay between the key parts of the parable—community, monitoring and assessment, environmental management, intergenerational asset transfers, and globalization—blinding us to a full explanation of unsustainability.

THE ECONOMICS OF INTERGENERATIONAL TRANSFERS

Some of the concerns identified in the parable can be addressed through a general equilibrium economic framework in which the effects of different distributions of property rights across generations, or different levels of transfers from one generation to the next, can be explored. Even though resource and environmental debates have been over the rights of future generations—over the responsibilities of this generation to care for the next—the partial equilibrium models of environmental and resource economists implicitly assume that the current generation never considers the intergenerational distribution of rights to resources. The general equilibrium framing allows an economic exploration of the interrelations between allocative efficiency, the conventional turf of economists, and distributive equity—the questions of changes in rights, social obligations, or other manifestations of caring for others across generations.

The relation between allocative efficiency and the intergenerational distribution of resource and environmental rights is illustrated in Figure 2 (see Bator 1957). The line labelled U—the utility, or well-being, possibility frontier—indicates the highest utility possible for people in each future generation, given the utility of people in the current generation and vice versa. Each point on this frontier results from an efficient allocation of resources between uses. Inefficient points lie within the frontier U. From an interior point, it is possible to increase the well-being of either generation or both by establishing institutions that move society to the frontier. Clearly, there are many places a society could move to *on* the frontier—many possible efficient allocations. Each point on U, as well as each point within the frontier, is

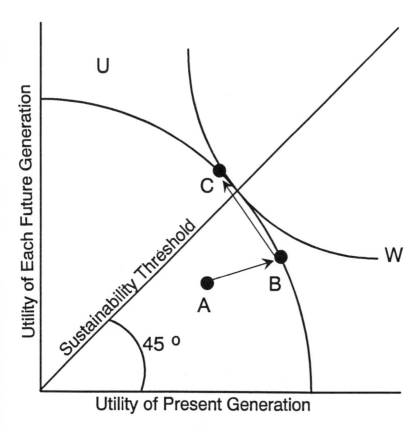

Figure 2.

determined by the distribution of rights to productive assets, including natural assets, between generations. Sustainability entails being on or above the 45-degree line. This line denotes that each future generation has equal or higher well-being or utility than the current generation. Note that both efficient and inefficient points can be sustainable.

By making its economy more efficient, society can move to the possibility frontier *U*. An economy, having become efficient, is not necessarily sustainable. Indeed, unless future generations acquired additional resource rights in the process of making the changes leading to greater efficiency, a previously unsustainable economy will still be unsustainable, just more efficiently so. Achieving sustainability requires a "northwest" movement along the possibility frontier *U*. Since each point on *U* is efficient, criteria beyond economic efficiency are necessary for selecting a new position on *U*. Economists represent such external criteria by a social welfare function illustrated by W in Figure 2. The point where W is tangent with the possibility curve identifies the highest level of welfare that can be reached given the utility possibility frontier. If society "wants" to act sustainably, its W will be tangent to U above the sustainability threshold represented by the 45-degree line indicating sustainability.

The issues are presented in Figure 2 in as simple a form as possible. Sustainability is a matter of equity, the distribution of rights, between generations, not a matter of the efficient use of resources. The relationships between the efficient use of resources and the intergenerational distribution of rights to resources have been more fully elaborated with simulation models of overlapping generations (Howarth 1990; Howarth and Norgaard 1990; Norgaard 1992a; Norgaard and Howarth 1991).

The environmental, resource, and development economic literature to date, even the most recent literature on sustainability, draws on models and reasoning that largely ignore intergenerational equity. The emphasis of this literature is on institutions for internalizing externalities, institutions that move the economy from an interior, inefficient position, such as that at Point A in Figure 2, to a position such as Point B on the possibility frontier. Institutions to improve efficiency move the economy toward U, the utility possibility frontier. However, a society that accepts the obligation of sustaining itself over generations must strive to operate at or above the 45-degree line. To assure sustainability, each generation must transfer sufficient assets to the next generation so that the next generation is as well off as it is. If the economy is not sustainable, then assuring sustainability requires intergenerational commons or other institutions that move the economy from a position such as Point B in Figure 2 and maintain it in a position such as Point C. Such institutions are either not discussed in the literature, or are discussed after presenting a model that does not illustrate the problem (for an early example, see Dasgupta and Heal 1979; for a more recent one, see Pearce and Warford 1993).

Resource economists have developed an extensive literature on the "optimal" exploitation of stock resources over time (Devarajan and Fisher 1981), based on a model of Harold Hotelling (1931). The foregoing general equilibrium framing shows that what economists have called "optimal" is simply the efficient solution based on the current distribution of rights between generations or obligations by one generation for the next (Howarth and Norgaard 1990). The efficient use of resources over time is different at Point B and at Point C. Environmental economists have similarly developed an extensive literature on the valuation of nonmarket environmental services and techniques that are now being put into practice by government agencies (Cropper and Oates 1992). Environmental valuation also assumes the current distribution of rights between generations or obligations by one generation for the next. Environmental valuation as now practiced implicitly assumes that society is not considering whether it prefers to be at a position such as Point

C rather than Point B. The values of environmental services are different at each point on the utility possibility frontier (Norgaard 1992a; Howarth and Norgaard 1992).

Economists have long recognized the perversity of discounting the benefits received and costs borne in the future (Ramsey 1928; Markandya and Pearce 1988), and have derived numerous arguments for using lower discount rates in order to protect future generations. But the problem is simply that economists have considered all decisions with respect to the future as investment decisions. Discounting is used for investment analysis—an efficiency decision. The decision to affect the level and nature of transfers to the next generation is not an investment decision, and so the benefits of such a transfer are not discounted. On the contrary, rather than trying to protect the future by reducing the discount rate, our models show that one of the outcomes of choosing to protect the future, by moving from Point B to Point C through increased transfers, is that the discount rate for efficiency calculations becomes lower (Howarth and Norgaard 1990, 1992).

While environmental and resource economists often *discuss* and *express concern* about the well-being of future generations, the models they use do not include the option of affecting their well-being through redistributing rights. Economists can argue that they have been thinking about equity issues for decades. Policy development and project decisions, however, follow from the patterns of thinking in their formal models, not from their musings interspersed in various texts.

Switching from a partial to a general equilibrium framing of the future affects our interpretation of how institutions manage common property and how the transformation of these institutions may have affected sustainability. Economic insights into commons institutions have mostly been rooted in efficiency interpretations rather than equity explanations precisely because the partial equilibrium models of economics do not facilitate formal thinking about equity. The general equilibrium model does. To what extent did commons institutions in the past prove fit because they facilitated intergenerational transfers and hence the sustainability of the societies that adopted them? Even asking the question as an evolutionary one forces us into a generation-to-generation survival perspective rather than the customary static-allocational perspective of the dominant economics. To what extent are institutions, environmental and otherwise, currently being designed to assure asset transfer? The introductions to environmental legislation frequently contain grand statements about protecting posterity. To what extent has economic reasoning rooted solely in efficiency analysis worked against such "common" sense during the latter half of this century?

ECONOMIC INDICATORS OF RESOURCE SCARCITY

While some economists certainly have worried about the future, most hold progressive beliefs about technological change and people's eventual control over nature. The future will be better than the past, so we do not need to worry about the future, or at least the future should be discounted by the rate of increase in well-being over time. Economists have bolstered their progressive beliefs with analyses of resource prices which show that prices have, for the most part, declined over time. If resources are becoming cheaper and cheaper, they argue, surely they are not becoming scarcer and scarcer. A short elaboration on prices and market theory is therefore in order.

Prices equate supply and demand for currently available goods, equilibrating markets so that neither surpluses nor shortages occur. The flexibility of prices is the great strength of the market system. Both supply and demand curves for each product are a function of the prices of other goods in other markets, and so markets are constantly responding to each other. Prices adjust systemically. Demand is a function of tastes and income as well as institutions. Both demand and supply are intimately related to the distribution of natural, human, and human-produced resources throughout society; to institutions affecting how resources can be used; and to people's information about the availability of resources, existent and potential technologies, and future needs. In summary, prices are flexible, systemic, and related to tastes, resource distribution, institutions, human knowledge of resources and technologies, and expectations with respect to each of these for the future. Or, even more precisely, prices are equilibrating mechanisms within and between markets where markets themselves are artifacts of human values, knowledge of resource availability, and social structure.

At the same time, it is important to keep in mind that prices are not simply social artifacts, but are *historical* social artifacts. Oil prices today reflect the depletion allowances, expensing of intangibles, prorationing institutions, import quotas, and transport regulations that affected how we developed, used, and grew dependent upon oil over the past. Oil prices today also reflect our historical beliefs about the scarcity or abundance of oil and our historical lack of knowledge about the environmental consequences of its use.

While nearly all economists would agree with the foregoing description of the systemic, social, and historical nature of prices, the vast majority of economists also appeal to market prices as evidence of the "real" availability of resources and environmental services, ignoring their social nature. This contradiction has become deeply embedded in economic thinking. The literature on economic indicators of resource scarcity provides an excellent example.

Over the last three decades, resource economists have developed an extensive literature on the theoretical advantages and disadvantages of alternative economic indicators of long-run natural resource scarcity and have undertaken detailed empirical analyses (Barnett and Morse 1963; Brown and Field 1978; Smith 1979; Hall and Hall 1984). The indicators include the historical trends in extraction costs, the rents earned from resource extraction, the costs of exploration, and resource prices that are the combination of each of the separate cost components. While the choice of indicator makes some difference, there is general agreement among natural resource economists and the profession at large that the indicators show that long-run resource scarcity declined from the late nineteenth-century into the late 1960s or early 1970s. The findings are dramatic: The classic study by Barnett and Morse (1963) indicated a fourfold decline in the difficulty of accessing resources. The conceptual elaborations and discussions of the empirical findings are thoroughly presented in leading treatises (Dasgupta and Heal 1979; Fisher 1981) and texts (Tietenberg 1992; Pearce and Turner 1990) on resource economics. Both the conceptual arguments and empirical findings, especially the longer trend of apparent decreasing scarcity, have been used to justify laissez-faire policies with respect to the use of resources (Simon and Kahn 1984). In spite of the less optimistic recent trends in the indicators, development economists (such as those who work for the World Bank) still tend to cite the long trend when confronted by environmentalists.

Though this line of reasoning is well established in economics, the arguments that economic indicators can inform us of whether resources are scarce or not are logically fallacious (Norgaard 1990). The arguments derive from two theories as to how resource allocators behave and thereby affect the generation of economic indicators over time. David Ricardo argued that farmers would use the best land first and that, as demand grew, they would expand their activities to lower quality land that required more labor and capital per unit of resource produced. From this simple and reasonable theorizing has come the cost indicator of resource scarcity and the classic empirical analysis by Barnett and Morse (1963). Harold Hotelling (1931) developed a more elaborate argument, especially appropriate for depletable resources, arguing that profit-maximizing producers would equate the return realized through holding units of the resource for future extraction to the return available from extracting the resource and investing the net revenue earned from the sale in the capital market. If the return on holding the resource is higher than interest rates in capital markets, the resource owner should hold the resource; if it is lower, the owner should extract the resource. Accordingly, when owners are extracting along an equilibrium path, the rent earned on resource extraction would increase over time at the rate of interest. If this were not so, they would be choosing to extract at a faster or slower rate, changing the path. Hotelling's argument requires that resource owners not only be aware of the qualities of different resources but that they also know the total stock of resources, future demand, and the prospects for new technologies. These assumptions have been thoroughly explored in the theoretical literature on how resource allocators "should" allocate resources over time, as have the implications of alternative assumptions.

The "theoretical" literature on resource scarcity, however, is surprisingly vacuous with respect to the assumptions behind the theory. Without going into the respective theories in detail, the important point is that the theories of how resource allocators behave assume that allocators are well informed of the nature of resource scarcity. Both Ricardo and Hotelling's theoretical models can be reduced to the following argument:

Premise 1.   If resources are scarce,
Premise 2.   If resource allocators know resources are scarce,
Premise 3.   If the knowledge of resource allocators affects their economic decisions, and
Premise 4.   If allocators' economic decisions affect economic indicators,
Conclusion: Then economic indicators will reflect this resource scarcity.

Economists have run this argument backwards in an effort to determine whether resources are scarce, the initial premise of the behavioral argument, by looking at resource indicators, the conclusion of the behavioral argument. The problem is that their analyses have ignored the second premise. Clearly, whether or not the argument can be run backwards, it is logically fallacious to ignore one of the premises.

Beyond this fallacy lies an obvious contradiction. The analyses have been undertaken to address the contentious public issue whether resources are scarce or not using models based on the assumption that resource allocators know whether resources are scarce or not. Clearly, if resource allocators are informed of scarcity, economists could simply ask them. If allocators are not informed, their behavior does not produce indicators that reflect scarcity. Barnett and Morse (1963), for example, argued that their findings refuted Ricardo's assumption of resource scarcity, but their findings could also simply refute the assumption of informed allocators.

Remember that, for economies too large to assess directly, intergenerational commons institutions require knowledge of the mix of resources themselves and a model to help interpret the meaning of the mix. While Dasgupta and Heal (1979) recognized that institutions to collect and disseminate information were probably necessary for the market to work, economists in practice frequently argue that prices provide all the signals that resource allocators need.

Considering the interaction between price trends and institutions adds a further interesting twist. If resources were becoming increasingly scarce, people concerned about the future would devise institutions to reduce resource use now and to extend use into the future. Or, if resources were becoming more abundant, existing institutions to protect future generations might be relaxed. Institutions affect scarcity. And yet no analysis of resource price trends has ever addressed how institutions over the past have changed. The dynamic of ignoring institutions is perverse. What if resource prices have not indicated scarcity because intergenerational commons institutions have protected future generations? By current economic mislogic, scarcity is not a problem, justifying the further relaxation of the institutions that have kept scarcity from being a problem! Or worse, what if resource prices were declining because intergenerational commons institutions that protect the future were steadily being relaxed? Using decreasing prices as a guide would justify their further relaxation. Recall that the parable with which we started portrayed exactly this situation. Local intergenerational commons institutions were breaking down as the geographical scope of the economy expanded with globalization while new, more global, intergenerational commons institutions were increasingly difficult to put into place. This brings us to the next dimension along which economists have let the assumptions of modernity and their roles in modern society derail their own logic.

TRANSACTIONS COSTS, DISTANCING, AND INSTITUTIONAL FAILURE

Economists have long argued that trade is good, more of it is even better, and governments should not intervene to constrain market transactions. Based on the logic of exchange, economists have provided strong justification for and generally favored the globalization of the world's economies through the expansion of the institution of the market.

At the same time, economists recognize that market exchanges entail transactions costs: the costs of receiving a potential gain, contracting with other parties, and enforcing a contract. For individual goods traded in markets, transactions costs are relatively low and sufficiently overcome by the transactors to complete an exchange. To some extent in the markets for all goods, however, there are some benefits and costs associated with the exchange that are external to the transacting parties and fall on external parties. Where transactions costs are sufficiently low for the external parties, they can become internal parties and influence the exchange. The problem of market failure exists when these transactions costs are prohibitively high and those external parties experiencing benefits or costs from the exchange remain external and do not affect the exchange. Similarly, for commons institutions, it is the transactions costs of communicating and agreeing between individuals and enforcing agreements that ultimately determine whether commons institutions arise and are sustained for the management of environmental resources and the attainment of other collective goals.

While it is well-recognized that high transactions costs prevent the success of commons institutions and the internalization of externalities, why there are transactions costs and what makes them change are rarely discussed by economists. Economists systematically address the symptom of externalities, but do not ask from whence externalities come. Ironically, the arguments for trade and the development of externalities are closely interrelated. Understanding transactions costs, or distancing associated with trade, identifies these connections.

The term *distance* helps us to understand the interrelationships between trade and transactions costs (Giddens 1990). Distance can be physical, social, or both. The subsistence community at the beginning of our parable could easily observe the effects of their interactions with nature, easily interpret the nature of problems, and easily communicate with each other and agree on a collective action. Their number, cultural homogeneity, geographic scope, and the relative character of the technologies they had available to them kept everything "close" and transactions costs low. The geographic expansion of exchange increases physical distance. With greater distance, it is more difficult for people to see the consequences of their actions. Those who see the consequences are in one place, those who can do something about it are in another, and the distance between them makes communicating and agreeing on a collective solution difficult. Specialization, which goes along with increased trade, increases social distancing by reducing shared experiences and ways of seeing the world. The parable started with a world of generalist farmers and ended with a world of academics distanced by their disciplines, of bankers with amazing international camaraderie, of communications specialists who care little about the substance of their message, of doctors and dentists with specialities of their own, of engineers who think physics can and should be used to override ecological and sociological problems, and so on through the alphabet. Specialization not only makes communication difficult; specialization makes it difficult to perceive problems that defy specialties (Norgaard 1992b). And as trade expands, existing national and cultural borders are crossed, further adding to the difficulties.

The likelihood that adequate intergenerational commons institutions evolve are a function of the size of the community. The difficulties of negotiating an agreement among individuals are a function, in part, of the number of connections between individuals. Two people have 1 connection, 3 people have 3, 4 people have 6, and 5 people, as evidenced by Figure 1, have 10, a progression generated by the formula $(n)(n-1)/2$, which increases geometrically. To the extent that groups already exist and have appropriate communication hierarchies, then the costs of transacting individually can be lowered. But the appropriateness of a communication hierarchy depends on whether the groups' prior ordering of interests and knowledge to be communicated fit the new problem. In any case, the geographical expansion of trade increases the number of individuals in the area over which commons institutions are now needed but, with a greater number of people, forming and maintaining commons are more difficult.

As trade expands it creates new problems, and challenges the communication systems of existing groups. Existing commons institutions become obsolete as the geographic scope of effects, beyond the market that they managed, expands beyond their existing boundaries. Thus, communities that have some autonomy, and are not constantly being challenged by strong external forces but rather are evolving largely through internal dynamics, are more likely to develop and sustain viable institutions to encourage individuals to transfer appropriate levels of assets. Such autonomy has not been a characteristic of the past few centuries of globalization. Thus there is good reason to be concerned that the rise of trade and the geographic expansion of economic activity have broken down the institutions of many separate communities that facilitated asset transfer. This globalization has also worsened the conditions for new institutions to arise as the expanding number of people who must come to terms geometrically increases the cost of coming to a new agreement.

In summary, the increased material consumption of current generations attributed to the gains from trade may well have been facilitated by the breakdown of commons that facilitated the transfer of assets to future generations and the absence of their replacement on a larger scale. While economists' promotion of exchange and specialization advances the markets for particular goods, it increases transactions costs and promotes the conditions for externalization of other goods through the failure of existing commons institutions and through a net increase in the externalization of environmental and other goods. Economics, by not using its own understanding of transactions costs more fully and acknowledging the problem of distancing, has unwittingly promoted two inextricably linked phenomena, both of which lead to more consumption in the present, but one of which results in less consumption in the future. There no doubt are gains from specialization and expansion of the market for the particular goods traded. At the same time, both specialization and geographic expansion increase the transactions costs for effects that are associated with exchange but not included, by the very same increased transactions costs, in determining an exchange. The negotiations to "free" trade in North America were prolonged by the difficulties of making new international agreements to cover the expanded context of environmental and social problems. To the extent that externality-resolving institutions have not expanded in scope and adjusted as fast as have trading patterns, the gains from trade are less than expected, perhaps even negative, because the economy is working less efficiently than presumed. Equally important, however, is the absence of discussions concerning intergenerational equity and institutions to facilitate transfers of assets to future generations. Whereas "environmental externality" is now very much a part of the vocabulary of international discourse, the concepts of intergenerational commons and the transfer of assets to future generations are not a part of trade negotiations.

THE INDETERMINACY OF WHO SHOULD BE FREE TO CHOOSE

The logic of exchange, Adam Smith's great discovery, has been used to promote free trade for two centuries. The logic is simply that *when two parties who are free to choose actually choose to enter into an exchange, it is because the exchange makes each party better-off.* Based on this impeccable logic, economists have long intoned that governments should not restrict opportunities for people to make themselves better-off through trade. Indeed, for two hundred years the political agenda of economics—to empower individuals and corporations and restrain governments and other forms of collective action— has been bolstered, if not driven, by the logic of exchange. The logic is faultless under the assumption of informed, utility-maximizing parties and no effects beyond the two parties. But the political agenda of free trade for individuals and corporations unfettered by taxes or other trade controls imposed through collective choice does not logically follow. The problem, quite simply, is that the logic of exchange is indifferent to how the parties conducting an exchange are defined. It is true whether the parties are individuals, communities, bioregions, or nations. If it is true for nations, why should nations not be "free to choose" or be free to choose to affect the choices of individuals and corporations through taxes, quotas, or other controls? Some criterion beyond economics is needed to determine which parties are free to choose under different circumstances. The logic of exchange would then be operational but not particularly policy-relevant. The policy problem remains one of deciding when individuals, groups, communities, or the state should be entrusted with decision-making authority, the central issue of politics for millennia.

Had the atomistic premise of natural philosophy not so readily transferred to, and proved to be as fit as, individualism in Western social thought, we might today presume that communities, bioregions, nations, or even spatially-overlapping cultural groups should be free to choose. The difference between individual and community interest, of course, is intimately tied to the systemic character of environmental systems. Nature cannot readily be divided and assigned to individuals. For this reason, collective management or collective limitations on individual choice are frequently appropriate. But the fact that the logic of exchange is indeterminate with respect to how we define the parties also tells us that commons institutions do not have to be justified on the ground that individual behavior imposes costs on others. People may simply prefer to work together in common and share the fruits of their efforts in common. We do not need the failure of the logic of exchange to justify common activity since the logic of exchange is equally applicable to groups.

"Free to choose" as individualist ideology, and its use to justify the expansion of exchange across communities, thus facilitate new opportunities for externalities along the lines developed in the previous section. Externalities arise as we respond to individualist ideology combined with the logic of exchange, expand the geographic boundaries of our activities, and let commons institutions along existing boundaries decay or become obsolete.

THE COEVOLUTION OF ECONOMISM

Economists are proud that neoclassical economics is considered the physics of the social sciences. It is the most theoretically well developed and stable, both the most mathematical and the most empirical, and the most emulated. The assumptions and methods are thoroughly explored and widely shared; indeed, they are frequently adopted by scholars within anthropology, political science, and sociology. It is the only social science for which there is a Nobel Prize. Marxist scholars continually remind us that, by the very nature of its assumptions and the structure of its model, neoclassical economics supports the status quo. To argue that neoclassical economists have not properly followed their own logic correctly or completely, however, is rare. And yet the problems identified in the previous four sections pervade economics, from its theories in academe, through its practice in public decision making, to its use in political discourse. I have labelled the existence, indeed the vibrant life, of incorrect and incomplete economic logic as "economism." How economism arose to become the secular religion of modernity, displacing earlier understandings with respect to how people and people, as well as people and nature, should interact, is more than a minor curiosity. It is an important part of a broader explanation of the breakdown of intergenerational commons, and thereby of the problem of unsustainability. Let us return to a coevolutionary framework.

Economics, like the other social sciences, established itself in the last century and coevolved in the midst of technological and social transformations complementing overarching beliefs about progress (Nisbet 1980). Progressivism as a philosophy of social organization, most explicitly formulated by Auguste Comte (1848), was incorporated into both Marxist and liberal theory during the third quarter of the nineteenth century. Comte and his followers thought that not only could natural scientists actually know reality but that social systems could likewise be understood positively as being made up of phenomena apart from human values and apart from the patterns by which people think, design, and act. Comte envisioned that the methods of science, by serving the process of social decision making, would free society from the irrationalities of established religions and the tyrannies of arbitrary political powers. As a well-established system of beliefs, progressivism became firmly embedded in social discourse and the design of institutions. In this vision, the collaboration between science, technology, and government took on increasing importance in the final quarter of the nineteenth century. The social scientists who fit the times and thrived assumed the modern vision of progress and the role of facilitating progress through science, engineering, and rational social organization and decision making. Those who questioned the changes underway were unfit at the time.

The idea of progress also included the belief that Western science, as an increasingly right way of knowing that was constantly validated by the wonders of new technologies, would inevitably be adopted by all cultures. This would reduce cultural differences and lead to a merging of all people into a global humanity. Scientific merging was an appropriation of Christian beliefs about moral progress. Cultural merging was rooted in millenarian beliefs and the long-standing argument that, as God revealed himself to more and more people, all would converge to one, highest morality. Robert H. Nelson (1991) argues that economists appropriated Christian beliefs about moral progress and universal adoption, transforming it into material progress and growth for all. At the same time, Nelson argues that economics retains a contradictory mix of communitarian ideals from Catholicism and individualist ideals from Protestantism with respect to social obligation. The idea of progress and progressive beliefs about social obligation influence the assumptions used by economists and the role economists play in public decision making, much as Newton's mechanics influenced their pattern of thinking.

The practice of economics and the political and organizational contexts in which economists work have always coevolved with social concerns. Early economists, including Adam Smith, Thomas Malthus, John Stuart Mill, and Karl Marx made philosophical contributions to a broad social moral discourse. At the same time, Adam Smith rationalized how people acting in their individual interest act in the collective interest, while David Ricardo justified why landlords should earn a rent from the mere holding of land. During the Great Depression, economics addressed whether and how economies could be stabilized and structured to maintain full employment. Similarly American economists assumed the role of econocrats charged with making decisions on behalf of society as they joined the federal and state agricultural agencies established on the progressive model after the Civil War, the water and forestry agencies established at the turn of the twentieth century, and the soil and land management agencies established during the Great Depression. Later, economists joined the international development agencies established after World War II, and the environmental and energy agencies set up during the 1970s.

Those with scientific and technical expertise had a special responsibility to see that the political process was not only appropriately informed but that the agenda was appropriately narrowed. Politics, though not democracy, was pictured as crass, chaotic, and corrupt. Technocrats and econocrats were rational public servants. Economists filled a critical niche in these agencies. Their justifications for and methods of using economic values allowed the agencies to go beyond mere technical design and to make choices on the public's behalf without having to constantly return to legislative bodies for advice. Indeed, legislatures increasingly mandated that decisions be made through economic reasoning (Nelson 1987). To fit this role, economists had to take the distribution of rights as fixed so that there would be but one efficient solution, a single economic answer (Bromley 1990). Similarly, economists, in order to continue to fit their mandate within progressive governmental structure, retained positivism and other modern assumptions about the nature of science long after many researchers in the other social sciences—disciplines that had not acquired a formal role in the progressive institutional structure— had abandoned them (McCloskey 1985; Norgaard 1989).

During the second half of the twentieth century, with few exceptions economists have simply been concerned with improving material well-being. Furthermore, most economists felt that improving the material well-being of this generation would improve the well-being of subsequent generations. With concerns thus defined, economists were asked to assist in a determination of how current well-being could be improved most rapidly. Economics transformed from being a contribution to social and moral philosophy, to a discussion of the stability of economic systems, to an exercise in efficiency analysis by econocrats on behalf of the public. Economism acquired dominance especially rapidly as economists acquired econocratic power during this last phase. The academic economic literature and discourse lost almost all of its earlier breadth while better mathematical models and econometric techniques for estimating parameters were valued highly. The economics of political discourse was reduced to free trade rhetoric, the economics of secondary education to market mechanics, and the economics of environmentalism to getting prices right and valuing environmental services in dollar terms.

Economism also proved fit in a much broader coevolutionary process. The tenets of modernity were confirmed, at least in the medium run, by increasing material abundance. New fossil fuel-based technologies increased the productivity of labor and land. Increased specialization and trade reduced production costs. Cultures did seem to be merging as economic globalization spread modern technologies and tastes. Resources appeared to be increasingly accessible through new technologies, at least to those at the front of the modernization process, and this increased access became extrapolated into the future. With the rise of economic development as a goal throughout the world, economists acquired power in international agencies (Pechman 1989). Belief in the overarching role of economic progress in overcoming material want eventually put economists at the top of the technocratic progressive priesthood (Nelson 1991). In short, the modern view of the world which bent economics into economism could readily be appealed to as an empirical fact, not simply a world view. Reality coevolved with progressive beliefs such that they became reality, at least for many people for the time being. Thus economists can appeal to their role within progressive institutions as "the way things are" when justifying their arguments. From this inside vantage, economists at the World Bank with whom I have worked tend to dismiss the multiple efficient solutions of general equilibrium analyses, not as incorrect theory, but as theory the Bank will never use because it would entail appealing to political processes for moral guidance.

While the loss of ecological and social integrity have been identified by a few for a long time, it has only been in the last few decades that environmental and social critiques of progress and empirical evidence have affected the consciousness of many peoples. While environmental and resource economics had earlier beginnings, it did not really become a subdiscipline until this rather late date, effectively not until the 1960s. Environmental economics very quickly coevolved with the current environmental issues of the resource agencies established at the beginning of the progressive era in the late nineteenth and early twentieth centuries, and then with the new environmental bureaucracies established during the 1970s. Consequently, environmental economics coevolved tightly with the progressive world view, even more so than other subdisciplines of economics, in spite of the fact that many environmental economists have been personally very sympathetic with an environmental world view.

The current emphasis of environmental economists on determining dollar values for nonmarket goods, for example, clearly puts them in the role of scientific experts making superior technical decisions on the public's behalf in order to avoid the irrationalities of politics. When environmentalists have argued for the rights of future generations in political debates, environmental economists could have contributed to public understanding by showing how alternative distributions of resource rights would affect the efficient allocation of resources and thereby the mix of goods available for present and future generations. Instead, they erroneously argued for the efficient use of resources under the current distribution of intergenerational rights. When environmentalists have expressed their concern over long-run scarcity, environmental economists have analyzed the question using models that implicitly assume economic actors are aware of scarcity. And when environmentalists have expressed their concern over the spatial scale of economic activity, environmental economists have joined in the discussion with arguments that are based on the assumption that individuals rather than communities, regions, or nations should be free to choose.

While economic and environmental reasoning can be quite compatible, the neutral ground that environmental economists have tried to create is, in fact, very contradictory ground. Environmental economists, by espousing many aspects of an environmental world view, have disguised the economism inherent in their work. And yet environmental economists, by attempting to use economic reasoning to address major differences in world views, are more deeply embedded in economism than the profession at large. The use of partial equilibrium analyses and ceteris paribus assumptions, which take all the other prices in the economy as givens, is more or less appropriate for the smaller issues addressed by most of the profession. Partial equilibrium analyses make no sense at all when addressing overall sustainability, global climate change, and conflicts in worldviews. The techniques of environmental valuation to set prices right are derived from data and behavior produced by an economy gone awry. If the economy is not on the right course, it is inappropriate to use data generated by the economy to set it on course. To the extent that environmental economists have realized these problems they have tried to correct for them through ever more elaborate arguments, drawing themselves deeper into the quagmire of economism.

Economists will still appeal to their beliefs about resource abundance, the inevitability of the dominance of economics in modern political discourse, and the predetermination of their role as econocrats in modern bureaucratic organization. Hence the future will continue to unfold with an ever-tightening interaction between their understanding of economic rationality, specialization, globalization, and material abundance. But these beliefs that drive economic discourse and policy, best understood as economism, are simply nineteenth to mid-twentieth century beliefs about progress and modernity bolstered by partial or fallacious economic logic. As more people continue to question economism with increased sophistication (Sagoff 1988), and as environmentalism continues to hold its own against progressive beliefs, economics will open up again. Indeed, such an opening is already apparent.

The end of the twentieth century is an important watershed in public perceptions, a time when new understandings are still intermixed with old. On the one hand, we are in the midst of the final stages of economic globalization. On the other, global unity is threatened as nations individually reformulate how they wish to chart their progress. Even the idea of nations themselves— the cultural fragmentation of the Soviet Union and Yugoslavia and the cultural tensions in Canada and India being obvious examples—is threatened by a revitalization of cultural differences previously subdued by the promise of progress best accessed through strong nations. The modern vision of cultural merging facilitated a merging for several centuries, but the reality of cultural dissonance at the end of this century emerges through the vision nonetheless.

Similarly, environmental systems have refused to succumb to modern science and technology and continue to surprise us with outcomes no one foresaw. Economism facilitated development, but the reality of the destructive transformations of such development is not masked by economistic beliefs, not even to World Bank economists. The people who are either packed into cities or commuting 20 hours a week in order to gain a little space are now well aware of resource limits and environmental degradation. Population growth and agricultural modernization drive the poor in rural areas onto increasingly marginal lands, accelerating deforestation and soil loss. And our perception of environmental degradation is increasingly being matched by advances in environmental science, confirming the obvious and projecting new problems, in a coevolution of knowledge and perceptions that challenges the fitness of progressivism and economism within it. A projected six-fold increase in atmospheric carbon over the next century threatens life as we know it.

Yet, concerns over climate change are still intermixed with arguments that we need not worry about the impacts of such change on our descendants since technological change will make them better off than we are. Few see the irony of extrapolating into the future the historic globalization that broke down the commons by which we managed environmental systems and passed assets to the future, or the irony of extrapolating historic technological change driven largely by fossil fuels when it is the same fuel technologies that are causing climate change. Being more globally competitive and applying modern science more systematically may save us. At the same time, the superiority of modern science and progressive social organization are discredited by our inability to foresee the environmental and social consequences of development. The sustainable development discourse is as replete with contradictions as the term "sustainable development" itself.

Concerns over sustainability, both of communities and of environmental systems, are having a significant new effect on the coevolution of economics. The economism that largely evolved since World War II is clearly at odds with these increasing concerns over the plight of our progeny. These new concerns are drawing economics back into discourse with moral philosophy (Sagoff 1988; Howarth and Monahan 1992). Complementing these new concerns are new economic arguments, including those derived from game theory, evolutionary thinking, and the significance of chaos (England 1994), that are challenging established models. The Society for the Advancement of Socio-Economics has been formed to link economists with sociologists to expand our economic understanding of socioeconomic systems (Etzioni 1988, 1993). Economists are actively participating with anthropologists, geographers, and sociologists in the Association for the Study of Common Property. The International Society for Ecological Economics consists of ecologists and economists exploring new ways of understanding the interplay between economic and ecological systems (Costanza 1991). Economics is beginning to respond to the detrimental ways in which social and environmental systems have been transformed under economism. What is not clear is the extent to which the new economics will simply be an ecological economism that violates ecological and economic logic in order to patriarchically provide answers for society, or an ecological economics that combines ecological and economic understanding with democratic processes (Norgaard 1994).

CONCLUSIONS

Our descriptions and interpretations of commons institutions to date have largely been driven by the concept of market failure within a given time period. Our understanding of commons institutions is rooted in the opportunity to internalize external costs, thereby improving efficiency and goods production, through collective action. Our descriptions and interpretations of commons can be further elaborated through an understanding of additional limitations in economic reasons that have arisen because economics has coevolved with modern beliefs. I have elaborated these further fundamental arguments with respect to shortcomings in economic reasoning and how these shortcomings have proven fit through the last century. The connection between these shortcoming and our understanding of commons institutions, however, needs to be made more tightly.

First, because economics coevolved with progressive beliefs, economists have not developed their own models to illustrate how the distribution of assets across generations affects the efficient allocation of resources within generations. If progress will take care of our progeny and if progress is driven by the investments of current peoples, then it makes sense to think about the future in terms of efficient investments rather than in terms of the responsibilities of each generation to transfer assets to the next. Indeed, driven by their belief in progress, economists have gone one step further and falsely argued that economic indicators show that resources are becoming increasingly available so concern for the future is unwarranted. This aspect of economism seems to have had two effects on our interpretation of the commons. First, like the undeveloped economic theory from which our interpretations have drawn, our descriptions and interpretations of commons have not stressed their intergenerational and distributive nature. There are occasional descriptions of social norms in cultures that are not fully Westernized and which promote intergenerational redistribution, but these descriptions are not interpreted in terms of intergenerational economics and how commons institutions facilitated intergenerational transfers and hence sustainability. Second, our understanding of the unsustainability of modern socioeconomic systems has not been tied to the breakdown of intergenerational commons through globalization. The elaboration of this point ties into a second aspect of economism.

Economics coevolved with progressive beliefs which, on the one hand, stressed the individual and, on the other, stressed how all would merge into one global culture based on Western knowledge. This stress on the individual at one extreme and the global at the other left little room for thinking about communities and nations. Indeed, economic reasoning was illogically turned against any collective organization, viewing globalization as merely individuals connected by markets. This stress on individuals, markets, and globalization has worked directly against the elaboration of commons institutions in the theoretical literature of economics and in political economic discourse, making commons less fit in the coevolutionary unfolding of modernity. More specifically, however, economics has developed without spatial or organizational dimensions that can shed light on our understanding of commons institutions. The spatial expansion of markets across communities might best have been accompanied by a spatial expansion of commons institutions across communities. Spatially more-encompassing commons institutions are not needed simply to fulfill the tasks of community-based commons institutions but also to handle new externalities that arise with trade. At the same time, with trade the need for some old commons institutions fade away. Spatial expansion generates new opportunities for externalities that are not internalized because of distancing, both physical and social. Globalization, in short, breaks down existing commons institutions, in part by making them obsolete and subject to natural decay and, in part, by increasing distancing within communities and breaking down their ability to sustain commons institutions. At the same time, globalization entails the need for new commons institutions on a larger scale, but collective action on larger scales is increasingly difficult, hence less likely or less complete.

As in the linkage between our understanding of commons and the economic concept of market failure, it is by converse reasoning that knowing more about economics enriches our understanding of commons institutions. Knowing that economics has not pursued its own theory with respect to intergenerational equity and has falsely argued that resources are becoming more available helps us better understand how commons institutions may have addressed precisely what economics has underplayed or denied. Understanding more fully how economics has ignored, even falsely pursued, the spatial and organizational dimensions of its own theory helps us see how commons institutions may have arisen in an earlier patchwork quilt of coevolving cultures and ecosystems and declined under the globalizing unfolding of modernity. And this interplay gives us a richer perspective on the extension of globalization currently underway through the North American Free Trade Act and the Uruguay Round of the General Agreement on Tariffs and Trade, and thereby the prospects for sustainability.

ACKNOWLEDGMENTS

Many participants of the 3rd Common Property Conference of the International Association for the Study of Common Property, held in Washington, D.C. in October 1992, provided helpful comments on a less inclusive draft with the title "Institutions for Assuring Our Common Future." Lee Freese and two Editorial Advisors for this series provided critical insights leading to the complete overhaul of the first attempt at a comprehensive draft completed in early 1994. Richard Howarth must be acknowledged for his contribution to the intergenerational arguments in this paper. Space does not allow for the reacknowledgment of all those who have contributed to my prior work over the past fifteen years on coevolution that has been melded into this paper. Nancy A. Rader provided much appreciated assistance through persistent questioning and red ink on an earlier draft.

REFERENCES

Barnett, H. and C. Morse. 1963. *Scarcity and Growth: The Economics of Natural Resource Availability*. Baltimore, MD: The Johns Hopkins University Press.

Bator, F. 1957. "The Simple Analytics of Welfare Maximization." *American Economic Review* 47: 22-59.

Bromley, D.W. 1989. *Economic Interests and Institutions: The Conceptual Foundations of Public Policy.* Oxford: Blackwell.

————. 1990. "The Ideology of Efficiency: Searching for a Theory of Policy Analysis." *Journal of Environmental Economics and Management* 19(1): 86-107.

Brown, G. and B.C. Field. 1978. "Implications of Alternative Measures of Natural Resource Scarcity." *Journal of Political Economy* 86: 229-243.

Comte, A. 1848. *A General View of Positivism.* Paris: Hertford.

Costanza, R., ed. 1991. *Ecological Economics: The Science and Management of Sustainability.* New York: Columbia University Press.

Cronon, W. 1983. *Changes in the Land: Indians, Colonists, and the Ecology of New England.* New York: Wang and Hill.

Crosby, A.W. 1972. *The Columbian Exchange: Biological and Cultural Consequences of 1492.* Westport, CT: Greenwood Press.

————. 1986. *Ecological Imperialism: The Biological Expansion of Europe, 900-1900.* Cambridge: Cambridge University Press.

Cropper, M.L. and W.E. Oates. 1992. "Environmental Economics: A Survey." *Journal of Economic Literature* XXX: 675-740.

Daly, H.E. and J.B. Cobb, Jr. 1989. *For the Common Good: Redirecting the Economy Toward Community, the Environment, and a Sustainable Future.* Boston: Beacon Press.

Dasgupta, P.S. and G.M. Heal. 1979. *Economic Theory and Exhaustible Resources.* Cambridge: Cambridge University Press.

Devarajan, S. and A.C. Fisher. 1981. "Hotelling's 'Economics of Exhaustible Resources': Fifty Years Later." *Journal of Economic Literature* XIX: 65-73.

England, R.W., ed. 1994. *Evolutionary Concepts in Contemporary Economics.* Ann Arbor: University of Michigan Press.

Etzioni, A. 1988. *The Moral Dimension: Toward a New Economics.* New York: Free Press.

————. 1993. *The Spirit of Community: The Reinvention of American Society.* New York: Simon and Schuster.

Feeny, D., F. Berkes, B.J. McCay, and J.M. Acheson. 1990. "The Tragedy of the Commons—22 Years Later." *Human Ecology* 23(2): 1-19.

Fisher, A.C. 1981. *Resource and Environmental Economics.* Cambridge: Cambridge University Press.

Giddens, A. 1990. *The Consequences of Modernity.* Stanford, CA: Stanford University Press.

Guha, R. 1990. *The Unquiet Woods: Ecological Change and Peasant Resistance in the Himalaya.* Berkeley: University of California Press.

Hall, D.C. and J.V. Hall. 1984. "Concepts and Measures of Natural Resource Scarcity with a Summary of Recent Trends." *Journal of Environmental Economics and Management* 11: 363-79.

Hardin, G. 1968. "The Tragedy of the Commons." *Science* 162(December 13): 1243-1248.

Hotelling, H. 1931. "The Economics of Exhaustible Resources." *Journal of Political Economy* 39: 137-175.

Howarth, R.B. 1990. "Economic Theory, Natural Resources, and Intergenerational Equity." Ph.d. Thesis, Energy and Resources Program, University of California at Berkeley.

————. 1992. "Intergenerational Justice and the Chain of Obligation." *Environmental Values* 1: 133-140.

Howarth, R.B. and P.A. Monahan. 1992. "Economics, Ethics, and Climate Policy." Energy and Environment Division, Lawrence Berkeley Laboratory, University of California at Berkeley.

Howarth, R.B. and R.B. Norgaard. 1990. "Intergenerational Resource Rights, Efficiency, and Social Optimality." *Land Economics* 66(1): 1-11.
———. 1992. "Environmental Valuation Under Sustainability." *American Economic Review* 82: 473-477.
Marglin, S.A. 1963. "The Social Rate of Discount and the Optimal Rate of Investment." *Quarterly Journal of Economics* 77: 95-111.
Markandya, A. and D. Pearce. 1988. "Environmental Considerations and the Choice of the Discount Rate in Developing Countries." Environment Department Working Paper No. 3. Washington, DC: World Bank.
McCloskey, D.N. 1985. *The Rhetoric of Economics*. Madison: University of Wisconsin Press.
Nelson, R.H. 1987. "The Economics Profession and Public Policy." *Journal of Economic Literature* XXV(1): 49-91.
———. 1991. *Reaching for Heaven on Earth: The Theological Meaning of Economics*. Savage, MD: Rowman and Littlefield.
Nisbet, R. 1980. *History of the Idea of Progress*. New York: Basic Books.
Norgaard, R.B. 1981. "Sociosystem and Ecosystem Coevolution in the Amazon." *Journal of Environmental Economics and Management* 8: 238-254.
———. 1988. "Sustainable Development: A Co-evolutionary View." *Futures*(December): 606-620.
———. 1989. "The Case for Methodological Pluralism." *Ecological Economics* 1: 37-57.
———. 1990. "Economic Indicators of Resource Scarcity: A Critical Essay." *Journal of Environmental Economics and Management* 18: 19-25.
———. 1992a. "Sustainability and the Economics of Assuring Assets for Future Generations." Policy Research Working Paper No. 832. Washington, DC: The World Bank.
———. 1992b. "Environmental Science as a Social Process." *Environmental Monitoring and Assessment* 20: 95-110.
———. 1994. *Development Betrayed: The End of Progress and a Coevolutionary Revisioning of the Future*. London: Routledge.
Norgaard, R.B. and R.B. Howarth. 1991. "Sustainability and Discounting the Future." In *Ecological Economics: The Science and Management of Sustainability*, edited by R. Costanza. New York: Columbia University Press.
Ostrom, E. 1990. *Governing the Commons: The Evolution of Institutions for Collective Action*. Cambridge: Cambridge University Press.
Pearce, D.W. and R.K. Turner 1990. *Economics of Natural Resources and the Environment*. Baltimore, MD: The Johns Hopkins University Press.
Pearce, D.W. and J.J. Warford 1993. *World Without End: Economics, Environment, and Sustainable Development*. Oxford: Oxford University Press.
Pechman, J.A., ed. 1989. *The Role of Economists in Government: An International Perspective*. New York: New York University Press.
Polanyi, K. (1944) 1957. *The Great Transformation: The Political and Economic Origins of Our Time*. Boston: Beacon Press.
Ramsey, F.P. 1928. "A Mathematical Theory of Saving." *Economic Journal* 38: 543-559.
Sagoff, M. 1988. *The Economy of the Earth*. Cambridge: Cambridge University Press.
Shiva, V. 1988. *Staying Alive: Women, Ecology, and Development*. London: Zed Books.
Simon, J.L. and H. Kahn, eds. 1984. *The Resourceful Earth: A Response to Global 2000*. New York: Basil Blackwell.
Smith, V.K. 1979. "Natural Resource Scarcity: A Statistical Analysis." *Review of Economic Statistics* 61: 423-427.
Tietenberg, T. 1992. *Environmental and Natural Resource Economics*, 3rd ed. New York: Harper Collins.

Weiss, E.B. 1989. *In Fairness to Future Generations: International Law, Common Patrimony, and Intergenerational Equity*. Dobbs Ferry, NY: Transnational Publishers.

Worster, D., ed. 1988. *The Ends of the Earth: Perspectives on Modern Environmental History*. Cambridge: Cambridge University Press.

RECYCLING:

CONSERVING RESOURCES OR ACCELERATING THE TREADMILL OF PRODUCTION?

Adam S. Weinberg, Allan Schnaiberg, and Kenneth A. Gould

ABSTRACT

This paper draws attention to the sociopolitical causes and consequences of recycling policies. We argue that recycling policies, like other "environmental" policies, are actually implemented to reflect the dominance of sociopolitical interests. Central to our argument is the increasing liquidity of capital, the transnational scope of politics, and the interconnectedness of ecosystems. Recycling policies reflect these forces, and also have consequences at many levels of the world economic system. They have arisen primarily as political responses to social complainants, not as corrections to the disorganization of the natural environment. By not grasping the global dimensions to human ecology, locally-based citizen action groups have pushed for recycling programs that fuel the very processes that their communities are concerned about. Additionally, they have failed to mobilize in ways that could bring about significant social and

Advances in Human Ecology, Volume 4, pages 173-205.
Copyright © 1995 by JAI Press Inc.
All rights of reproduction in any form reserved.
ISBN: 1-55938-874-9

ecological change. We conclude this analysis by suggesting that the environmental movement could mobilize more fruitfully by developing a human ecological critique. A new political economy could draw on a rich theory of the relationships between garbage and human institutions, the local and the global, and the economic and the ecological order.

INTRODUCTION: CONTEXTUALIZING RECYCLING

Recycling is currently in vogue. We all do it, and we all feel good for having done it. And yet, few of us give much thought as to how it came to be that we did it. Why *do* we do it (Derksen and Gartrell 1993)? And, does carrying it out do any good?

In this paper, we use the example of recycling to argue that good environmental initiatives developed by a well-organized, well-funded, and good-intentioned environmental movement may be fueling the very social and ecological processes they seek to tame. We trace this consequence to the absence among activists, public policy "experts," and politicians, of a theory about humans and the environment. We challenge the all-too-commonplace assumption that recycling represents a sociopolitical ideal, in which local government agencies, environmental movement organizations, and large-scale capital owners have negotiated a mutually acceptable alternative to solid waste disposal through burial in landfills, or through incineration (cf. Moberg 1991). Instead, we develop an alternative social analysis of recycling policies. We analyze the political-economic consequences of recycling, and the actual interests of major actors that support recent increases in local curbside and other recycling programs.

In part, we draw attention to the *sociopolitical* causes and consequences of such policies, in an effort to better understand the *ecological* costs and benefits of recycling. We argue that recycling policies, like other "environmental" policies, are actually *implemented* to reflect the dominance of sociopolitical interests (Lowi 1979). Our view is that these policies are primarily political responses to social complainants (Spector and Kitsuse 1977), rather than rational planning responses to correct the actual disorganization of the natural environment. Furthermore, these political policies cannot be understood as local. The liquidity of capital, the globalness of politics, and the interconnectedness of ecosystems means that policies have consequences at *many* levels of the world economic system.

Environmentalists have largely missed this interpretation because they lack a theory of the global sociopolitical dimensions of human ecology. The consequence has been the formation of citizen action groups that lack any understanding of what they are seeking to alter, and fail to maximize the strength of a movement that currently encompasses at least 12,000 grass-roots groups, 150 national social movement organizations, 14 million American members, and a budget of $600 million a year (Sale 1993). These groups have pushed for recycling programs that fuel the very processes the communities are concerned about, or they have failed to mobilize in ways that could bring about significant social and ecological change. We conclude this analysis by suggesting ways that the movement could mobilize in more fruitful ways by developing a human ecological critique of the political economy that would draw on a rich theory of the relationship between garbage and humans, the relationship between the local and the global, and the relationship between the economic and the ecological.

In making this critique we are extending and applying the model of the treadmill of production introduced by Schnaiberg in earlier writings (1980, 1983a,b, 1986, 1990, 1991a,b, 1992a; Schnaiberg and Gould, 1994), and updated in this series last year (Schnaiberg 1994). The model is presented in the following section.

SOME INITIAL COMMENTS: THE TREADMILL OF PRODUCTION

We start with two sets of generally accepted scientific principles about thermodynamics that govern all production practices. First, matter cannot be created or destroyed. Matter cycles through the global environment. It can be chemically or otherwise physically transformed, but all the original materials are preserved in some form, without any being lost or created. Second, as energy is altered from its potential energy form (for example, coal or oil) to more socially useful forms of kinetic energy (for example, combustion to drive turbine) there is a loss of organization, or an increase in entropy. Energy is reduced from organized chemical forms into randomized heat. This randomized heat is less readily usable in social production. In a sense it is spent energy. It is still energy, but its form has been changed from potential resource to disorganized resource.

The first principle of thermodynamics is referred to as the law of conservation of matter. Unused matter does not disappear as it is changed or transformed within the production process. Instead, unused matter takes the form of additions to ecosystems. Pollution and solid waste are the societal labels assigned to this type of transformed matter. The second principle of thermodynamics is referred to as the law of entropy. All production processes rearrange matter in ways that decrease the amount of available ordered energy. Natural resource depletion is the common label given to the social problems that arise from this principle.

Starting with these natural laws, we observe that all production processes include additions to (pollution) and withdrawals from (resource depletion)

Table 1.   The Treadmill of Production

---

1.   Producers accumulate wealth through ownership of economic organizations which successfully use ecological resources to expand production and profits.

2.   Workers increasingly move away from self-employment into organizations where they must rely on expanded production to maintain jobs and wages.

3.   Accumulated wealth is allocated into newer technologies, which replace labor with physical capital. This generates profits for wealth-holders who can sustain and expand their ownership in the face of growing competition from other wealth-holders.

4.   Governments must facilitate expanded accumulation of wealth, which is accepted as the only way to maintain "national development" and "social security."

5.   The net result of the above processes is that to sustain a given level of social welfare ever-greater ecological withdrawals and additions are needed.

6.   The ecological obverse of No. 5 is the increasing *likelihood* of an industrial society creating ecological disorganization as economic pressures push toward greater extraction of market values from ecosystems.

7.   Extending No. 6, societies are placed into an increasing *vulnerability* to socioeconomic disorganization as their ecological "resource base" itself becomes disorganized.

Source: Adapted from Schnaiberg (1980, 1986, 1994) and Schnaiberg and Gould (1994).

ecosystems. Likewise, all production processes will to some extent lead to ecosystem disorganization. The proper starting point for all environmental analyses lies with assessing the social implications of production processes. Within a highly advanced capitalist mode of production (political economy), the social implications of these laws are captured with the concept of the treadmill of production (Schnaiberg, 1980, 1986, 1994; Schnaiberg and Gould 1994). The treadmill is outlined in Table 1.

The logic of Table 1 is that in a liberal capitalist political economy (the treadmill of production), most participants are committed to some form of economic expansion. Ecosystems are a pivotal part of this process because they can be converted by participants through market exchange into profits. These profits can then be reinvested through the purchase of productive physical capital into more profit, which can then be used to purchase more productive physical capital, and so forth. At each stage of this acceleration the technological change raises the capital-intensification of the treadmill (and lowers its employment capacity). Thus, greater ecosystem access is needed to "efficiently" operate this equipment to generate exchange values and eventually profits. In other words, more ecosystem resources are needed because there is more productive physical capital to produce more goods. This new productive physical capital becomes more efficient and can generate more products in a given time. Expanded ecosystem use is driven by three other factors as well. Increasingly, a growing share of national production is needed to repay capital owners. Production must then generate enough surplus to: (1) support this outlay to capital owners, (2) provide enough additional exchange values and social surplus to supply an adequate level of wages to maintain consumer demand, and (3) generate enough tax revenue to cover social expenditures of the state. By increasing exchange values, the environmental demands of the treadmill are increased.[1]

Historically, three groups have battled over the effects of this process on ecosystems. Capitalist producers have sought to maintain it, for they are highly conscious of their material need for natural resources. They use all their assets to capture exchange values in markets, and to influence the state to maintain the flow of, and access to, these resources.[2]

Environmentalists have fought to slow down the treadmill, reform it, or dismantle it. These efforts, however, are hindered by the unique mix of use values and exchange values among American environmentalists. Environmentalists, like most people, have a diverse network of use-value interests in ecosystems. Most of these involve access to natural resources for either biological sustenance (like air to breathe and water to drink), or recreational purposes. Contrarily, environmentalists also have exchange value orientations. As workers, their companies depend on access to resources; and as tax payers, they worry about the costs of safe waste or sewage disposal and the costs of growing local regulatory bureaucracies. In our own fieldwork, we have each worked with local groups that fight for environmental causes while also fighting for lower property taxes. Thus, American environmentalists have diverse, conflicting, and unclear attitudes about environmental protection issues (Gould 1991a). Simply put, they are part of the treadmill.

The state plays the role of mediator in these conflicts. Consequently, its most severe internal conflicts revolve around environmental issues. Its constituencies are on all sides of every issue. The state is both a facilitator of capital accumulation and a social legitimator of the socioeconomic structure for the citizenry (O'Connor 1973, 1988). In its role as facilitator of a prosperous economy, the state needs unlimited access to ecosystem elements for exchange values. In its role as distributive justice legitimator, it must maintain resource levels for use value.[3]

Environmental conflicts arise when these three groups struggle to control and shape the access of ecosystems within the treadmill of production to fit their mixture of use and exchange values. The history of these conflicts is really one of emerging dialectical conflicts. Here, the dialectic has two parts: (1) with few exceptions, ecological systems cannot meet both exchange value needs and use value needs; and (2) the treadmill of production places primary emphasis on exchange value, but it is use values that are a social necessity for all classes and groups. Thus, use values are shared by a much broader constituency.

The tensions arising from this dialectic can be managed with three possible political-economic syntheses. First, there is what we will call the *economic* synthesis. Here, the state fosters capital accumulation, primarily supporting the exchange values of ecological systems. Only severe ecosystem disorganization is attended to, and only when it threatens productive systems or political legitimacy. State-based environmental policies are localized and short term. Second, there is what we will call the *managed scarcity* synthesis. Here the state attempts some minimal regulation of access to ecosystems. State agencies attempt to balance environmental exchange values and use values (Hawkins 1984) in a way that maintain levels needed for future uses. Third, there is what we will call the *ecological* synthesis (Schumacher 1973). Here the state is truly concerned with ecological protection. It emphasizes use value over exchange value (O'Connor 1988). The initiatives that arise to "safeguard" the environment shape these syntheses. That is, whatever synthesis is chosen to manage the dialectical tensions will determine the presence and form of environmental initiatives. States choose among these syntheses to manage dialectical tensions based on the interaction of three sets of factors: (1) the interests of various social, economic, and political actors, (2) the power that each of these groups has to push their interests in various economic, political and cultural arenas, and (3) the institutional structural arrangements that reflect these interests and powers.

Given the three sets of factors that shape the synthesis, we can argue that, when accounting for environmental initiatives, what becomes paramount is this: How do the motives (consciousness) and power (control capabilities) of various participants shape the dynamics of political-economic conflicts and lead to a particular synthesis emerging as dominant over others? The historical manifestations are a strong economic synthesis and, most recently, a weakly managed scarcity synthesis. We base this on the following: Most classes, groups of people, and institutions experience and define scarcity as increased difficulty in attaining their use values or exchange values from ecosystems. At the early stages of the conservation movement, the conflicts were between competing capitalist and precapitalist producers (Hays 1969). The goal was sustained-yield production.

Sustained-yield is a management approach that ensures private capital interests access to adequate supplies of natural resources for exchange value utilization—with little or no concern for negative impacts on ecosystems' capacities to support use values. With the rise of organizations devoted to environmental preservation, a more complex set of conflicts was introduced. But the conflict was still confined to the dominant economic class because the preservation movement itself was elitist, emerging from the economic concerns of the wealthiest socioeconomic strata. Thus, an economic synthesis still dominated the management of the dialectic.

Since the 1970s this has changed. The growth of the modern environmental movement has challenged dominant capitalist producers. This in turn has generated a more complex conflict around surplus distribution (Dowie 1992;

Gould, Weinberg, and Schnaiberg 1993; Morris 1992), and a shift from the economic to a weak form of managed scarcity synthesis. In this version of managed scarcity, regulations have most often been designed to preserve corporate access to productive resources for a longer time. Essentially, the state substitutes a longer-term view of sustained yield for the short-term calculus underlying political resistance by capitalist managers and stockholders. This view serves the capitalist class in the future, although it may impose burdens on particular producers in the present.

The shift to a managed scarcity synthesis, and the management of the tensions through increased environmental regulation, have produced varied responses. Producers have had mixed reactions. Most producers have duly resisted it. Other producers, however, have extracted new exchange value by providing clean up services and other regulatory functions. Environmentalists have praised the growth in regulation, and have called for more regulation, while simultaneously struggling to argue that the regulatory state will never manage the dialectic. The state has found itself increasingly responsible for managing a tension that cannot be managed to the satisfaction of any class, group, or institution. Thus, it has taken steps and institutionalized actions that ensure its survival (Landy, Roberts, and Thomas 1990).

Finally, communities have resisted the siting of waste storage facilities, the building of on-site incinerators, and the creation of new flood ways or water processing facilities. They see these implementation devices as detracting from their use value (they destroy the air they breathe, or are sited on places they recreate on), or they resent having to pay higher local taxes to fund these projects. Not surprisingly, these costs tend to fall on lower-class or minority communities (Bullard 1990; Bryant and Mohai 1992). On the other hand, communities have resisted environmental regulation and remediation that are perceived to be threatening to local employment options. Communities have also resisted the expansion of private capital investments, even in the face of increased ecological and public health damage (Gould 1991a).

To understand how these theories get played out in practice, we turn to the rise of modern recycling initiatives.

A SOCIOLOGICAL NARRATIVE ON
HOW RECYCLING CAME TO BE

An Overview: What Happened?

Recycling policies emerged in a historical context in which the treadmill of production has increased its dependency on discarding most producer and postconsumer wastes.[4] Such actions stimulate demand for new disposable products and also reduce some labor costs of production and distribution by using machine packaging and disposability. Incineration, landfill, and other modes necessary to deal with growing waste volumes have produced growing ecological additions of water and air pollution, and taken productive land out of alternative uses. In turn, these outcomes have diminished the use values of local ecosystem resources for local community groups, some of whom have become mobilized in opposition to this process.

Under the Reagan and Bush administrations this process intensified. Dominant capital interests were able to place market or *exchange value* considerations uppermost on our political agenda (Bachrach and Baratz 1962, 1963, 1973; Greider 1992; Philips 1989). United States producers operated in a world system that stressed growing changing competitiveness, and shifting capital and natural resource flows (Lipietz 1987; O'Connor 1988). The Reagan and Bush administrations helped producers compete by allowing them to deflect the focus of the Resource Conservation and Recovery Act (RCRA) of 1976 from *recycling within the production process* (which was seen as too costly) to *improved disposal of industrial wastes*, through landfills and incinerators (which was seen as less costly).

The call from the administration and major producers for more landfills and incinerators was met with hostility from local communities. To some extent, communities' fears stemmed from the coalescence of local pollution from existing landfills, and the subsequent heightening of communities' consciousness about *toxic* waste pollution. National publicity about toxic hazards at Love Canal and other sites increased such local concerns (Szasz 1990; Brown and Mikkelsen 1990; Schnaiberg 1992a).[5] From this rising concern with toxic industrial wastes, local communities formed NIMBY (Not In My Back Yard) opposition groups which joined forces with environmental organizations to oppose *all* landfills and incinerators. This gave rise to the LULU (Locally-Unwanted Land Uses) movement.

As the LULU movement spread, a "landfill crisis" emerged. Existing landfills were "filling up" (e.g., Papajohn 1987; Tackett 1987; Swanson 1990, 1991a, 1991b; Bukro 1989). And NIMBY-type groups had been able to stop the construction of new landfills and the expansion of existing ones. Likewise, they were able to channel local protests and fears toward local governments, which controlled some portion of the land used for landfills, incinerators, and other alternatives to recycling (Schnaiberg 1992a). Consequently, local governments become focal points and mediators of these conflicts. The response to these pressures varied widely. Their concerns were split between supporting citizen constituencies, and supporting dominant economic interests which support the state and its transfer payments to constituents.[6]

Despite the ambivalence to act, local governments (municipalities) had to do something. First, they feared that NIMBY constituents would withdraw political support for those administrations that failed to adopt some type of palatable policy. Second, the Reagan-Bush administrations shifted responsibility into regional, state, and local arenas, making it *their* responsibility.[7] Third, industrial producers were placing pressure on local and other governments (Lowi 1979) to maintain low-cost ("cost-effective") waste disposal, in order not to increase corporate costs in a time of increased world-systemic competitive pressures (Szasz 1990; Blumberg 1980).

Despite the urgency, local governments were befuddled as to how to proceed. Almost any local "solution" would likely increase costs for the economic actors involved with generating consumer goods. These solutions were politically unfeasible as they would alienate powerful allies, shrink the tax base (as profits decreased), and lead to a loss of jobs (again, as profits decreased). Likewise, landfills (like the littering of bottles, cans, and paper), had high social visibility (Schnaiberg 1995). Local governments knew that anything with high visibility was likely to draw local mobilization. Local government and industrial leaders managed these tensions by borrowing an old concept from the successful Keep America Beautiful campaign by using the principle: "out of sight, out of mind" (Szasz 1990).[8] Garbage, landfills, and "resource conservation" became merged in a dramatically new program of "curbside recycling."

Recycling became socially constructed as the "magic hope" that would solve the "landfill crisis" (Gutin 1992). According to predictions by public policy experts, recycling would reduce local waste disposal costs, allowing communities to recapture some exchange value of this waste as these materials were sold to private sector organizations that would remanufacture new goods from these wastes.[9] Recycling would be the first stage in moving wastes into a more market-driven commodity than was the case for landfills or incinerators. In the latter, municipalities paid contractors to somehow move wastes "out of sight." The rhetoric of recycling, dominated by the economic ideologies of Reaganism, was that recycling would be "cost-effective" or "profitable" for everyone, a utopian solution to the waste problem. Local governments would sell their curbside-collected wastes to recyclers, thereby making money instead of spending money on waste disposal. Not only would local citizens (including NIMBY participants) have fewer pollution problems as landfills somehow became less prevalent in the local ecosystem, but they would also be rewarded by lower tax bills for waste disposal. All of this would stimulate the treadmill while pleasing environmentalists, for wastes would be recycled instead of dumped into local land and water ecosystems.

What Might Have Been? Reuse versus Remanufacturing

The relationship between garbage and humans takes one of two forms: reuse and remanufacturing.

Reuse

The reuse path prevails in lower income communities in the United States, European, and Third World societies. In the United States, the range of reuse activities includes what we might call *social reuse*: activities that are more oriented to use values of consumers. Included are garage sales (run by individuals), rummage sales (run by churches and other nonprofit organizations), and thrift stores (run for profit or by nonprofit service organizations). For most of these activities, prices are set by the consumers' capacity to pay, and the use value of the goods to consumers.

In addition to this user-oriented mode of reuse, we can outline a mode of *market reuse* of consumer (and some producer) cast-off goods, which involves price setting based more on exchange value considerations of the sellers. Included are traditional antique dealers and newer antique malls, conducted house sales, and some used appliance, furniture and automobile agencies (including sales of previously rented goods).

Both of these paths to recycling reduce material use, maximize the reutilization of materials previously involved in production or consumption, and typically involve more labor intensive processes than do remanufacturing. For example, in poorer communities, paper sacks, and glass and plastic containers are resold. (In other settings, consumers essentially short-circuit the reuse cycle by essentially not using packaging, as when they use string or other durable bags instead of both "paper or plastic.") Some firms may be more sparing of energy and materials in production, and reintroduce into production lines those materials that have been discarded or rejected. Most importantly, from a social distributive perspective, the common denominator in many of these reuse processes is *higher input of lower skilled labor*. Workers sort, move, rework, reclassify, and rethink how to reuse discarded production and consumption byproducts. The following account provides one example of early market reuse from the first quarter of the twentieth century in Chicago, detailed in Eastwood (1992, p. 28, emphasis added):

> Another specialized form of junk peddler ... started out with a horse and wagon, but instead of collecting junk from ordinary consumers, he concentrated on collecting the waste from manufacturers in the area, particularly those producing mattresses, pillows, and other sleeping equipment. As his business flourished, he acquired a warehouse and a truck to bring materials for storage, and his sons entered the business....[T]he importance of these peddlers in recycling materials cannot be overestimated. Instead of waste collecting in landfills, much could be reused, while at the same time, employment was available for countless immigrants when they needed it.... The regression in this form of recycling [occurred] when synthetics replaced natural fibers, such as wool, cotton, and jute, and the scrap from soft goods could no longer be effectively reprocessed.

This type of policy is generally more socially progressive than remanufacturing. It affords more labor participation opportunities for workers with lower education and lower skills than remanufacturing. Both policies involve some exchange values, of course, since all goods tend to be distributed in some form of marketplace. However, the reuse model is dominated by social use value interests—sometimes because original consumers donate these goods for resale, or merely discard them for scavengers to pick up. Generally, the criteria for reuse are more heavily dominated by what utility social actors can derive from *using* the previously discarded materials, than by what they can remanufacture for a profit. In part, this is indicated historically by the fact that most reuse has not been mandated by state policy, but spontaneously generated by consumers and social intermediaries (e.g., flea market "dealers"). This is sharply distinguished from the major role of U.S. government agencies in the past five years in mandating "recycled content" in goods to be marketed. In overview, then, reuse is a somewhat less "commodified" way of dealing with waste production and disposal than the present system of remanufacturing. Although there *are* markets to bring reuse sellers and buyers together, the material outcomes are much less dictated by the profitability criteria of dominant economic organizations (often negotiated with state agencies) than by the use values anticipated by consumers entering small-scale markets. Another way of viewing this is that reuse markets are actually closer to an ideal "free market," unmediated by external forces controlling market conditions.

The social organization of labor occurs in different sites and modes of production to accomplish reuse. For example, a flea market is one way of reusing consumer products. It requires labor in transporting, sorting, and marketing in open-air or closed settings—often on state leased property. Low-income scavengers frequently perform similar services for production organizations, transporting discarded materials from one user to another. Labor for the sorting of materials tends to be utilized earlier in the production process, by the first user, to separate reusable wastes from nonreusable ones.

Many years ago, a colleague gave us an example about food wastes in Hong Kong. Traffic is heavy there throughout the night, he said, because intermediaries move unused food from one level to the next lower one in the hierarchy of food services. Street stalls are at the bottom, and first-class tourist hotels at the top of this hierarchy. By contrast, in American society, it is only the homeless and the very poor—whose labor is *un*paid—who scavenge for wastes from many of these restaurants. Hence, while the end-user of recycled goods may still be capital-intensive, the *process* of organizing goods for reuse entails a relatively high labor-to-capital ratio. Both large European flea markets and Third World human sorting of "tips" or dumps are examples of this latter approach.

Remanufacturing

In contrast to reuse, consider the "recycling" that has evolved in the United States. While some of the producers' less visible efforts may involve processes similar to those above, they usually involve higher capital-to-labor ratios in production operations. This new path has come to dominate our concept of "recycling," as Javna (1991a) suggests:

Old clothes can't be recycled the way bottles and cans are. You can't melt down an old pair of bell-bottoms and come up with new blue jeans. But they can be reused. And why should they be? First, it saves resources.... Reusing clothes can save landfill space.... By donating clothes to non-profit organizations.... you provide clothes for disaster victims and the homeless, and you're redistributing them into your community. Your second-hand clothes are important to people in Third World countries.

Ironically, this advisory column must educate readers that a *non-remanufacturing* path to recycling actually *exists*. This points to the dominance of remanufacturing in American recycling policies and markets (Swanson 1990). The clothing example above provokes interest, since there are in fact market intermediaries who are already selling used clothes in resale shops. By contrast, a recent voluntary movement in the United States has begun to recruit commercial caterers to donate their leftover foodstuffs to the poor and homeless, paralleling the clothing donations noted above.

Generally, labor and capital are used quite differently in the dominant remanufacturing path of U.S. recycling. For example, a firm may use engineering design labor to redesign a materials flow system. It would then purchase and install expensive equipment, to recover liquid wastes that were formerly disposed of. Less labor—especially low-skilled labor—is involved than in the case of reuse. In other producer and consumer recycling, we seem to be moving toward collection and mechanized processing to centrally relocate recyclable materials in preparation for remanufacturing. Increasingly, the state is subsidizing this effort, primarily through curbside collection from consumers. Discarded materials are picked up at residences, sorted, and transported to either for-profit business intermediaries, or directly to remanufacturers. The state may also subsidize the marketing of remanufactured goods by (1) favorable tax treatments; (2) mandating recycled (i.e., remanufactured) materials in the state's own purchasing (even if it is less economic or of lower quality than products which use virgin materials); or (3) legislating that other producers must incorporate in their products some mandated level of recycled/ remanufactured materials .

Though lower-skilled labor is involved in some of this sorting in preparation for remanufacturing, two realities must be noted. First, the preparation for remanufacturing is becoming more capital- than labor-intensive. Scavengers used to collect aluminum cans and bottles with carts or bicycles. Today, municipalities with curbside collection are outlawing such scavengers and replacing them with trucks and trailers used for pickup. Further, the intermediaries now involved with municipalities in processing for remanufacturing are becoming more capital-intensive. They increase their use of machines for sorting, crushing, and packing as the volumes of collected materials grow, and the specifications of some remanufacturers become more rigid (West and Balu 1991). This displaces low-skilled labor, which operated with low levels of capital. As the state coerces and seduces producers into using more recyclables in their production, we find an increasing capital intensification of the remanufacturing processes.

The distributive reality is that remanufacturing is paralleling manufacturing, in terms of capital-to-labor ratios. Recycling-remanufacturing is becoming, in other words, more "rationalized," thereby commodifying wastes (Schnaiberg 1990) in terms of rationalized exchange values. (Note that this differs sharply from reuse, which often involves extensive bargaining and negotiating in the absence of such highly rationalized exchange value systems.) Thus, we melt aluminum cans in standard furnaces, and establish paper mills to disaggregate and reaggregate newsprint and other recycled papers. The patterns of withdrawals (especially energy) and additions resemble those of manufacturing. As an example, Gould (1991a, 1991b, 1991c) notes the water pollution in the Great Lakes produced by a paper recycling plant in one of his community sites.

Gould's work points to another paradox of the treadmill and the relations of state and capital interests. In remanufacturing, the state often colludes with capital interests in disregarding water pollution to avoid interfering with local capital accumulation. Waste recycling in turn leads to new waste disposal problems, which arise from the remanufacturing processes themselves. Equally important, there is a selective private sector response to recycling, dictated primarily by profitability. Everyone wants aluminum cans today, and virtually no one wants newsprint, which is defined as a "glut." A glut may be defined from a use value perspective as an ecological resource, but one that from an exchange value view lacks profitability. Again, the state is ambivalent here. While the state could instantly transform the glut into a valued commodity by outlawing virgin paper products, it is reluctant to impose new capital requirements on manufacturers. This is especially true in tough competitive times—particularly, during a recession. Nor does the state propose to reuse papers through more labor-intensive processes. For example, street vendors in the poorer European countries and Third World use old office and notebook papers to vend nuts and other dry foods.

From Past Practices to Current Policies: The Rise of Recycling in Chicago

The sharp distinctions between reuse and remanufacturing paths to recycling are partially blurred in extant communal programs of recycling-remanufacturing that grew out of earlier social movement efforts. The Resource Center in Chicago, headed by Ken Dunn, is one such program. It emerged 20 years ago in a low-income area near the University of Chicago. It relies on local labor, in large part, and welcomes local scavengers. The Center is skeptical about the more capital-intensive curbside recycling programs currently being proposed by the Chicago sanitation agency:

Now that recycling is on the city's political agenda, Dunn and the organization that
embodies his vision stand at a critical juncture. No longer confronted by indifference on
the part of the city, they must now contend with competing interests and agendas.... Dunn
and other critics counter that the studies on which the city plan is based are biased and
flawed.... At stake, as Dunn sees it, is not only the future of the Resource Center but also
the potential of *recycling as a vehicle for social change* (Kalven 1991, p. 23; emphasis added).

Two contrasts between the Chicago program and the Resource Center
emanate from recycling goals and means. The city program aims for reduction
of landfill needs, due to the rising costs of landfills, and the political resistance
to landfills by NIMBY protesters. In contrast, Dunn's program was initially
aimed at resource conservation. His concern lay with reducing ecosystem
withdrawals. To accomplish his goals, he relied on concepts that he had
developed in his Peace Corps experiences of preserving Brazilian rain forests.

The recycling process currently proposed by the City of Chicago involves
the use of a single bag for all recyclables. This entails less labor and more
machine separation at city sorting yards. But Dunn and others estimate that
it also involves high losses of recyclables before remanufacturing. Conversely,
the Resource Center uses much hand labor to separate materials brought in
from pushcarts and truckloads of wastes. Eventually, most of this sorted
material does go into remanufacturing, which often involves machine
compression. This Center forwarded 24,000 tons and generated $2 million in
gross revenues in 1990. Yet Dunn attempts to attract local unskilled and
impoverished labor in an attempt to enhance community development along
with the remanufacturing process.

Use value recycling programs such as Dunn's, many of which were initiated
by earlier social and environmental movement activists, provide a hybrid model
between the two major paths to recycling. While most of the materials gathered
will be remanufactured (for exchange as well as use value) rather than reused,
the *process* by which the gathering and sorting occurs is more labor-intensive
and use value oriented. The sorting sites themselves, for example, use
communally gathered and socially discarded materials (such as old van bodies)
as part of their structures. Socially discarded workers often constitute the labor:

Many of those who have found a livelihood with the Resource Center are from the
impoverished surrounding neighborhoods. "Most people assume that day laborers or
unskilled people are stupid and don't care," Dunn says, "but these guys really work hard.
Their production is phenomenal."

With the exception of a few brightly colored pieces of machinery, everything in sight
is recycled—used and reused and used again. It is a strangely consoling—and even, in its
way, a beautiful—place. In this setting, man-made materials take on an almost organic
quality-perpetuated, reincarnated, giving ongoing life by the care conferred on them. And
the postures of the workers, winnowing through these artifacts, suggest both the hard labor
and the dignity of farmers bringing in the harvest. (Kalven 1991, p. 23).

Ironically, though, because the Resource Center ultimately gathers local wastes for remanufacturing, it too competes with other "free-lance" local gatherers. Poor and street people in the University of Chicago area struggle with each other (and with Dunn's vans) for aluminum cans, and other more valuable recyclables which they can also "cash in" at the Resource Center. Therefore, the exchange value portion of this communal operation leads to some of the same negatively redistributive features as those of municipal curbside collection. This testifies powerfully to the dominance of the logic of the treadmill of production (Schnaiberg 1980, 1994). It indicates just how socially different, in terms of the *relations* of production, are the remanufacturing-recycling approaches, as *forces* of production, from the previous local technology of reuse recycling.

If this communal exception only proves the rule of social *un*consciousness about the social and ecological impacts of remanufacturing-recycling, then what are our options with regard to state organized recycling?

The Local and Multinationals: Utopias versus the Dystopias

Two features made municipal curbside recycling seem realizable as a local solution to the "local landfill problem." The first was that recyclers—many of whom were large manufacturers who processed raw materials such as major aluminum and paper mills—would make sufficient profit through this recycling-remanufacturing (Schnaiberg 1983a,b, 1990, 1991a,b, 1992, 1995; Underwood 1991; Young 1991; Bukro 1991a). Yet, this condition has always existed, begging the question why had not this program been introduced earlier? The second, and previously missing ingredient included in the new recycling coalition (Staggenborg 1989), was the idea of municipal curbside collection. By collecting wastes from dispersed households (and some production sites), and concentrating them in some municipal area, curbside recycling reduced the costs of primary resource extraction for large-scale recyclers (Bunker 1985). The wastes collected through curbside programs became commodities. For local governments, the environmental (use value) gains from moving wastes away from landfills and incinerators were to be matched by negotiating a municipal profit (exchange values) from curbside collection. Local governments, therefore, had become willing players in new waste markets. Local city governments did so because they believed recycling would rapidly yield either of the following two outcomes.

First, the proceeds from sales of recyclable goods would provide a municipal fiscal surplus, over and above all the costs of curbside recycling (what we might call the "strong" promise); or, second, the sales of recyclable goods, coupled with the reduction of waste disposal costs entailed in curbside diversion of disposable wastes, would together reduce the total municipal costs of all their waste treatment activities, compared to the prior waste disposal system (the "weak" promise).

Alas, the strong promise has not materialized in succeeding years. Municipalities have spent more on curbside recycling that they can recover in sales of recyclable materials (e.g., Gold 1990; "Facing the Recycling Facts" 1991). Moreover, although the evidence is not as unambiguous—due, in part, to municipal accounting—it appears that the weak promise has also failed to be realized. Why? The simplest analytic answer is that municipalities have moved, in their contemporary recycling policies, away from areas of potential advantage (cf. Logan and Molotch 1987; Rudel 1989) where their politics (use value oriented, in part) can regulate local markets and ecosystem access. Instead, they have become actors in new market systems (primarily exchange value oriented) for wastes.

This simple explanation for the increasingly painful reality that recycling *does not* "pay for itself" (Belsie 1991) lies in the complement to municipal curbside recycling, namely, the desire of remanufacturers to extract profits from the remanufacturing process itself. In this new version of the American dream, profitability would once more activate this system. But profitability depends on reducing the remanufacturing costs sufficiently below market prices, so as to extract profit (Bukro 1991a). In this network, municipalities are weak players, and large-scale remanufacturers are powerful market players. Not only do recyclers frequently have market negotiation experience over much of the twentieth century (e.g., Bunker 1985; Szasz 1990), but they have at least oligopolistic (if not near-monopolistic) control over the remanufacturing process. That is, there are many municipalities eager to start curbside recycling, and only a few large-scale recyclers willing to bid on most of the collected waste materials. Historically, the reasons for this situation relate to the substitution of energy and chemicals for raw materials and human labor in the production process (Schnaiberg 1980: chs. 3, 4). As Eastwood (1992) recently noted, Jewish peddlers in Chicago once collected with a horse and wagon the waste products from bedding manufacturers (as well as postconsumer "junk"). Unfortunately, their recycling business collapsed when synthetic fibers replaced natural ones. Presumably, the costs of cleaning and sorting synthetic fibers were less than the manufacture of "virgin" polyesters and the like, so that manufacturers bought such virgin materials from chemical multinational corporations rather than from small-scale local recycling-reprocessors. This was a profit-driven calculus, after all. The local recyclers had little market power to compete with large-scale fiber manufacturers. Since the tempo of the treadmill of production began increasing (Schnaiberg 1980, ch. 4), this process has been repeated many times.[10]

The net result of this historical process is that in the later 1980s, when "recycling" was hailed as the new panacea for municipal solid waste treatment, municipalities confronted much tougher bargainers in the private sector than they had anticipated. While municipalities had a complex mixture of use value (legitimacy) *and* exchange value (citizens' tax reductions and new corporate tax revenues), the remanufacturers were primarily concerned with the "bottom line" of profitability. Remanufacturing of aluminum, glass, steel, or paper involves capital outlays that are beyond the capacity of smaller scale firms, due to the economies of scale (Belsie 1991; Gold 1990). Although corporations were also attacked for their part in the landfill and waste disposal crises, they were often able to use advertising and public relations in their "green marketing" imagery (Young 1991; Bukro 1991b; Stevenson 1990; Holusha 1991; Belsie 1991) to citizen-consumers. They thus diverted these attacks, without having to quickly invest scarce capital into recycling facilities (Stevenson 1990; Bukro 1991a; Holusha 1991).

In practice, what did this disparity between the economic power of municipalities versus remanufacturers entail? At one extreme is the newsprint "glut" (Belsie 1991). Municipalities continued to collect discarded newsprint, even though recycling intermediaries could not find buyers. Frequently, cities simply dumped this "glut" in landfills (where paper already constitutes nearly 80% of volume). The use value of newsprint is high, but the exchange value is low. Paradoxically, this process has reduced wastepaper prices so much that the United States is currently shipping this paper to South Korea. This relieves Korean politicians from having to approve the cutting of some forests symbolically planted after the Korean War to sustain their industrial expansion. The newspaper glut is a pure market definition. There's too much supply of "recycled" newsprint, and too little demand. The potential demand doesn't seem high enough yet to encourage paper corporations to invest in new recycling mills (Belsie 1991).

Thus, citizens deposit their newsprint into municipal containers, where it is whisked "out of sight" by municipal trucks, which then dump their newsprint in landfills because of "market conditions." At the other extreme, corporations engage in "green marketing" in which they advertise often exaggerated claims about the "recycled" (i.e., remanufactured) content of their products. In this way, the corporations increase their market power by holding down demand for recycled goods, thereby decreasing the value of municipally collected waste materials. This marketing ploy has led to actions by attorneys-general of a number of states to enforce new regulations about what "recycled content" actually means, in terms of the minimum content of the product constituted by recycled materials (Holusha 1991).

In both these extremes, the actual recycling-remanufacturing process *does* occur. In addition, major remanufacturers use their market power to enhance profits by reducing the costs of their "raw materials:" municipally collected curbside wastes. The prices they pay are dictated by their production and market situation, not by the environmental or political legitimacy, or the use value considerations that led to curbside recycling. As a result of this, recent critics have suggested (e.g., "Facing the Recycling Facts" 1991) that some big cities stop curbside recycling because it's "too costly."

Others cities, such as Evanston, Illinois, try to control more of the remanufacturing process—and thereby increase profits—by setting up municipal facilities for processing (West and Balu 1991). This is exactly the response of many Third World primary product producers (Bunker 1985), who have tried to move farther into the processing arena, with mixed success.

Changing world system conditions have increased this domestic contradiction between municipality curbside recycling and the private sector. The market for recycled aluminum is becoming attenuated by the policies of the former USSR and its successor states. These states have become so desperate for foreign exchange that they have been dumping metals on world markets at "bargain basement rates," thereby depressing prices for both virgin and recycled metals (Arndt 1992). Thus, the future of our "resource management" is increasingly moving away from political control over markets (Lindblom 1977) toward the control of local (and national) politics by major market actors—a more typical treadmill scenario.

The Institutionalization of A Bad Policy:
The Ambivalent State and The Misled Movement

As noted at the start of this paper, state agencies have not organized recycling primarily to attend to constituents' use values and thereby enhance their social legitimacy. Although the political *rhetoric* often focuses on this level, the actual organization of recycling has primarily supported increased rates of capital accumulation. Instead of carefully weighing the social and ecological dimensions of a materials policy (Schnaiberg 1990), most state agencies have patched together a set of waste treatment "programs." This has pacified many of those environmental organizations which in the 1960s and 1970s offered the primary social complaints that solid waste was a social problem (Spector and Kitsuse 1977).

In light of our analysis of the treadmill of production above, and the corresponding pressures on *all* levels of government to maintain the "growth machine" (Logan and Molotch 1987), it is not surprising that recycling in the U.S. context devolved into a *de facto* economic policy, within a legitimated framework of an apparently *de jure* environmental policy (Bachrach and Baratz 1962, 1963, 1973; Crenson 1971). In other words, it is not surprising that we have emerged with local *exchange*-value solutions to local *use*-value protests.

As we have argued earlier (Schnaiberg 1990), in the 1980s the strongest push for recycling came from local, NIMBY-type political resistance to local landfills, due to fears of toxic and other pollution. Such local movements generally had little general critique of materials usage in America. Local and regional government agencies, rather than national ones, attended to these problem definitions in the 1980s, and were even more likely to respond to immediate and localized issues. Most common among their goals was to "reduce landfill usage," in order to "extend landfill lifetimes." The prime constituents that the state responded to—other than local NIMBY groups— were economic elites who were concerned about the increased costs for business that a landfill limitation would produce (e.g., changes in manufacturing or in waste treatment).

This nonredistributive political context (Lowi 1972) resulted in the state developing pragmatic recycling policies that retained a patina of environmental legitimacy. They used the *rhetoric* of environmental movement organizations from the 1960s and 1970s. To a considerable extent, contemporary environmental movements have actively or passively colluded with this misspecification of policy impacts (Bachrach and Baratz 1962, 1963, 1973). The movements could now claim that they had achieved some policy gains during the 1980s, a decade in which they were frustrated by Reagan's anti- environmentalism. In this acquiescence, they have abandoned broader and perhaps utopian goals of environmental justice or sustainable development (Schnaiberg 1991a, 1995).

The future expansion of community recycling programs is uncertain. Recessions may increase local willingness to accept new landfills (Goering 1992) because of a desire for new tax revenues and employment. Environmental movement organizations may thus have failed to sustain resistance to the coordinated efforts of state agencies and capital interests to promote capital accumulation (Gould et al. 1993). They have at least acquiesced in the dismissal of many social justice and environmental protection objectives, some of which were crudely articulated by local NIMBY protests (Bullard 1990; Schnaiberg 1991c; Brown and Mikkelsen 1990; cf. Szasz 1990; Gould et al. 1993).

TOWARD A STRUCTURAL THEORY OF HUMAN ECOLOGY: SCARCITY AND LIQUID CAPITAL

Environmental movements are often naive about the fields of political forces surrounding local decision makers. They are even more naive about realizing that these forces arise from dominant economic interests (Logan and Molotch 1987; Rudel 1989). This naivete has often led to ceding the local political conflict to capital accumulation interests (Skocpol and Amenta 1986), accepting recycling as a "good start in the right direction." Environmentalists should have been chary of *any* remanufacturing process in recycling.

We need a way of thinking that includes the potentials and pitfalls, the local and global, and the present and past—a systematic analysis that asks: What drove the programs? What were the social and ecological consequences? And what alternatives existed? To do this we need to start with a better theory of scarcity and an understanding about the liquidity of capital in the 1990s.

Elaborating A Concept of Scarcity

The scarcity of ecosystem elements has been heightened and fundamentally changed by the historical reliance of the state on managing the dialectical tension through an economic synthesis (which exerts a strong institutional bias in favor of exchange values over use values). We see this through the example of recycling.

Fortunately, this bias can be offset. The treadmill of production is made by humans and can be changed by humans. Disruption of ecological use values, disseminated scientific information about the hazards of certain practices, and the rise of a social movement industry, all have the potential to provide key political conditions under which use values may predominate over exchange values in specific instances (Skocpol 1980; Buttel 1985, 1986). These factors led the United States forward in the 1960s, and again in the 1980s, from an economic synthesis toward a more managed scarcity synthesis. Consequently, the problem of scarcity has·become increasingly problematic today. Various groups, classes, and institutions develop competing and conflicting claims over what constitutes scarcity and what resources are actually scarce.

Under a period of managed scarcity, the ecological system continues to deteriorate. For some, this represents a potential source of exchange value. One clear example is the opportunity posed to recycling firms. Firms which can "dispose" of garbage will be highly profitable. (Waste management firm stocks have done very well in the last 10 years.) Furthermore, all those actors whose occupational interests are with these firms also share some exchange value interests. Thus there is a large industry of high-tech firms, university research labs, and trade associations that have a vested exchange value interest in ecosystem disorganization being recognized and dealt with. Thus, some ecosystem scarcity is an economic necessity.

From this we can conclude that scarcity is an interactive outcome derived from ecological properties of ecosystem elements and social users' criteria for use. This becomes further compounded by relative cost. For users with either small volumes of need or readily available monetary resources, the scarcity experienced for a given degree of ecosystem disorganization will be smaller. These inherent inequalities of fiscal resource distribution further bias policy making toward capitalist class segments.

For others this scarcity is the problem. At another ecological extreme, there is a growth industry with exchange value interests in the preservation of ecosystems for sport, recreation and tourism. For example, the producers of camping equipment and the employees of federal parks (state actors) derive exchange values from the desirability of recreational areas to be visited. The sociopolitical concept of scarcity is compounded by historical forces. Simply put, larger-scale production has diminished other users' exchange values and use values by withdrawals (harvesting of resources) and additions (pollution) to ecosystems (Hays 1969; Schnaiberg 1980, 1994).

It is important to realize that political conflicts over environmental resources initially arose from tensions within the historically dominant economic synthesis. Reform legislation emerged during the Johnson and Nixon administrations, and was implemented during the Nixon, Ford, and Carter administrations. These administrations were attempting to move from an economic synthesis toward a managed scarcity one without altering the basic tenets of the treadmill of production (Landy et al. 1990). While they changed policy, and made minor revisions in the arrangements of production, they left intact the class structure and institutional arrangements that create and reproduce the treadmill (Buttel 1985; O'Connor 1988).

In taking this approach to environmental protection, state policies changed both the degree and the costs of access by producers to ecosystem elements. This "solution" produced new scarcities (Gould et al. 1993). Ecosystem resources were not able to satisfy all users, especially as they competed to use or exchange a given ecosystem element that was in more demand but less supply. The shift from an economic to a managed scarcity synthesis did not eliminate dialectical tensions. The same conflicts recurred as classes, groups, and institutions competed for access to common ecosystems elements.

In other words, the strategies for setting the public agenda which emerged in the 1970s to deal with this problem were short-term, and relied on the cheapest methods (see Schnaiberg 1994, p. 41, Table 1). There is a variety of consequences of this strategy. Most significantly, consciousness patterns were altered. Conflict arose around assertions about problem severity. Environmentalists argued that ecosystem disorganization was a matter of survival, while producers argued that there was no problem. Environmentalists attempted to raise consciousness in order to develop broader constituencies and build networks. Producers tried to lower consciousness by suppressing information, or overloading people with information.

Next, the conflict moved to the cause of the problem. Environmentalists argued that the problem was caused by careless production decisions, while producers denied any contribution or minimized their contribution. Usually this evolved into a claim that the problem was a generalized outcome of all production or of industrialization itself. Producers made this claim by using academic research on population and consumer influence out of context.

These two strategies were further compounded by cost-benefit allocations. Environmentalists minimized consciousness about the amount and allocation of costs. The scenario they described projected certain, substantial and egalitarian-diffused social benefits from environmental protection. Producers played the opposite role. They emphasized the certainty and large scale costs of environmental protection and regulation, and the uncertainty, inequality, and modest social returns on environmental investments.

Finally, a fourth strategy emerged in which the cost-benefit allocations were inverted. Here, all sides agreed that protection was a social and economic good. Exchange value gains by corporations could be viewed as consistent with environmental protection goods.

Over the past 20 years, this scenario has played itself out in almost every environmental conflict. As the tiers converge on each other, the typical pattern of conflict emerges. Generally, producers' objectives in these conflicts involve maximizing their physical and financial accessibility to ecosystem elements. This is done to extract maximum exchange values from these transactions. Environmentalists generally seek to maximize their access to ecosystem elements for their use values. State agencies face a different situation. They confront the above conflicts of interests directly and differently. They confront them directly as all sides ask for and expect support for their claims. They confront them differently as they operate in local, regional, and national economic contexts that are diverse and volatile. These agencies seek to maintain social use values, while not impinging on producer exchange values.

The end result is always exchange value answers to use value problems.

Capital Flows and Production Transformations: The Global Dimension

Three facets of environmental degradation are central to this analysis. First, most environmental degradation is an outcome of a broader *extralocal* system, the economic treadmill of production. By extralocal we mean that operations occur locally as outcomes of decisions, arrangements and practices at the local, regional, national, and increasingly, international levels.

Second, the treadmill of production is essentially a *market-oriented* arrangement of economy and polity; thus decisions by producers at each of these levels are aimed at generating profits.[11] That is, growth and profitability dominate the private goals of investor-owners (seeking maximization of share values) and managers (seeking maximum of net revenues).

Third, the treadmill is central for both the economy and the polity. Maintaining the treadmill stands uppermost on the public agenda. As such, economic growth has become *the* most pressing item on the agenda of most industrial nations of the North, and of most industrializing nations of the South (e.g., Greider 1992). When social concerns are raised, the policy discourse revolves around how to increase tax revenues to support social programs. We speed up the treadmill in order to correct problems caused by the historical acceleration of the treadmill. Moreover, even when other local concerns weigh on the minds of some local or regional business owners or managers, most of these "social" considerations are outweighed by the fact that the dominant market actors depart substantially from a free market form of exchange (Granovetter 1985, 1990). This ideal type of economic competition includes requirements such as equal access to information and other elements of production. But the reality is that successful, economically powerful organizations protect their interests by controlling access to many kinds of social and economic resources, making it more difficult for new and smaller social and economic organizations to compete with them on a level playing field (Yonay 1991).

The consequence of these three facets is that powerful multinational organizations now operate in markets freed of locations. Commercial activities are no longer tied to specific features of a given place—a given community, terrain, *or* ecosystem. In recent decades, we have approached this ideal of capital liquidity through the transformation of many economic outcomes into electronic exchanges that are communicated globally through computers and satellites, and the computerization of a network of stock and banking centers. While goods and many services must still move by conventional means of transportation, the market transactions (exchange values) that dictate the flow of capital resources between buyers and sellers has become increasingly divorced from the geographic and physical realities of the place of production, packaging, trans-shipment, and unloading. The increasingly abstract but "rationalized" quality of economic development uses exchange (market) values as the central indicator, to be monitored and maximized by all those involved in directing the treadmill. Such globally mobile capital makes it increasingly difficult for local, regional and national governments to control their own economies and natural environments. Increased capital fluidity (and the increasing pace at which it can be pumped through electronic highways) is leading to a very real erosion of state power on all levels. This is an ominous development for the future of national environmental policies and democratic input in national decision making. The recent controversy over the potential ecological and economic impacts of NAFTA on the United States is a manifestation of the conflict between free markets and national autonomy. If, globally, "stateless money" threatens the power of national governments, we can expect even greater and faster disempowerment of decision makers at the regional and local levels. This process leads us to the international arena as the last level at which democratic controls may be exerted on the global treadmill of production.

Details of production and transportation, including extraction of raw materials as inputs and dispersal of waste by-products, still need to be dealt with by engineers and lower-level workers. But the management of enterprises, industries, and national treadmills became increasingly concerned only with fiscal considerations—the so-called "bottom line" of the modern period. As Veblen (1947) noted in *The Engineers and the Price System*, the rising control of production decision-making by accountants rather than engineers represented a qualitative shift in modern industry. His prescient analysis was among the first documentation of the roots of the treadmill of production.

USING THE THEORY:
ORGANIZING WITHIN THE TREADMILL OF PRODUCTION

Environmental groups could have taken an alternative path (and still can in the future). Establishing coalitions with local NIMBY groups and social welfare movements (local, regional, and national), they could have mobilized to monitor, evaluate, and critique proposals for alternative waste policies in a coordinated and sustained fashion (Schnaiberg 1991c, 1992b; cf. Staggenborg 1989; Bullard 1990; Logan and Molotch 1987; Gould et al. 1993). Rather than episodically and separately offering caveats about some policies and programs, a coordinated socioenvironmental coalition might have exerted a sustained division of political labor in offering an ecologically and socially grounded alternative policy.

This could have partly offset the dominating political influence in communities of many multinational organizations' capital accumulation interests. As with the NIMBY groups, the increasing universality of coordinated resistance would pressure local government elected officials and agencies to reassess their relative attentiveness to use value groups, rather than to continue to respond to exchange value institutions (O'Connor 1973; Skocpol and Amenta 1986).

Our alternative model of socioenvironmental mobilization is one of local embeddedness in larger extralocal networks (cf. Granovetter 1985). Most simply put, mobilization must occur in ways that track the scale of capital accumulation and allocation. Regulation of local environmental usage must be extralocal in order to come closer to effective control over resource extraction. That is, extralocal mobilization is a *necessary condition* for social control over ecological degradation, although there is no guarantee that it will be a *sufficient* condition.[12]

These mobilization efforts seek to change the agenda of the state and economic leaders towards realizing such social distributive goals (Lowi 1972). They would do this by revising the signs and symbols by which policymakers, politicians, producers, and the public talk and think about initiatives (Weinberg 1994). One example of such an interpretation is the following.

Much has been written in recent years about how "excessive packaging" in retail supermarkets and other shops generates large amounts of solid waste for landfills. However, few analysts have traced the historical underpinning of this packaging "revolution." Observers have noted that consumers express preferences for the health and convenience features of prepackaging, particularly when both spouses work and want to reduce the time needed for shopping. This suggests that consumers will resist older forms of bulk marketing that require less packaging (Schnaiberg 1991a). However, the history of packaging is not solely determined by such functional consumer preferences. Packaging is one of the "four P's" of marketing. It is one element of producer persuasion aimed at consumers (Schnaiberg 1980, ch. 4; 1991a). Therefore, these marketers will resist some forms of packaging control.

Still another major function for retail *pre*packaging is the reduction of wage labor needed by retail outlets. Clerks once had the responsibility to sort and package goods at the retail level, since they were "agents" of management who had considerable discretion. Shop owners needed to pay these workers enough to ensure their trustworthiness (Shapiro 1987). Besides monitoring pilferage and damage by customers (especially in food stores), these clerks had to avoid the temptation to pilfer small items themselves. Clerks in many modern retail shops have far less discretion. They pass bar-coded, prepackaged goods over computer screens which automatically record prices and tally bills. (Many stores with larger items also have magnetic tags which set off door alarms if the items are removed from the shop—though such tags do not generate a solid waste problem.) Today's agents of management thus have far less opportunity to pilfer and steal prepackaged goods, and to cheat customers, than did earlier generations of retail clerks.

Managers and owners can now "serve" customers while paying far lower wages for their clerks. *Ceteris paribus*, then, profitability is higher with prepackaging, as both the discretion of wage laborers and their wages are thereby reduced. Yet the *ceteris* is neither *paribus* as far as ecological withdrawals and additions are concerned, nor as regards the distribution of wage income. Modern clerks do not generally earn a "family wage," regardless of whether they are male or female workers. Consequently, recruitment of retail clerks has increasingly focused on younger workers (with the exception of some recent efforts to hire the retired). Further, this lack of a family wage is one reason why two wage earners are needed to approach a wage sufficient for them to raise children. This is yet another example of how the negative externalities of production are passed along from production organizations into both the social (familial) and ecological spheres. In order to increase profits in the face of increased competition, retail operators have reduced wage costs, and increased solid waste generation through extensive prepackaging. Thus, retailers will join some consumers and many producer marketing departments in resisting serious limitations on packaging, thereby impeding the kind of material policies that van Vliet calls for above.

This type of mobilization toward institutional reanalyses suggest as structural alternatives some combination of the following:

1. *Obtain municipal and state subsidies for communal waste collection systems.* This could include more favorable contracts for nonprofit organizations; lease arrangements for uses of municipal vehicles in off-hours for waste collection; tax credits or subsidies for local communal waste collectors.

2. *Place legal restrictions limiting waste sorting to communal nonprofit organizations.* Possible inclusions are local underwriting of waste sorting land areas and more labor-intensive sorting at such sites. With some reorganization, it may be more cost-effective than current arrangements if reduced local social expenses (such as unemployment and welfare costs) are integrated into the balance sheet of this communal system.

3. *Intervene in the broader remanufacturing process with local labor* (*ideally, in nonprofit organizations*) *to recycle local tax revenues in support of the local community.* These efforts can organize some local remanufacturing, or at least more involvement of local labor in packaging, transportation, and marketing of remanufactured goods (e.g., through setting up communal local marketing organizations for some consumer or business service products).

4. *Increase the social visibility of contracts between state agencies and remanufacturers and recycling haulers.* This would determine how socially effective the local government agencies are in recycling income back into the community in the process of reducing waste dumping or incineration.

With such sustained resistance, some socially progressive and more ecological goals of recycling, including reuse (Schnaiberg 1991c), could have been used to temper current capital-intensification of remanufacturing programs. The United States might have emerged into the 1990s reusing both valuable aluminum cans *and* discarded paper, regardless of the market prices of each.

The absence of this strategy has led us into futile debates about "paper or plastic?" in local supermarkets. Ironically, even at this mundane level, environmentalists have failed to follow through with the social reuse alternative of "neither." This option of reusable containers is being utilized by fewer than 2 percent of national respondents in a recent survey sponsored by The American Paper Institute ("Paper Sacks Plastics" 1992). Moreover, by employing underutilized local labor pools, "uneconomic" waste could have been turned into "socially usable" reused *or* remanufactured goods (van Vliet 1990, pp. 32-33; West and Balu 1991; Kalven 1991; Swanson 1992). The movements lent social legitimacy to current recycling programs and capital accumulation by failing to organize coordinated and sustained resistance to them (Gutin 1992).

CONCLUSION: CHANNELING SOCIAL RESENTMENTS

Discontent with state costs for recycling is rising. This has been particularly acerbic in an era of recession and state indebtedness. Critics (e.g., Gold 1991;

Schneider 1991; Swanson 1991a) *have* noted that municipal costs of recycling exceed revenues from remanufacturers. One logical approach would call for higher fees from remanufacturers (an exchange value orientation). Another would reason that the negative environmental externalities justify these net costs (a use value orientation [e.g., van Vliet 1990, pp. 32-33]). But the most frequent argument is that this "unprofitability" of waste collection calls into question the social value of waste collection programs. These critics suggest scaling down the extensity and intensity of collections. A recent New York Times editorial ("Facing the Recycling Facts" 1991) put this argument most directly:

> Recycling is obviously a laudable goal. It conserves materials at little cost to the environment. But until recycling generates its own revenues, the increased expenses of collection, like rising landfill costs, will have to be paid by cutting other city programs. [The Sanitation Commissioner] is right to go slowly.

This response suggests that recycling has been significantly transformed from its ideological origins in the environmental movement. Essentially, the editorial above reflects the dominance of exchange values, and the concomitant decline of earlier use value arguments such as those of environmental movements (cf. Bukro 1991a). Once again, markets are elevated and dominate political decisions about waste processes (Lindblom 1977; Young 1991; Swanson 1991b). From this position, only those elements of solid waste that generate profits should be recycled. The rest should be disposed of in other "more economic" ways. If landfills are too politically risky, then perhaps incineration or shipment abroad should be tried. Environmental and NIMBY groups are likely once again to be duped into accepting and perhaps supporting a bad policy.

Using the treadmill of production, we have offered an alternative model of socio-environmental mobilization, where the local is understood to be embedded in the extralocal so that coalitions of local and national social movement groups would mobilize to track the scale of capital accumulation and allocation, and so that the regulation of local environmental usage would be extralocal in order to come closer to effective control over resource extraction. Finally, we have suggested a model of mobilization in which the agenda of the state and economic leaders would be focused more directly toward achieving social distributive goals.

NOTES

1. To some extent these factors also contribute to recent increases in the U.S. national debt (Barlett and Steele 1992; Phillips 1989)

2. For example: Jeffrey Birnbaum (1992) has estimated that there are over 80,000 lobbyists in Washington, D.C. representing private industry. Many of these people each year will work in some capacity to maintain open access to any ecosystem resources that can be converted into profits.

3. This internal conflict can be seen most clearly in the internal fighting within the Environmental Protection Agency (EPA), and between the EPA and the Department of Commerce (Landy et al. 1990; Yeager 1991).

4. An interesting side note to this changing history is the beverage container industry. Over the last two decades manufacturers of beverage containers have taken three strong stands with regard to their containers. In the late 1960s and early 1970s, they helped to spawn an early "cosmetological" social movement that was interested in "Keeping America Beautiful." From the mid-1970s to the mid-1980s they spent millions of dollars opposing container deposit ("bottle bills") and other legislation designed to facilitate container reuse. Starting the mid-1980s they became among the most enthusiastic industrial supporters of recycling (Schnaiberg 1975). This historical juxtaposition alone should challenge our assumption that recycling represents the imminent dominance of (environmental) politics over economic markets (Lindblom 1977).

5. This was either an "epidemic of reports," as seen by conservative politicians, or a "report of an epidemic," as seen by activists (e.g., Brown and Mikkelsen 1990).

6. Modern structural theories of the state have moved well beyond the earlier academic consensus around a pluralistic model of mediation (Buttel 1985). Three major perspectives on the advanced industrial state have emerged in the past twenty years, each of which has some relevance for this chapter. Instrumentalist views (Miliband 1969) conceptualize the state as an agent of the interests of the capitalist class. The activities of the dominant class of capitalist producers are reflected by state actors and agencies. A revision of this perspective by Poulantzas (1973a, 1973b) envisioned the state as a reflection of the entire class structure of advanced industrial societies. This structural concept of the state theorized that the major goal of the state apparatus was to reproduce the capital logic of the society, with a broader and longer-term perspective than that imposed by the immediate interests of any segment or fraction of the capitalist class itself. The newest reformulation of the state, most widely expressed in the work of Skocpol (1979, 1980) and her students (Evans, Rueschemeyer, and Skocpol 1985; Skocpol and Amenta 1986) offers a more complex and dynamic view of the state. State actors and agencies are conceptualized as having some autonomous interests of their own. This becomes an additional factor in determining state actions. As well, this concept of a state-logic argues that the state's policies are more volatile than suggested by the earlier conceptualizations. The state, embedded in national and world-systemic contexts, produces a historical and comparative variability across time and states. This is due to the opportunities and constraints offered to state actors, and to various classes and class segments in advanced industrial societies.

7. Technically, the provisions of the Resource Conservation and Recovery Act (RCRA) of 1976 gave the federal government the pretense for doing something. The Reagan-Bush Administrations chose to do nothing.

8. Many of the beverage container manufacturers who had collaborated on the Keep America Beautiful, Inc. campaigns of the 1960s and early 1970s (Schnaiberg 1973) successfully dealt with visible litter by distributing municipal containers widely enough to "keep litter in its place." They provided one model of successfully dealing with local social complainants (Spector and Kitsuse 1977). On the other hand, their efforts in the 1970s and 1980s against "bottle bills" strongly suggest that a *reusable* (refillable) container approach was deemed too cost-*in*ffective for these beverage container industries.

9. Ironically, in many municipalities such as Los Angeles, this was actually a reintroduction of much earlier programs of *garbage separation* that local citizens had eventually voted against because of its inconvenience (van Vliet 1990). These earlier programs predated most modern environmental movements, and were introduced to reduce waste disposal costs (thereby reducing local taxes for this purpose).

10. In recent years, for example, the sports-shoe industry has moved away from rubber and leather components to synthetics. In the process, it has made expensive (and profitable) "athletic shoes" unrepairable, thus displacing many shoe-repair workers throughout our cities. As Eastwood

(1992, p. 28) notes, during the 1920s there were small-scale recyclers who remained in business by finding specific market niches. These included auto junk yards, scrap metal dealers, flea market agents, and the like (Schnaiberg 1991c). These were deviant activities of scavenging, which was often labor-intensive—though scavenging was sometimes also capital-intensive, in order to process heavy materials such as auto bodies for the steel industry. Some environmental activists, in the interests of resource recovery (e.g., Kalven 1991) continued and expanded such activities through labor-intensive, semivolunteer efforts that were often countercultural. However, they too had to operate within the remanufacturers' market systems, in order to sell most of what they collected (Swanson 1992).

11. While these production practices produce social goods (jobs) and service political needs (tax revenues), these are indirect consequences that do not enter into the decision-making process of private-sector corporations (Schnaiberg and Gould 1994, chs. 3 and 4).

12. We realize that the logic of this is simple to specify, but difficult to operationalize in reality. Any local economic system that is subject to external economic forces cannot control these external forces. Generally, these forces can usually only be challenged at the same level that such forces are marshalled at, although they may be challenged at the next lower level of social aggregation, under some special conditions. For example, the international flow of capital should ideally be controlled by an international body, such as the United Nations, the Geneva Agreement on Tariffs and Trade, the World Health Organization, or the like. In the complexity of the real world, however, most of these international bodies are subject to vetoes and withdrawals by nation states. While this is contrary to the increased ideological support of "free trade," most structural analysts are aware that trade has historically seldom been free for most smaller economic organizations, but is distorted by a variety of national (and eventually, even local) influences, as well as the powerful global influence of many multinational firms.

REFERENCES

Arndt, M. 1992. "Russia Goes from Military to Metal Threat." *Chicago Tribune* (February 2), p. C1.

Bachrach, P. and M. Baratz. 1962. "The Two Faces of Power." *American Political Science Review* 56: 947-952.

_____ . 1963. "Decisions and Nondecisions: An Analytic Framework." *American Political Science Review* 57: 632-642.

_____ . 1973. *Power and Poverty: Theory and Practice.* New York: Oxford University Press.

Barlett, D. and J.B. Steele. 1992. *America: What Went Wrong?* Kansas City: Andrews and McNeel.

Belsie, L. 1991. "Cities Avidly Recycle, But Market is Weak." *Christian Science Monitor* (July 16), p. 9.

Birnbaum, J. 1992. *The Lobbyists: How Influence Peddlers Get Their Way in Washington.* New York: Times Books.

Blumberg, P. 1980. *Inequality in an Age of Decline.* New York: Oxford University Press.

Brown, P. and E.J. Mikkelsen. 1990. *Toxic Waste, Leukemia, and Community Action.* Berkeley: University of California Press.

Bryant, B. and P. Mohai, eds. 1992. *Race and the Incidence of Environmental Hazards: A Time For Discourse.* Boulder, CO: Westview Press.

Bukro, C. 1989. "The True Greenhouse Effect: In 1990s, Environment May be Politically Explosive Issue." *Chicago Tribune* (December 31), p. 4.1

_____ . 1991a. "From Coercion to Cooperation." *Chicago Tribune* (November 17), pp. 6-8 Ecology-Special Report 1991.

_____ . 1991b. "Shopping for an Ideal." *Chicago Tribune* (November 17), pp. 24-25, Ecology-Special Report 1991.

Bullard, R. 1990. *Dumping in Dixie: Race, Class, and Environmental Quality*. Boulder, CO: Westview Press.

Bunker, S. 1985. *Underdeveloping the Amazon: Extraction, Unequal Exchange, and the Failure of the Modern State*. Urbana: University of Illinois Press.

Burton, D. 1986. "Contradictions and Changes in Labour Response to Distributional Implications of Environmental-resource Policies." Pp. 287-314 in *Distributional Conflicts in Environmental-Resource Policy*, edited by A. Schnaiberg, N. Watts, and K. Zimmermann. Aldershot, England: Gower Publishing.

Buttel, F. 1985. "Environmental Quality and the State: Some Political-Sociological Observations on Environmental Regulation." Pp. 167-188 in *Research in Political Sociology*, edited by R. Braungart and M. Braungart. Greenwich, CT: JAI Press.

_____ . 1986. "Economic Stagnation, Scarcity, and Changing Commitments to Distributional Policies in Environmental-resource Issues." Pp. 221-238 in *Distributional Conflicts in Environmental-Resource Policy*, edited by A. Schnaiberg, N. Watts, and K. Zimmermann. Aldershot, England: Gower Publishing.

Catton, W. and R. Dunlap. 1989. "Competing Functions of the Environment: Living Space, Supply Depot, and Waste Repository." Paper presented at conference on Environmental Constraints and Opportunities in the Social Organization of Space, International Sociological Association, University of Udine, Italy, June.

Crenson, M. 1971. *The Un-Politics of Air Pollution: A Study of Non-decisionmaking in the Cities*. Baltimore, MD: The Johns Hopkins University Press.

Derksen, L. and J. Gartrell. 1993. "The Social Context of Recycling." *American Sociological Review* 58(June): 434-442.

Devall, B. 1980. "The Deep Ecology Movement." *Natural Resources Journal* 20: 299- 322.

Dowie, M. 1992. "The New Face of Environmentalism: As Big Environmental Organizations Dodder, the Movement's Energy Shifts to the Grass Roots." *Utne Reader* (July/ August): 104-111.

Eastwood, C. 1992. "Sidewalk Sales: Remembering the Heyday of Jewish Street Peddlers in Chicago." *JUF News* (May): 22-33.

Evernden, N. 1985. *The Natural Alien*. Toronto: University of Toronto Press.

Evans, P., D. Rueschemeyer, and T. Skocpol. 1985. "On the Road to a More Adequate Understanding of the State." Pp. 347-366 in *Bringing the State Back In*, edited by P. Evans, D. Rueschemeyer, and T. Skocpol. New York: Cambridge University Press.

"Facing the Recycling Facts." 1991. *The New York Times*, (January 3).

Feshbach, M. and A. Friendly, Jr. 1991. *Ecocide in the USSR: Health and Nature Under Siege*. New York: Basic Books.

Gamson, W. 1975. *The Strategy of Social Protest*. Homewood, IL: Dorsey Press.

Goering, L. 1992. "Garbage Anyone? Landfill Crisis Goes in the Dumpster." *Chicago Tribune* (February 9).

Gold, A. 1990. "Study says Recycling Effort Could Fail in New York." *New York Times* (October 12), p. B1.

Gould, K. 1991a. "The Sweet Smell of Money: Economic Dependency and Local Environmental Political Mobilization." *Society and Natural Resource3* 4: 133-150.

_____ . 1991b. "Money, Management, and Manipulation: Environmental Mobilization in the Great Lakes." Ph.D. dissertation, Department of Sociology, Northwestern University, June.

_____ . 1991c. "Putting the [W]R.A.P.s on Public Participation: Remedial Action Planning and Working-class Power in the Great Lakes." Paper presented at the annual meetings of the American Sociological Association, Cincinnati, August.

Gould, K. and A. Weinberg. 1991. "Who Mobilizes Whom? The Role of National and Regional Social Movement Organizations in Local Environmental Political

Mobilization." Paper presented at the annual meetings of the American Sociological Association, Cincinnati, August.

Gould, K., A. Weinberg, and A. Schnaiberg. 1993. "Legitimating Impotence: Pyrrhic Victories of the Environmental Movement." *Qualitative Sociology* 16: 207-246.

Granovetter, M. 1985. "Economic Action and Social Structure: The Problem of Embeddedness." *American Journal of Sociology* 91: 481-510.

_____ . "The Old and the New Economic Sociology: A History and an Agenda." Pp. 89-112 in *Beyond the Marketplace: Rethinking Economy and Society*, edited by R. Friedland and A.F. Robertson. New York: Aldine de Gruyter.

Greider, W. 1992. *Who Will Tell the People? The Betrayal of American Democracy*. New York: Simon & Schuster.

Gutin, J. 1992. "Plastics a Go-go: The Joy of Making New Useless Junk Out of Old Useless Junk." *Mother Jones* (March/ April), pp. 56-59.

Hawkins, K. 1984. *Environment and Enforcement: Regulation and the Social Definition of Pollution*. Oxford: Clarendon Press.

Hays, S. 1969. *Conservation and the Gospel of Efficiency: The Progressive Conservation Movement 1890-1920*. New York: Atheneum Books.

Holusha, J. 1991. "Friendly? Fine Print Isn't Enough When Evaluating Products for Effects on the Planet's Health." *Chicago Tribune* (February 10), p. 15.10

Hooks, G. 1990. "The Rise of the Pentagon and U.S. State Building: The Defense Program as Industrial Policy." *American Journal of Sociology* 96: 358-404.

Javna, J. 1991. "Recycling Old Clothes can Help People in Third World Countries as well as the Environment." *Chicago Tribune* (July 14), p. 15.17.

Kalven, J. 1991. "Trash Action." *University of Chicago Magazine* (April): 17-23.

Landy, M., M. Roberts, and S. Thomas. 1990. *The Environmental Protection Agency: Asking the Wrong Questions*. New York: Oxford University Press.

Lindblom, C. 1977. *Politics and Markets: The World's Political-Economic Systems*. New York: Basic Books.

Lipietz, A. 1987. *Mirages and Miracles: The Crises of Global Fordism*. Translated by D. Macey. London: Verso Books.

Logan, J. and H. Molotch. 1987. *Urban Fortunes: The Political Economy of Place*. Berkeley: University of California Press.

. Lowi, T. 1964. "American Business, Public Policy, Case-studies, and Political Theory." *World Politics* 16: 677-715.

_____ . 1972. "Four Systems of Policy, Politics, and Choice." *Public Administration Review* 32: 298-310.

_____ . 1979. *The End of Liberalism*, 2nd ed. New York: W.W. Norton.

Mankoff, M. 1972. *The Poverty of Progress: The Political Economy of American Social Problems*. New York: Holt, Rinehart and Winston.

Miliband, R. 1969. *The State in Capitalist Society*. New York: Basic Books.

Moberg, D. 1991. "Garbage: The City's Blue-bag Recycling Program Stinks." *Chicago Reader* (September 20): 20-29.

Morris, D. 1992. "The Four Stages of Environmentalism." *Utne Reader* (March/ April): 157, 159.

O'Connor, J. 1973. *The Fiscal Crisis of the State*. New York: St. Martin's Press.

_____ . 1988. "Capitalism, Nature, Socialism: A Theoretical Introduction." *Capitalism, Nature, Socialism* 1: 11-38.

Papajohn, G. 1987. "Garbage Becoming Crunching Problem." *Chicago Tribune* (April 12), p. 2.1

"Paper Sacks Plastics in Great Bag Bout." *Chicago Tribune* (April 26).

Phillips, K. 1989. *The Politics of Rich and Poor: Wealth and the American Electorate in the Reagan Aftermath*. New York: Random House.

Poulantzas, N. 1973a. "The Problem of the Capitalist State." Pp. 238-253 in *Ideology in Social Science*, edited by R. Blackburn. New York: Vintage Books.

————. 1973b. *Political Power and Social Classes*. London: New Left Books.

"Recycling: How to Throw Things Away." 1991. *The Economist* (April 13), pp. 17ff.

Rudel, T. 1989. *Situations and Strategies in American Land-Use Planning*. Cambridge: Cambridge University Press.

Sale, K. 1993. *The Green Revolution: The American Environmental Movement 1962-1992*. Hill and Wang.

Schnaiberg, A. 1973. "Politics, Participation and Pollution: The 'Environmental Movement'." Pp. 605-627 in *Cities in Change: Studies on the Urban Condition*, edited by J. Walton and D. Carns. Boston: Allyn and Bacon.

————. 1980. *The Environment: From Surplus to Scarcity*. New York: Oxford University Press.

————. 1983a. "Redistributive Goals versus Distributive Politics: Social Equity Limits in Environmental and Appropriate Technology Movements." *Sociological Inquiry* 53: 200-219.

————. 1983b. "Soft Energy and Hard Labor? Structural Restraints on the Transition to Appropriate Technology." Pp. 217-234 in *Technology and Social Change in Rural Areas*, edited by G. Summers. Boulder, CO: Westview Press.

————. 1986. "Reflections on Resistance to Rural Industrialization: Newcomers' Culture of Environmentalism." Pp. 229-258 in *Differential Social Impacts of Rural Resource Development*, edited by P.D. Elkind-Savatsky. Boulder, CO: Westview Press.

————. 1990. "New W(h)ine in Old Bottles: Recycling the Politics of Recycling." Paper presented at the annual meetings of the American Sociological Association, Washington, DC, August.

————. 1991a. "The Political Economy of Consumption: Ecological Policy Limits." Paper presented at the annual meetings of the American Association for the Advancement of Science, Washington DC, February.

————. 1991b. "Saving the Environment: Whose Investment? Whose Return?" Keynote presentation, McKee Symposium, Michigan State University, East Lansing, May.

————. 1991c. "Recycling vs. Remanufacturing: Redistributive Realities." Paper presented at the annual meetings of the American Sociological Association, Cincinnati, Ohio, August.

————. 1992a. "Oppositions." *Science* 255: 1586-1587.

————. 1992b. "Accepting the Political Limits of Environmentalism: Towards a Model of Sustained Resistance." Lecture presented at the Business School, University of Valencia, Spain, March 26.

————. 1994. "The Political Economy of Environmental Problems and Policies: Consciousness, Conflict, and Control Capacity." Pp. 23-64 in *Advances in Human Ecology*, Vol. 3, edited by L. Freese. Greenwich, CT: JAI Press.

————. 1995. "How I Learned to Reject Recycling, Part 2: Paradoxes and Contradictions— A Contextual Analysis." *Blazing Tattles* 4(1): 1, 3-7.

Schnaiberg, A. and K. Gould. 1994. *Environment and Society: The Enduring Conflict*. New York: St. Martin's Press.

Schneider, K. 1991. "As Recycling Becomes a Growth Industry, Its Paradoxes Also Multiply." *New York Times* (January 20), p. E.6.

Schumacher, E.F. 1973. *Small is Beautiful: Economics as if People Mattered*. New York: Harper & Row.

Shapiro, S. 1987. "The Social Control of Impersonal Trust." *American Journal of Sociology* 93: 623-658.

Skocpol, T. 1979. *States and Social Revolutions*. New York: Cambridge University Press.

————. 1980. "Political Response to Capitalist Crisis: Neo-Marxist Theories of the State and the Case of the New Deal." *Politics and Society* 10: 155-201.

Skocpol, T. and E. Amenta. 1986. "States and Social Policies." *Annual Review of Sociology* 12: 131-157.

Spector, M. and J. Kitsuse. 1977. *Constructing Social Problems*. Menlo Park, CA: Cummings.

Staggenborg, S. 1989. "Organizational and Environmental Influences on the Development of the Pro-choice Movement." *Social Forces* 68: 204-240.

Swanson, S. 1990. "Recycling Suffers Growing Pains." *Chicago Tribune* (December 9), p. 1.1.

_____ . 1991a. "Recycling Grows Into a Way of Life." *Chicago Tribune* (June 16), p. 1.1.

_____ . 1991b. "The No. 1 Second City." *Chicago Tribune* (November 17), pp. 21-22, Ecology-Special Report 1991.

_____ . 1992. "Trash Means Cash for Some: Poor Picking Up Needed Money by Scrounging Alleys." *Chicago Tribune* (April 12).

Szasz, A. 1990. "From Pollution Control to Pollution Prevention: How Does It Happen?" Paper presented at meetings of the American Sociological Association, Washington, DC, August.

Tackett, M. 1987. "Little Town that Roared Savors Victory over Waste Dumper." *Chicago Tribune* (July 5), p. 1.4.

Underwood, E. 1991. "Accessories for Recycling go Upscale." *Chicago Tribune* (June 30).

van Vliet, W. 1990. "Human Settlements in the U.S.: Questions of Even and Sustainable Development." Paper presented at colloquium on "Human Settlements and Sustainable Development," University of Toronto, Toronto, Canada, June.

Veblen, T. 1974. *Engineers and the Price System*. New York: Viking Press.

Weinberg, A.S. 1994. "Environmental Sociology and the Environmental Movement: Towards a Theory of Pragmatic Relationships of Critical Inquiry." *American Sociologist* 25(1): 31-57.

_____ . 1991. "Community Right to Know and the Environment: Reconceptualizing the Law." Paper presented at the annual meetings of the American Sociological Association, Cincinnati, August.

West, M. and R. Balu. 1991. "City to Pay $1.5 Million for Recycling Center." *Daily Northwestern* (May 7).

Yeager, P. 1991. *The Limits of Law: The Public Regulation of Private Pollution*. New York: Cambridge University Press.

Yonay, Y. 1991. "When Black Boxes Clash: The Struggle Over the Soul of Economics, 1918-1945." Unpublished Dissertation, Department of Sociology Northwestern University.

Young, D. 1991. "Green is Also the Color of Money." *Chicago Tribune* (November 17), pp. 16-18, Ecology-Special Report 1991.

J A I   P R E S S

Advances in Human Ecology

Edited by **Lee Freese,** *Department of Sociology, Washington State University*

This series publishes theoretical, empirical, and review papers on scientific human ecology. Human ecology is interpreted to include structural and functional changes in human social organization and sociocultural systems as these changes may be affected by, interdependent with, or identical to changes in ecosystemic, evolutionary, or ethological processes, factors, or mechanisms. Three degrees of scope are included in this interpretation: (1) the adaptation of sociocultural forces to bioecological forces: (2) the interactions, or two-way adaptations, between sociocultural and bioecological forces; (3) the integration, or unified interactions, of sociocultural with bioecological forces.

The goal of the series is to promote the growth of human ecology as an interdisciplinary problem solving paradigm. Contributions are solicited without regard for particular theoretical, methodological, or disciplinary orthodoxies, and may range across ecological anthropology, ecological economics, ecological demography, ecological geography, biopolitics, and other relevant fields of specialization.

Volume 1, 1992, 234 pp. $73.25
ISBN 1-55938-091-8

JAI PRESS INC.
55 Old Post Road # 2 - P.O. Box 1678
Greenwich, Connecticut 06836-1678
Tel: (203) 661- 7602   Fax: (203) 661-0792

J A I

P R E S S

Research in Philosophy and Technology

Edited by **Carl Mitcham,** *Science Technology and Society Program, Pennsylvania State University*

European Editor: **Walter Ch. Zimmerli,** *Technische Universitat Braunschweig.*

Review Editor: **Leonard J. Waks,** *Pennsylvania State University*

REVIEWS: "...Reflecting a sudden burst of interest in this subject over the past decade, the essays attempt to answer the question What would constitute an adequate philosophy of technology?...the collection offers an introduction to the subject that will be useful to specialists and nonspecialists alike."

--Science

"...a series which has been overdue and is bound to be a significant factor in the development of this field."

--Dialogue

Volume 14, Technology and Everyday Life
1994, 351 pp. $73.25
ISBN 1-55938-712-2

CONTENTS: General Editors Introduction. THEME SECTION. Guest Editors Introduction, *George Allen.* Altered States: Images of Technology in Two Prime Time Syndicated Television Series, *Mark Giese.* Albert Borgmann and John Dewey on Everyday Technolgy, *Peter Limper.* Don Dellillo and Daniel Boorstin: White Noise as an Illustration of Technology and Democracy, *Kathryn A. Walterscheid.* Parenting Technology, *Elizabeth Dodson Gray.* Challenging Technology, *David Strong.* The Technology-Culture Spiral: Three Examples of Technological Developments in Everyday Life, *Ingo Braun.* The Match and Other Agents of Liberation: The Role of Technology in the Social Thought of Louise Otto, *Ingrid H. Soudek, and Kathryn A. Neeley.* Technology: Artistic Medium and Muse, *H. Wendell Howard.* Whitehead and Heidegger on Technological Goodness, *Joseph Grange.* Making the Everyday, *George Allan.* CONTEMPORARY DISCUSSION. Bacon and Pascal on Mastery Over Nature, *Douglas Groothuis.* Enlightenment and Technology: Outline for a General Ethics of

Technology, *Heiner Hastedt.* Technology as Art and the Spheres of Freedom and Necessity, *Fred Evans.* Middle Level Theory in Elluls Thought: Where Theory and Practice Meet, *Daryl J. Wennemann.* Instrumental Realism and the Idea of Embodied Knowledge, *Don Ross.* Artificial Intelligence and Human Personality, *Albert Borgmann.* REVIEW SECTION. Explaining Medical Technology, *Joseph D. Bronzino, Vincent H. Smith, and Maurice L. Wade.* Medical Technology and Society: An Interdisciplinary Persepctive. Toward Civilization Change, *Andrew Feenberg.* Critical Theory of Technology. Reviewed by Paul T. Durbin. The Magic of Technology, *Juan David Garcia Bacca,* De magica a tecnica: Ensayo de teatro filosofico-literario-tecnico. Reviewed by *James A. Lynch.* Myths of the Future, *Peter Schwartzz,* The Art of the Long View. Reviewed by *Darryl Farber.* Evolutionary Theory and Technology, George Basalla, The Evolution of Technology. Reviewed by *Juan F. Ilerbaig.* Science, Technology, and Power: Further Than Foucault, *Stanley Aronowitz,* Science as Power: Discourse and Ideology in Modern Society. *J.R. Ravetz,* The Merger of Knowledge with Power: Essays in Critical Science. Wolfgang Sachs, editor, The Development Dictionary: A Guide to Knowledge as Power. Reviewed by *Carl Mitcham.* Understanding Risk, *H.W. Lewis,* Technological Risk. *Deborah Mayo and Ranchelle Hollander,* editors, Acceptable Evidence: Science and Values in Risk Management. *K.S. Shrader-Frechette*, Risk and Rationality. Reviewed by *Paul B. Thompson.* Constructivist STS. *Dennis W. Cheek,* Thinking Constructively about Science, Technology and Society Education. Reviewed by *William F. Williams.* Author Index. Subject Index.

Volumes 9-14 were edited by Frederick Ferré,
Department of Philosophy, University of Georgia

Supplement 3, Technologys School:
The Challenge to Philosophy

by **Leonard J. Waks,** *Temple University*
1995, 270 pp. $73.25
ISBN 1-55938-956-7

CONTENTS: General Editors Introduction. Foreword. Preface. INTRODUCTION: TECHNOLOGY, EDUCATION, AND THE MODERN STATE. PART I. EDUCATION AS THE TECHNOLOGY OF LEARNING. Part I. Introduction. Educational Objectives and Existential Heroes. Curriculum as Engineering Design. Curriculum Philosophy and Accountability. The New World of Technology in American Educational Policy. PART II. PHILOSOPHIES OF EDUCATION IN THE TECHNOLOGICAL SOCIETY. Part II. Introduction. John Dewey on the School and Social Progress. A.S. Neils Summerhill: Education as Anti-Technology. Jacques Ellul on Human Techniques as Oil in the Mega-Machine. Ivan Illich and Deschooling Society. PART III. DEMOCRATIC EDUCATION AND THE CRISIS IN TECHNOLOGY. Part III. Introduction.

J
A
I

P
R
E
S
S

J

A

I

The Responsibility Spiral: A Framework for STS Education. STS Education and Citizen Participation. Technological Literacy for the New Majority. STS Education and the Paradox of Green Studies. Value Judgment and Social Action in Technology Studies. PART IV. PHILOSOPHY AS CRITICISM OF TECHNOLOGY AND EDUCATION. Part IV. Introduction. Public Philosophy and Social Responsibility in Technological Society. Three Contexts of Philosophy of Education: Intellectual, Institutional and Ideological. STS as an Academic Field and as a Social Movement. Bibliography. Index.

Also Available:
Volumes 1-13 (1979-1993)
  + Supplements 1-2 (1984-1988) $73.25 each

P

R

E

S

S

JAI PRESS INC.
55 Old Post Road # 2 - P.O. Box 1678
Greenwich, Connecticut 06836-1678
Tel: (203) 661- 7602   Fax: (203) 661-0792

Knowledge and Society

Edited by **David J. Hess** and **Linda L. Layne,**
Rensselaer Polytechnic Institute

REVIEW: "... Jones has successfully complied a list of contributions that treat a number of diverse topics in a generally competent, interesting and thorough manner. This is an important book ..."

-- Sociology & Social Research

Volume 9, The Anthropology of Science and Technology
1992, 254 pp. $73.25
ISBN 0-89232-973-4

CONTENTS: Preface, *David J. Hess and Linda L. Layne.* Introduction: The New Ethnography and the Anthropology of Science and Tehcnology, David J. Hess. I. RECONSTRUCTING MEDICAL SCIENCE AND TECHNOLOGY. Of Fetuses and Angels: Fragmentation and Integration in Narratives of Pregnancy Loss, *Linda L. Layne.* The Technocratic Body and the Oragnic Body: Cultural Models for Womens Birth Choices, *Robbie E. Davis-Floyd.* Blaming the User in Medical Informatics: The Cultural Nature of Scientific Practice, *Diana E. Forsythe.* II. SCIENCE AND TECHNOLOGY AT LARGE. Multiple Contexts, Multiple Meanings: Scientists in the European Space Agency, *Stacia E. Zabusky.* CAD/CAM Saves the Nation? Toward an Anthropology of Technology, *Gary L. Downey.* Severing the Ties: Fragmentation and Dignity in Late Modernity, *Paul Rabinow.* III. DISCIPLINE, CULTURE, AND POWER. The Anthropology of the Academy: When we are the Indians, *Roberto Kant de Lima.* Disciplining Heterodoxy, Circumventing Discipline: Parapsychology, Anthropologically, *David J. Hess.*

Also Available:
Volumes 1-8 (1978-1989) $73.25 each

FACULTY/PROFESSIONAL discounts are available in the U.S. and Canada at a rate of 40% off the list price when prepaid by personal check or credit card and ordered directly from the publisher.

JAI PRESS INC.
55 Old Post Road # 2 - P.O. Box 1678
Greenwich, Connecticut 06836-1678
Tel: (203) 661- 7602   Fax: (203) 661-0792

J A I   P R E S S

J A I   P R E S S

JOURNAL OF SOCIAL AND EVOLUTIONARY SYSTEMS

Editor
Paul Levinson

The *Journal of Social and Evolutionary Systems* is an interdisciplinary quarterly concerned with the unity, analogy, and relationships, theoretical and practical, between biological dynamics and mechanisms such as evolution, natural selection, and individual development, and social activities including technology, economics, politics, ideologies, literature, art, customs, and culture. As such, the Journal embraces such disciplines as theoretical biology, evolution theory, developmental psychology, artificial intelligence, cognitive and physical anthropology, paleontology, philosophy of science and technology, evolutionary epistemology, history of ideas, literary and film criticism, media theory, sociology, cosmology, and systems theory, and seeks thereby to help elucidate the human place in the cosmos.

Subscribers: Biologists, psychologists, anthropologists, paleontologists, sociologists, and students who specialize in social and evolutionary systems.

Subscription Rate
(all subscriptions are for the calander year only)

Volume 18 (1995)   **Published Quarterly**
Institutions: $225.00
Personal: $90.00
Volumes 13-17 $225.00 per volume
Please add $20.00 for Canada and Foreign; $40.00 for Airmail